Fieldwork and Families

Fieldwork and Families

Constructing New Models for Ethnographic Research

EDITED BY

JULIANA FLINN

LESLIE MARSHALL

JOCELYN ARMSTRONG

UNIVERSITY OF
HAWAI'I PRESS
HONOLULU

© 1998 University of Hawai'i Press
All rights reserved
Printed in the United States of America
03 02 01 00 99 98   5 4 3 2 1

Library of Congress Cataloging-in-Publication Data
Fieldwork and families : constructing new models for ethnographic research / edited by Juliana Flinn, Leslie Marshall, and Jocelyn Armstrong.
   p. cm.
  This work grew from a session at the 1991 annual meeting of the Association for Social Anthropology in Oceania (ASAO) in Victoria, British Columbia, in 1991.
  Includes bibliographical references and index.
    ISBN 0-8248-1928-4 (alk. paper). — ISBN 0-8248-1988-8 (pbk. : alk. paper)
    1. Anthropologists—Oceania—Family relationshiips—Congresses.
2. Ethnology—Oceania—Field work—Congresses. 3. Anthropologists' spouses—Oceania—Congresses. 4. Children of anthropologists—Oceania—Congresses. 5. Family—Oceania—Social conditions—Congresses. I. Flinn, Juliana, 1950-   . II. Marshall, Leslie B.
III. Armstrong, Jocelyn. IV. Association for Social Anthropology in Oceania. Meeting (1991 : Victoria, B.C.)
GN662.F54 1998
306'.0995—dc21   97-18075
                                                              CIP

University of Hawai'i Press books are printed on acid-free paper and meet the guidelines for permanence and durability of the Council on Library Resources

Designed by Josie Herr

Contents

Preface   VII

Introduction   1
The Family Dimension in Anthropological Fieldwork
Juliana Flinn

CHAPTER 1   Fieldwork and a Family   22
Perspectives over Time
Ruth Gallagher Goodenough

CHAPTER 2   Both Ways through the Looking Glass   35
The Accompanied Ethnographer as
Repositioned Other
Sheila Seiler Gilmore

CHAPTER 3   The Anthropologist, the Mother,
and the Cross-cultured Child   45
Lessons in the Relativity of Cultural Relativity
Heather Young Leslie

CHAPTER 4   Through the Eyes of a Child   60
A Gaze More Pure?
Barbara Burns McGrath

CHAPTER 5   Family and Other Uncontrollables   71
Impression Management in Accompanied Fieldwork
Jocelyn Linnekin

CHAPTER 6   Field and Family on Pohnpei, Micronesia   84
Glenn Petersen, Victoria Garcia, and Grace Petersen

CHAPTER 7   Single Woman, Married Woman, Mother, or Me?   96
Defining Family and Identity in the Field
Juliana Flinn

CHAPTER 8	Dancing to the Music of Time Fieldwork with a Husband, a Daughter, and a Cello *Karen Sinclair*	110
CHAPTER 9	Border-crossing in Tonga Marriage in the Field *Tamar Gordon*	130
CHAPTER 10	Fictive Families in the Field *David R. Counts and Dorothy Ayers Counts*	142
CHAPTER 11	The Inadvertent Acquisition of Kinship during Ethnographic Fieldwork *William R. Thurston*	154
CHAPTER 12	Shifting Stances, Differing Glances Reflections on Anthropological Practice in the Marshall Islands *Laurence Marshall Carucci*	169

Reflections on Families and Fieldwork 190
Anne Marie Tietjen

Fieldwork Relations and Ethnographic Presence 198
Michèle D. Dominy

References 211

Index 225

Preface

The impetus to act on occasional casual conversations we had all had over the years occurred in a tavern in Victoria, British Columbia, Canada, during a typical lively postsessions dinner at the 1991 annual meeting of the Association for Social Anthropology in Oceania (ASAO). Sean Rodman had joined his anthropologist parents, William Rodman and Margaret Rodman, and some others of us for the meal. His reminiscences of times in Vanuatu with his parents were so compelling that Leslie Marshall was persuaded it was time for some organized discussion of the place of family in ethnographic fieldwork. Later that evening, she and Julie Flinn planned the formal recruiting of others to extend their personal discussions.

We cast our nets throughout the ASAO community and encouraged spouses and children as well as the anthropologists to join us for the first ("informal") session in 1992. Although the final written collection includes only a few contributions by nonanthropologist family members, they were well represented in the intense discussions at the series of three annual sessions described by Julie Flinn in the introduction, and several gave presentations at the second ("working") session. Interest in our topic seemed high both in the sessions and in the hallways afterward, where many who were involved in other sessions and thus could not join the group discussions were moved to share their stories of family and fieldwork with us. Far beyond the meetings, insightful exchanges continued over the Internet. And the children who participated in the working session had their own more candid informal discussion on fieldwork experiences while their parents were otherwise occupied.

The participants and audiences for the sessions shifted over the years, as some (mostly spouses and children) had more pressing demands for their attention and dropped out, and as others (including a spouse) enthusiastically joined in the final effort as we moved toward a cohesive set of papers for publication. In our determination to create a tightly woven, highly interrelated work, Jocelyn Armstrong and Leslie Marshall withdrew as contributing authors to become editors only, and Julie Flinn took on the task of writing an introduction.

In addition to the chapter authors, we would like to recognize the contributions of the participants in one or more of the sessions. The following people contributed papers (field site and topic in parentheses):

- Jocelyn Armstrong (New Zealand Maori: Fieldwork with and without Family in New Zealand)
- Richard Feinberg, Nancy Grim, Joe Grim Feinberg, Kate Grim Feinberg (Solomon Islands and North Solomon Islands: Fieldwork and Family in the Solomon Islands)
- Nancy Grim (Solomon Islands and North Solomon Islands: Fieldwork in the Solomon Islands as an Anthropologist's Spouse)
- Eudene Luther (Western Samoa: His Mother's Son—Hell in Paradise)
- Kelsey Marshall (Chuuk and Papua New Guinea: Developmental Advantages and Disadvantages of Growing up in the Field)
- Leslie Marshall (Chuuk: Feathered Family—Pets and Fieldwork in the Pacific)
- Hazel Mason (Marshall Islands: Separation and Single Parenting Back Home)
- Channing Rodman (Vanuatu: A Brush with the Pigs—A Small Child's Experience on Ambae)
- Richard Scaglion, Kristina Scaglion Schempp (Papua New Guinea: Benefits of Attending Port Moresby High School)
- Diane Michalski Turner (Fiji: My Bifocals and My Fijian Baby)

For participation (both verbal and nonverbal) in discussions, we wish to recognize Michael Armstrong, Ann Chambers, Keith Chambers, Linley Chapman, Ann Chowning, Elaine Clark, Philip DeVita, Ceilidh Evans, Jane Goodale, Fanny Lawrence, Jeannette Mageo, Mac Marshall, Leonard Mason, Susan Pflanz-Cook, Margaret Rodman, Jehanne Teilhet-Fisk, and James Watson.

The diversity of this entire set of experiences makes a strong case for more public recognition than has been usual among Euro-American anthropologists of the frequent involvement of family in fieldwork. As others have recently been moved to do with regard to their local assistants, we need now to acknowledge very clearly that fieldworkers and families *together* construct a lot of ethnography. We are pleased to dedicate this volume to all the family members who have participated in fieldwork in Pacific societies in particular and to appreciate their various and always consequential contributions.

Juliana Flinn
Leslie Marshall
Jocelyn Armstrong

Fieldwork and Families

Introduction

The Family Dimension in Anthropological Fieldwork

JULIANA FLINN

We anthropologists all have our collection of stories from the field. We use them in class to educate and entertain our students. We regale friends and colleagues. We enlighten family members left at home. Anthropologists are not the only ones with stories; accompanying or visiting family members have their own. One arena for sharing these tales has been the Association for Social Anthropology in Oceania meetings, a setting that is small enough for the development of personal relationships and for the sharing of some of the more personal stories, the most poignant of which involve family issues.

Yet these are far more than mere stories. Sharing these experiences with other fieldworkers or family members who underwent similar experiences can prove therapeutic. It also provides opportunities for seeking advice. I myself have been consulted on several occasions about taking a small child or nonanthropologist spouse to the field. For most fieldworkers, this fortuitous and anecdotal advice is about the only guidance available. For many, it comes late —after the first research experience once they begin forming their professional networks. Some spouses, for example, have noted the absence of discussions in graduate school about the problems or research implications of accompanying the fieldworker. Those taking children may have considered health and education issues but not the impact on their research design or access to information. Those in the midst of decisions have had to act blindly and, for the most part, alone.

Personal, methodological, and theoretical issues are at stake, yet little serious, scholarly attention has been paid to them. Ethnographic fieldwork takes a person away from home for an extended period of time to a potentially dangerous and unhealthy place. As a consequence, it also forces some difficult family decisions: Shall I go alone or with my husband or wife? What about the spouse's own work left behind? What are potential consequences to the relationship regardless of the decision? What about children? Should they be left at home with one parent while the other pursues fieldwork? Should they be subjected to health and other hazards? Even though so many of us face these decisions, as have so many in previous years, where is the collective, scholarly discussion that might guide us? Where is some accumulated wisdom or experience? Where is some support or guidance? In what arenas are such discussions even considered legitimate topics when designing a research project? These family issues are treated as personal, not professional or academic. Not only does this situation deprive fieldworkers of valuable insights and some experience upon which to base a decision, but it also discourages analysis of the consequences for fieldwork and the research process. How ironic that claiming family ties with hosts is a way of asserting authority in conventional ethnographic writing, yet writing about accompanying family has not been considered of theoretical significance.

After listening to and recounting our own fieldwork experiences with family in informal conversations at ASAO meetings over the years, Leslie Marshall and I took advantage of the "ASAO process" for discussing and writing about topics of mutual concern. To the best of our knowledge, the process is unique in professional American anthropological circles. Interested parties meet for an "informal session" one year to explore a topic, assess interest, and formulate tentative common issues. Participants write papers for a "working session" the following year and spend an entire day in discussions, analyzing the papers in turn and then as a whole. Based on those discussions, participants revise and precirculate papers for a formal "symposium" the next year, during which the themes raised jointly by the papers are examined. Some kind of joint publication typically results.

Since Leslie Marshall and I had both worked in Chuuk in Micronesia as women, wives, and mothers, at times with a child, at times without, we inevitably began comparing experiences. The fact that Leslie went as a spouse of an anthropologist and I went as an anthropologist added an intriguing dimension to the discussions. She spoke of her feelings as the accompanying spouse; I spoke of the responsibilities I felt for my husband's experiences. We compared the experiences of having a toddler versus an older boy in the field. We spoke of factors that entered into our decisions and pondered the impact on the research. And we knew we were not alone; a number of our ASAO friends and colleagues had experienced fieldwork as part of a family.

An informal session that we convened in 1992 proved us right, although we also discovered that much is still too painful or personal for people to make public. Even with the publication of this book, much is left unsaid. Unwritten or only briefly recorded ordeals include resentment toward a spouse, insecurity in the face of a spouse's work and reputation, guilt about a child's experience in the field, and guilt about the experience of a child left at home.

The working session in 1993 included fieldworkers, spouses, and children, thus providing more than just the accounts of anthropologists. That session produced tears. Homesickness and a mother's lost hope of a year with her child, loneliness of fatherless children, yearning for simple touching and affection, frustration at an inability to return with family to a field site, falling in love, and worries about being unprofessional are some of the feelings that surfaced—or resurfaced. This proved to be therapeutic, with a sense of catharsis, although none of that had been planned. Informal discussions later revealed other therapeutic aspects surrounding our analyses of these experiences. I, for example, had initially found it painful but eventually cleansing to examine old diaries and letters concerning an ex-husband and former fieldwork companion. This process of writing and discussing our experiences helped bring people to terms with some events and feelings. Finding commonalities with others also helped many feel not so alone.

In addition, some participants for the first time had an opportunity to discuss these family-related issues in a professional forum rather than relegate them to personal problems or events inappropriate for academia. These are very real issues anthropologists face as they enter the field. Furthermore, we discovered we had more than a collection of cute stories and more than a therapy session; we had implications for methodology and the research process. Participants spoke of behavior, access to information, interpretations, and attitudes being shaped by their family situation in the field. The symposium provided an opportunity to examine further these issues and to critique the prevailing model of fieldwork and the production of knowledge in anthropology.

As conveners and organizers of the ASAO sessions, Leslie Marshall and I assumed the roles of editors of the symposium papers for publication. We later recruited Jocelyn Armstrong as third editor. A participant in all three ASAO sessions, Jocelyn shared with Leslie and me the experience of multiple field visits across an extended period under diverse family circumstances. She added experience of fieldwork in Polynesian sites and in non-Pacific settings.

Family and the Scientific Endeavor

Despite a number of edited books on personal aspects of anthropological fieldwork such as the presence of children (Butler and Turner 1987b; Cassell 1987b), the impact of gender (Bell, Caplan, and Karim 1993; Golde 1986; Whitehead and Conaway 1986), the value of long-term fieldwork (Fowler and Hardesty 1994), and learning through humbling or other unplanned experiences (DeVita 1990, 1992; Lawless, Sutlive, and Zamora 1983), none of these works has taken as its focus the anthropologist as embedded in a family. Before ever becoming involved in fieldwork, the anthropologist has a culturally constructed family of orientation and in many cases a family of procreation as well. Decisions about leaving family at home or taking family to the field shape field experiences and thus have an impact on the research process and production of knowledge. Once in the field, especially in Pacific kinship-structured societies, the anthropologist usually becomes attached to or otherwise acquires a family from within the society under study as well, and the local people tend to understand and interpret the anthropologist within a kinship framework.

Even in many of the articles discussing the impact of gender, it appears not so much the gender of the anthropologist that is most relevant to the local people as the anthropologist's status in a family. In the Whitehead and Conaway (1986) collection, for example, each contributor's discussion of gender seems more accurately a discussion of "unmarried female," "mother," "spouse," or other family status. Because of Euro-American biological folk models of gender and kinship, these are conflated topics in our society (Yanagisako and Collier 1987).

Our collection seeks to address this issue of the impact on research of family—socially constructed Euro-American family, whether left at home or accompanying the fieldworker, and acquired Pacific family. Fieldworkers' identities and roles are connected with their family positions and links, and this is especially the case, though not exclusively, when members of the family are part of fieldwork. Furthermore, these positions shape research. Many of the contributors to this volume, for example, clarify what they were in a position to know (or not know) because of their family position and presence of family members. Family attachments and status affect the ethnographic enterprise: how fieldworkers present themselves, the data they collect, their connection with the local community, and even their research topics, methods, and orientation. Not only who they are in terms of gender, age, personality, ethnicity, and the like, but also their family positions—especially when evident in the field—are essential to understanding the fieldworker as a "positioned subject" (Rosaldo 1989, 207) and social actor.

It is important to recognize that the Euro-American (Canadian and American of European ancestry) notion of the family is not a universal analytical category (see, for example, Schneider 1984). Some members of the symposium in which this volume originated discussed avoiding the use of the term "family" in our title for that reason. Indeed, some of the authors highlight the dangers of assuming too much similarity between our concepts and those of cultural others. Yet we retain the term because this book is about Euro-American researchers, reared in Euro-American families, making decisions about fieldwork with or without members of Euro-American families, and conducting their research with concerns for those members. We recognize that this family is a historical product and is rooted in cultural beliefs about it being natural, biological, resulting from sexual intercourse, and involving shared biogenetic substance (Schneider 1980). Even when recognizing the Euro-American family as a cultural, symbolic construct, anthropologists carry it to the field, especially when accompanied by family members. In fact, some of the contributors to this volume discuss their struggles in reconciling their own with their Pacific hosts' conceptions of family, because the Euro-American construct often fails to match what anthropologists find in the field.

To return to two published collections that are explicitly about children in the field (Butler and Turner 1987b; Cassell 1987b), we find that they discuss problems and benefits of children in the field and focus on whether or not the experience was a positive one. To a certain extent, at least some of the authors deal with the impact on the research process, especially on the ability to collect data and to develop rapport. Spouses are mentioned, but the focus is on children, not family.

Both collections were edited by women; both broke away from the convention of keeping discussions of children and family out of the professional realm. Butler and Turner view their contribution as acknowledging the reflexive process in anthropology; they argue for the value of including personal information and acknowledging feelings while explicitly rejecting the conclusion that such discussions mean abandoning objectivity. Although their collection acknowledges cultural constructions of social development and values, it nonetheless focuses on children rather than taking the family as the operant unit and exploring how much of the fieldwork process involves American cultural assumptions about spouses and families. Some recent attention is being paid to collaborative work of anthropologists with spouses, including the role of American gender role expectations (Gottlieb 1995; Kennedy 1995).

Other collections of personal accounts of fieldwork (such as Lawless, Sutlive, and Zamora 1983) contain articles that attempt to clarify method, demystify fieldwork, and acknowledge how much of the learning is informal and unplanned. These are significant perspectives because fieldwork is an experience, not just a set of procedures. Two collections specifically focus on how anthropologists can learn from such experiences (DeVita 1990, 1992). A fieldworker's personal, social, and cultural characteristics as presented by the fieldworker and interpreted by members of the local community become part of the packet of research strategies.

Furthermore, method shapes theory, and ethnography, with its emphasis on participant observation, is cultural anthropology's hallmark method. Rosaldo (1989) has written eloquently of the value of theoretical insights derived from personal experience in the fieldwork process, and Okely (1992) examines theoretical connections between the experience of fieldwork and the resulting analysis and ethnography. Yet despite the widespread use of this method that involves immersion in interpersonal relationships and blurs the lines between the observer and the observed, and despite the growing number of manuals on conducting fieldwork, firsthand accounts of the lived and felt experience of fieldwork and its impact on research often are still seen as marginal, "subjective," and therefore not fully accepted as professional or scholarly contributions, because the objective of the scientific endeavor is to describe the collective other as opposed to the unique researcher.

This attitude persists even though it has become fashionable to critique neopositivism in anthropology and to acknowledge reflexivity in ethnography. Interestingly enough, some of this criticism at the same time echoes positivist, scientific stances that demand clear statements of methodology. In anthropology this entails divulging personal details about fieldwork and the fieldworker. Myerhoff and Ruby (1982, 25–26), for example, discuss the obligations of all researchers to report on their methods, and they analyze the reluctance of anthropologists to do so: such disclosure would reveal how much of their own behavior, personality, and experiences must be taken into account as contributing to the production of knowledge, in seeming contradiction to the tenets of scientific methodology.

These problems are related to the very nature of ethnography. Marcus and Fischer (1986) discuss ethnography's alliance of observation with involvement in the daily life and experiences of local people, a very personal experience for the fieldworker but essential to the research process. Yet ethnographers have historically been reluctant (men more so than women) to reveal the details of this fieldwork and to discuss the impact of personal experiences on research; such revelations risk being construed as nonscientific, subjective, and unprofessional. Writing about the researcher; the researcher's feelings, emotions, and experiences; the researcher's relationships with others—this does not constitute "science" and "objectivity." Science focuses on what is researched, not who is researching. Ethnographic research is a "messy, qualitative experience in contrast to the positivist social-science vision of method" (Marcus and Fischer 1986, 22). The response on the part of ethnographers should be to include, not exclude, discussion of the details of fieldwork and of the process of the research.

Marcus and Fischer cite primarily male forefathers, however, such as Paul Rabinow and Louis Dumont, and present no challenge to the model of the fieldworker as a lone researcher. Bronislaw Malinowski, the purported pioneer of ethnographic fieldwork in the early decades of the century, is still with us: "Proper conditions for ethnographic work . . . consist mainly in cutting oneself off from the company of other white men" (Malinowski 1961, 6). There is certainly no discussion of the impact of families. Participants in this volume's symposium spoke of the model for fieldwork that involves a lone, male researcher—the model that has prevailed despite the fact that many fieldworkers are women, and many fieldworkers are accompanied. Scheper-Hughes (1987a, 217) is one of many who gives credit to Malinowski for promoting solitary fieldwork, and contributors to this volume elaborate on its mystique and purported value for anthropologists today. Even though many ethnographers have been female, and many have been accompanied by a spouse and/or children, the model remains one of a lone, male researcher. Rosaldo (1989, 30), for example, critiques that model of the "Lone Ethnographer" and discusses it as cast as male. He contends that in the older ethnographies, "'truth' was a manly, serious business; it was earnest, plain, and unadorned, not witty, oblique, and humanly engaging. The followers of classic norms paraded the banner of objectivism" (1989, 128). Furthermore, standards for fieldwork and for writing ethnography have been "scientific" and "objective," despite the recent emphasis on interpretive and humanistic endeavors. Positivism has remained a prevailing paradigm, and it is ideologically male (Harding 1986; MacKinnon 1987).

Bell (1993a) points out that despite a heightened interest in reflexivity and recognition of the value of interpretive stances, neopositivism retains a strong hold, especially since anthropology has not been able to come to terms with the tension between objectivity and subjectivity involved in fieldwork. Fieldwork involves a "set of personal relations" (Macintyre 1993, 47). As a participant, one must become immersed in another way of life and develop a network of interpersonal relationships, yet the observer role implies the scientific image of detachment and objectivity. Fieldwork is an intense, deeply emotional experience. Our involvement with fieldwork is not as some abstract, neutral, disinterested observer, but as someone of a particular age, gender, class, family background, personality, religion, and a host of other characteristics. The fieldworker may also be alone or accompanied, and in either case have family connections of various sorts back home if not in the field. Knowledge results from a process involving particular research questions and procedures, with certain personal and social characteristics, engaging in a network of relationships, and experiences that occur at a particular point in time; it is the "outcome of a socially and historically specific research process" (Schrijvers 1993, 143).

The rationality, objectivity, and detachment associated with "science" are at the same time traits associated with male gender ideology in our society (Harding 1986; MacKinnon 1987). Karim (1993, 82), for example, contends that she was told at the University of London School of Economics (a preeminent place of advanced education for generations of anthropologists) that "emotions and commitments" were not to be a part of anthropological work. In American cultural belief, emotion is associated with the female (Lutz 1988, 53–80), and emotion is also construed as irrational and subjective (and therefore not scientific). I remember being told by my professors that the research site should be chosen based on a rational decision about the most appropriate site, given my research topic. We have not read in most ethnographies, especially those written by males, about how the researcher's personality or life experiences influenced the choice of topic or site.

The "subjective" and "nonscientific" in our culture are associated with the female. It is not surprising, then, that women have been more willing to divulge these aspects and openly discuss their impact on research questions, site selection, and data collection. They have been less likely to retain the neutral and detached stance. Bell (1993a) contends this is because women can make no pretenses about their experiences and voices being neutral—certainly not gender neutral—and generalize from their experiences. "Female" is the marked, not the unmarked category. Women are more likely to realize they experience and write from a gendered perspective; this allows a recognition of the numerous other factors such as age and marital status that have an influence as well.

Furthermore, women in our culture are more likely than men to see themselves as part of a network of relationships (Gilligan 1982). The male identity is based more on a contrast between the self and the other, the female identity on connection and ties with others (Wolf 1992, 114). Women have been more responsible than men for family and family relationships. They have not kept the clean boundaries between family and work that men feel expected to maintain. It is not surprising, then, that women have been more willing to acknowledge and write about how their personalities and relationships affected the research experience, methodology, and data. These are basic questions about how knowledge is produced.

One would think, then, that women's voices would be prominent with the postmodern emphasis on reflexivity and that gender and other personal characteristics would be highlighted. Bell points out that this has not been the case, that in fact, "feminists' questions have been appropriated and their experimental moments erased" (Bell 1993a, 3). Despite a female tradition of analyzing the impact of one's personal situation in the field on the production of knowledge (see, for example, Bowen 1954, Briggs 1970, Golde 1986 [originally published in 1970], and Powdermaker 1966), reflexivity is hailed as new and innovative, with a male heritage. Furthermore, as participants in the symposium leading to this volume pointed out, the male voices in the reflexive mode focus on the self, the individual self in the field. Elsewhere, in a volume on the impact of gender on fieldwork, Back (1993, 215) writes of a colleague's story warning not to invite male anthropologists to visit because they would propound at length on the subject dearest to their heart—themselves. The voices in this volume (heavily female) write of connections with family.

Anthropologists previously tended to write abstractly of the "other" and attempted to remain "objective" and "scientific" even though fieldwork depends so much on interaction between fieldworker and local people—and often fieldworker family members as well. Certainly local people are constructing identities for the fieldworker and negotiating roles, and these may bear little resemblance to what the fieldworker has planned or attempted to present. Local people construct identities using their own cultural constructions, categories, and understandings (Keyes 1983); in societies that are primarily kin based (as in the Pacific), a social identity tied to a family status makes sense. Caplan (1993, 178) discusses the importance of "positionality" —who the researcher is in the eyes of the community and who community members are in the eyes of the researcher. The fieldworker attempts at least in part to become like the "other," and these attempts, too, relate to the fieldworker's connections (or lack of them) with family members. Furthermore, the fieldworker is both participant and observer, a part of local daily life yet an outside observer of it.

Wagley (1983, 13) describes how a fieldworker "loses objectivity and becomes entangled in the lives of the people." In fact, the more the fieldworker can become entangled, the more intensive the interaction with others becomes, the better the fieldworker can come to understand local cultural premises. Even the choice of field site tends not to follow the ideal model of a site best suited to the research question. Subjectivity is involved (Banks 1983), as is personality, even when being as inconspicuous as possible is the inclination (Flores-Meiser 1983). Taking family situations and needs into account is a similar consideration and another dimension to be reckoned with. Zamora (1983, 143) has called for an "anthropology of anthropologists" exploring the relationships between personal experiences in the field and research.

Hughes (1983, 89) acknowledges being less efficient because of normal family demands in the field but that this made him "more human," something he found more valuable than simple efficiency. Schrijvers (1993, 149) makes a similar comment about how revealing personal information about a divorce and her current partner not being the children's father made her look more like a "normal" human being. Cassell (1987a, 258–259) discusses how having children in the field makes it more difficult to hold back as much personal information; we are "observers observed" to an even greater extent because of the presence of others with us, and this may be a "more egalitarian way to conduct research" (1987a, 259), with more give and take on the part of both sides.

As fieldworkers, anthropologists tend to countenance behaviors in other societies they nonetheless do not want their children to learn. A conflict between roles as parents and as researchers can emerge. Scheper-Hughes (1987a, 229) and other contributors to the volume *Children in the Field* (Cassell

1987b) discuss this dilemma, which strikes at the core of anthropological values placed on cultural relativism and avoiding ethnocentrism.

The vision of the lone fieldworker is consistent with the more general Western notion of the person, which Geertz (1984, 126) describes as a discrete unit, emotionally and cognitively self-contained, and essentially separate from other such units. Feminist scholars have argued that this concept of the person, the "unencumbered self," is a male one in our society, whereas the "situated self," one that is situated in a network of relationships, is a female one (Benhabib and Cornell 1987, 12). Furthermore, following on the work of Geertz, Shweder and Bourne (1984) argue that the Western (male?) notion of the "egocentric" person differs from the "sociocentric" self, dependent on context, situation, and relationships, found in a number of other societies. The solitary ethnographer model suits the Western notion of the person, yet many of the peoples anthropologists work with have "sociocentric" views of the person, and they interpret fieldworkers accordingly. As members of kin-based societies, they are likely already to view fieldworkers as people connected with other people, especially to kin. The family model is closer to their reality than anthropology's lone fieldworker model. In many of the Pacific societies in which contributors to this volume have worked, a core aspect of a person's social identity is as a member of a network of kin, embedded in a relational field, and with family as a primary orientation (cf. Rudie 1993, 103).

Euro-American Families, Costs and Benefits for Research, and a Challenge to the Solitary Fieldworker Model

The contributors to this volume and the symposium participants include not just ethnographers but spouses of ethnographers and some children as well.[1] The ethnographers—all North Americans of European descent—range from young researchers who have recently completed dissertation fieldwork to senior fieldworkers with decades of research experience. Their work covers eight Polynesian, six Micronesian, and four Melanesian sites across the Pacific and includes both urban and isolated settings, and their experiences span four decades from the 1960s into the 1990s. In the joint analyzing of these experiences and the impact of family on research, three broad issues emerged: (1) the Euro-American socially constructed family and its impact on fieldwork; (2) costs and benefits of accompanied fieldwork; and (3) a challenge to the model of the lone, usually male, objective, culturally relative fieldworker.

Euro-American cultural notions of family[2] affect decisions about accompanied fieldwork, goals, expectations of possible benefits and problems, sense of personal identity, integration with the host community, willingness or ability to cross cultural borders, feelings of control or dependency, and role conflicts between "parent" and "researcher." For most Euro-Americans the term "family" has biological and essentialist connotations; although "family" is a social construct, most of us simply assume it is natural and inevitable. Most people believe, without question, for example, that a mother ought to raise her own child and not allow others to take over for extended periods of time. That was certainly behind the decisions of women to take their children, especially young ones, with them for fieldwork. In the words of a female symposium participant, "What kind of mother are you in middle-class American society to go off and leave your child? . . . You are consumed with guilt." Yet in the Pacific societies these women went to study, adoption and fosterage are common, and mothers often leave their children with other kin if they pursue employment or education.[3] Sheila Gilmore, for example, worried that her hosts would not understand her inability emotionally to endure a year-long separation from her daughter. Heather Young Leslie watched almost helplessly as her toddler was socialized by her hosts, and she even briefly considered allowing her child to remain permanently; the situations threatened her own sense of motherhood and challenged cherished notions of cultural relativity and objectivity. I discuss arriving in the field with American images of egalitarian marriages, and I explore the complexities of differing Euro-American class and ethnic family backgrounds on the part of husband and wife that shaped differential reactions to the field situation.

Given Euro-American beliefs about family and gender, men and women tend to undergo different pressures. Ruth Goodenough and Victoria Garcia, two female accompanying spouses, played appropriate cultural roles whether they remained at home with children or accompanied their husbands. Their roles as wives, mothers, and women remained unchallenged. Barbara McGrath's husband and my husband, however, as male accompanying spouses, were both challenged by friends, colleagues, and even family: what kind of a "man" leaves his work for such a long time to follow his wife? Furthermore, what kind of women and wives would we be if we either left our children at home or took them with us, leaving the father at home? Neither is culturally appropriate or sanctioned.

Cultural expectations of motherhood in the context of decisions about fieldwork easily induce feelings of guilt. Innumerable examples arose as symposium participants explored their experiences. They spoke of guilt at the thought of leaving a small child at home, even for a month; guilt at the thought of dragging a child to a possibly hazardous and unhealthy field site for the sake of an anthropological career; guilt at the thought of bringing a child back home again, away from security, a familiar culture, and close relationships; guilt at inabilities to control and socialize a child in the field; guilt at losing control and publicly yelling at a child. Heather Young Leslie berates herself for considering allowing her daughter to be adopted by a local family.

Wanting to maintain or create a "sense of family" played a factor in decisions about fieldwork. Participants and contributors seem to mean by this a sense of connectedness, bonding, and shared experiences; Euro-American families are supposed to be close physically and emotionally and share not just blood but also experiences. The Counts, for example, never questioned unaccompanied fieldwork; they were a family, so they conducted fieldwork as a family. The McGraths saw fieldwork explicitly as an opportunity to share an adventure together. Furthermore, for both Barbara McGrath's husband and mine, fieldwork was an opportunity for time with their children that fathers rarely have in the United States. When I took my son for a summer of fieldwork, and Sheila Gilmore took her daughter, both children at the time lived most of the year with their fathers, from whom we were divorced, so we both felt a need to use our time in the field to cement a sense of family, perhaps paving the way for a later change in custody. A male anthropologist who participated in our symposium discussions and who had conducted lone field research as a student spoke of attempts several years later for his wife and children to return with him so that the whole family would finally have a chance to share an experience that had been so pivotal in his life. Ruth Goodenough poignantly describes an opportunity to share fieldwork as a family after several previous solo trips by her anthropologist husband during which she and their children stayed at home.

Those accompanied to the field had the sense that they were more readily understood. Local people who have no understanding of "anthropologist" or "graduate student" believe they can understand "mother" or "father." Karen Sinclair and Barbara McGrath—to name only two—discuss a sense of shared motherhood that made them more accessible to local people. Furthermore, in these kin-structured societies, local people find a lone person quite problematic; a person without connections, especially in places with sociocentric notions of the person, is an enigma and perhaps not even human. Bil Thurston and Larry Carucci, two male anthropologists whose first fieldwork experiences were solo, both examine how members of their host communities negotiated and interpreted their identities and kin connections. The Counts point out that in their case—presumably a common one—it was more a matter of their hosts figuring out who they already were rather than creating connections. Perhaps because of the Euro-American family construct grounded in beliefs in biology and blood connections, anthropologists with Euro-American origins and background may fail to take these family connections acquired in the field as seriously as local people do. We may have a belief in kinship based on chronology and biology, but kinship in Pacific societies tends to be based on social action and behavior. The Counts learned the extent to which these connections are real when they accorded their graduate student, Bil Thurston, kin status. Tamar Gordon examines yet another type of family relationship acquired in the field when she married a Tongan she met while conducting her research.

Experiences in the field have in turn reshaped notions of family for some on their return. Victoria Garcia and I, for example, deliberately cultivated relationships with members of our (American) extended families. Victoria went even further by successfully recreating in suburban New Jersey aspects of the communal extended family environment she experienced and found rewarding in the field.

Contributors also analyze costs and benefits of accompanied versus lone fieldwork for the research, the fieldworker, the family members, and the hosts. These are hindsight analyses, however, because minimal rational cost/benefit analyses seem to have preceded fieldwork, in part because of lack of information about family in the field. Families facing such decisions make assumptions about potential problems and advantages but are then unprepared for problems such as Sheila Gilmore faced when her daughter became homesick. Some families seem to have deliberated more than others. The Counts, for example, simply assumed that the children "go where we go." It never occurred to them not to take their children, although they believed children should be at least two years old—old enough to have language skills enabling them to articulate where they hurt in the event of an accident or illness. (When their children were older, the Counts gave them a choice.) On the other hand, the Goodenoughs, with children of widely separated ages, carefully considered which children to take and why.[4] Despite carefully considered decisions—or the lack of them—there is also a considerable amount of arbitrariness as well. For Karen Sinclair, for example, it was the availability of last-minute, unexpected funds that enabled her child to accompany her.

Because of the nature of the discipline and the type of person entering the discipline, anthropologists perhaps tend to assume the fieldwork experience will be an enriching one for children.[5] One symposium participant expressed a common sentiment:

> I know many of us are committed to pluralism, to cultural relativism, to tolerance. We do not want our kids to grow up into little racists as we see so many Americans growing up. . . . So we think it is inherently an enriching, broadening experience to take them. So we do it. . . . Our commitment to that is a deep personal, ethical, moral commitment. . . . We rationalize it . . . whether we think it's good for our kids or not in terms of their personal development, their schooling, their relationships with their peers, their health. It's detrimental probably on a lot of counts, and yet we take them anyway, and I think it's because in the cost/benefit analysis, the personal and moral commitment to raising our kids to be tolerant, global citizens—that outweighs everything else. I think that is the bottom line for most of us as anthropologists, and that is why we would take them—even if there is malaria. We would rationalize it.

Many of the symposium participants attested to the fact that the experience was indeed an enriching one for the children as well as for their sense of family, and specific examples appear throughout the chapters in this volume. (Also attested to is resistance from parents, friends, and supervisors who viewed the family fieldwork prospect as bordering on child neglect. One symposium participant commented, "Our parents said, 'What kind of parents are you to take these children in where they are going to die?' and this sort of thing.") Several children seem to have thrived in the unfamiliar environments. In addition to the many examples in this volume, one symposium participant discussed how his daughter blossomed and flourished in part because of experiential learning in her New Guinea school, unlike anything she had experienced in school at home. Many of the children say they hope to return to the host community. The most intriguing case may be that of Emily Sinclair, now a young adult, whose sense of self and identity have been shaped since early childhood by her experiences with the New Zealand Maori, and for whom the field site has provided stability and a point of reference.

Yet no parent can count on a positive, enriching experience. Although none of the contributors experienced the death or serious injury of a child as some fieldworkers have (e.g., Hitchcock 1987), they confronted other problems. The Goodenoughs worried about children left at home and had to contend with their eleven-year-old son's deep dismay at being deliberately deceived by an adult. Karen Sinclair had to watch her daughter grapple with a growing awareness of her privileged class position. I worried about my eight-year-old son's lack of the privacy he valued and enjoyed at home.

The local community may incur costs as well. In many cases, the presence of children adds enormous responsibilities for the hosts. The Counts describe how incompetent they appeared to their hosts; not having the "sense God gave a goose," they were unaware of innumerable potential dangers to their children. Fieldworkers may enjoy the sense that their children can freely roam a village and wander from household to household, with local people ever watchful, but at the same time, it is a burden and heavy responsibility. Hosts can clearly become emotionally attached to the children as well. Karen Sinclair, for example, recounts Maori efforts to attend a concert featuring her grown daughter, whom they had known since childhood through a series of trips to the field. At the symposium, the Counts related the lament of one of their local friends: "I'm sorry you came, because you brought the children, and now you are taking them away, and we are not sure we will ever see them again."

Experiences of accompanying spouses varied considerably and in some cases involved role strains, especially in the face of Euro-American cultural expectations. For some contributors, both spouses in the relationship were fieldworkers (Young Leslie, Counts and Counts, Carucci), and Victoria Garcia and

Ruth Goodenough became fieldworkers. Barbara McGrath and some symposium participants spoke of "taking turns" with a spouse in terms of their professional development, with the accompanying spouses leaving their own work for a period of time because it was the anthropologist's turn. Some of these couples experienced conflicts because of expected gender roles in the field and what appeared to be an inegalitarian division of labor. Larry Carucci lamented the strains and inequalities stemming from his position as project director and greater familiarity with the local language culture compared with his future wife when they conducted fieldwork together. Some of the male accompanying spouses, such as my husband and Mike Sinclair, experienced a sense of being marginalized or anomalous, with no clearly defined role, although they each found a way to make at least a partial contribution, based on their own qualifications and experience, with my husband teaching English and Mike Sinclair assisting with some legal issues.

An advantage many authors discuss is a personal, psychological one, especially a healthier sense of self and identity. Tamar Gordon writes of emotional starvation when she was alone. Glenn Petersen and I write of a loss of sense of self during lone fieldwork, and the Goodenoughs describe feeling more like "whole human beings" when together as a family. Glenn Petersen most clearly points out, however, that there are likely to be costs; for him it was a loss of freedom in his work.

Several contributors analyze how accompanied fieldwork unmasks a researcher and hinders impression management. Barbara McGrath and Jocelyn Linnekin both cite embarrassing cases of losing control, yelling at their children, and thus acting in violation of cultural norms about appropriate behavior. Karen Sinclair describes Maori perceptions of her inadequacies as a mother and inabilities to handle her husband. Yet however disconcerting to the fieldworker, such incidents may actually serve to build rapport; Barbara McGrath, for example, describes a sense of shared motherhood that developed in the wake of her outburst. Victoria Garcia contends that local people appreciated the reciprocity involved in sharing two different behavioral systems and that it in no way inhibited good data collection for her to relax and be herself rather than strain to be as native as possible. Her "unmasking" proved to be beneficial. After experiencing fieldwork with a family, I found it disconcerting when it proved difficult to find ways of revealing myself when conducting lone fieldwork. Why do we all have the sense that "being ourselves" violated some canon of fieldwork? Expectations of objectivity and the neutral observer apparently still hold sway.

Even as accompanied fieldwork makes impression management more difficult, it can create contexts requiring it. Sheila Gilmore analyzes such a case, pointing out that accompanied fieldwork allows local people to witness interaction with children or spouses, interaction that may need to be explained.

Yet this explanation may well have to be an interpretation or translation into culturally appropriate terms.

Children, spouses, and relatives who accompany a fieldworker rarely have the same commitment as the fieldworker to suspending judgment and scrupulously following local conventions. Furthermore, they can be what Jocelyn Linnekin labels "uncontrollables." Losing control, especially yelling at children, was an almost universal (and unpleasant) experience among symposium participants. In the words of one symposium participant:

> If you have another person there, a lot of things are going to come out in the open that you didn't want necessarily to come out in the open, but you're going to react in some very spontaneous ways. Whether you like it or not, you've dropped a curtain.

All felt exposed. And not only was there the fear of losing rapport, but there was also concern about indulging in emotionalism and thus violating canons of objectivity and professionalism. Lone fieldwork can have its own cases of loss of control; Bil Thurston describes feeling completely out of control by being under the protection and direction of his hosts. He was not even allowed to cook for himself. For accompanied fieldwork, situations over which an ethnographer has no control are that much more likely to occur.

Although this unmasking seems to fly in the face of the detached observer stance, contributors found benefits for their research and they therefore challenge conventional models of fieldwork. Barbara McGrath discovered that her children's nonobjective and downright judgmental stances enabled her to derive some insights into Tongan culture. Karen Sinclair describes how she could no longer gloss over issues of social class in the face of her daughter's actions and attitudes. Valuable insights and closer relationships were typical results of this unmasking. Contributors discuss access to information made possible because of their family situation. In general, the sense was that fieldwork with a family humanized the fieldworker in a number of dimensions, both psychologically from their own perspective, as well as socially from their hosts' perspectives. Jocelyn Linnekin questions the very necessity of impression management, positing a possible connection with Western cultural beliefs. There is certainly an arrogance in the assumption that we are capable of successful impression management in the field even when alone and that local people are unaware or do not detect our efforts. It seems naive to believe that local people actually perceive us as we intend to be seen.

The point, however, is not that fieldwork with a family leads to better insights or better relationships, but that these cases certainly debunk old beliefs about the necessity of being thrown alone into the field to have one's old identity stripped and to contend with culture shock (alone) in order to develop a dependency on the local people and therefore produce good scholarship. We are all positioned in the field, as Bil Thurston and Larry Carucci point out; our hosts position us whether we arrive accompanied or not. Our age, gender, personality, and a host of other characteristics, including perceived family status, affect this positioning.

When discussing impressions of the fieldwork model received during graduate school, a consensus emerged: fieldworkers should spend a long time in the field, alone, and live in difficult situations. In fact, fieldwork that is too comfortable is less prestigious (and presumably produces less prestigious scholarship). Jocelyn Linnekin, for example, felt compelled to mention the discomforts and anxieties she experienced during fieldwork on Maui, the famed tourist paradise. According to the prevailing model, fieldwork that is accompanied presumably cushions the researcher from too much discomfort, provides emotional support, and entices the fieldworker away from work and language expertise. The best scholarship could be produced only under the difficult, anxiety-ridden situation, and anthropologists cloak their writing in this image. This is despite the fact that many anthropologists have been accompanied, although the only evidence is an acknowledgment thanking a spouse (typically a wife) for invaluable assistance. The cases in this volume clearly indicate that accompanied fieldwork provides a type of positioning in a society that provides for rapport with local people, access to valuable data, insights into emotions and attitudes, and a healthy sense of both self and family. As anthropologists we should continue to question the old model; these cases add another nail to the coffin of the "neutral, objective observer" and question other assumptions, such as the predilection for impression management and maintaining control.

Case Studies

Ruth Goodenough's chapter is from the perspective of a fieldworker's spouse who experienced both being left at home and being part of a family in the field. Her work offers insights into the benefits and costs, for both family and fieldwork, of decisions about accompanied fieldwork, especially some potential long-term effects. After three periods of fieldwork with the family left at home, Ruth Goodenough and the two younger children, both boys, accompanied her ethnographer husband, Ward Goodenough, to Chuuk in Micronesia. Two college-aged daughters remained at home in the United States, although the younger one remembered the earlier separations and initially asked to accompany her family. For all four family members in the field, the experience was a rewarding one, but the daughters left at home suffered a lack of emotional support, and the younger needed extensive counseling. The writing of this account led family members to examine some issues that had never before been discussed at length, enabling them to come to terms with events that took place decades earlier.

Whereas Ruth Goodenough writes of family left at home, Sheila Seiler

Gilmore writes of being forced to return home with family when a problem arose with her daughter and she had to make explanations to her hosts. She points out that accompanied ethnographers offer opportunities for hosts to see us interacting according to our own cultural rules. We become the other and may be called upon to translate our culture in a comprehensible way, with implications for the quality of field relations, perception of behavior, and data collection. Gilmore challenges the concept of the generic other and argues for a revised concept that is culturally specific. As a divorced woman and noncustodial parent, Gilmore faced these issues when she took her daughter to the field (planning a rich experience and hoping perhaps for an eventual change in custody as a result) and then had to explain to her Tahitian hosts an early return home when her daughter was unable to manage her homesickness.

Heather Young Leslie presents a case of husband and wife ethnographers with a toddler child in the field socialized to the local culture to an extent that threatened her sense of motherhood. Both spouses were engaged in doctoral dissertation fieldwork and took their eighteen-month old daughter with them to Tonga. Young Leslie entered the field committed to cultural relativism, and that commitment and belief in cultural relativism formed part of the basis for her concept of mothering. When her daughter became Tongan, however, and the role of "anthropologist" conflicted with that of "mother," Young Leslie was led to reexamine the concept of cultural relativism. She attempts a partial deconstruction of relativism as a concept and as a practice.

Barbara Burns McGrath presents a contrasting and much less angst-ridden Tongan case that enhanced rather than threatened the sense of family. McGrath's hidden agenda for her research in Tonga with her nonethnographer husband and three children—to have a positive experience as a family—was achieved. The presence of her family aided her research, especially her perspective on the emotional tone of Tongan life. She challenges the long-held but unspoken assumption that being accompanied jeopardizes the process of becoming an accurate observer of culture. In fact, since family members are not bound to be cultural relativists, their reactions push the ethnographer to decrease the distance between observer and observed.

Jocelyn Linnekin, Glenn Petersen and Victoria Garcia, Karen Sinclair, and I examine fieldwork over a number of years and in a variety of family configurations, accompanied and unaccompanied, with and without children. Linnekin compares the normative scenario of unaccompanied fieldwork in Hawai'i with fieldwork in Western Samoa accompanied by two children and visited by a sister. She points out that the presence of children makes it difficult if not impossible for the ethnographer to manage the impressions that others receive. Fieldwork with families, because it forces more honesty, points to a different research paradigm and challenges the inevitability and necessity of the ethnographer's impression management. The ethnographer's need to manage impressions may be culturally specific to Western fieldworkers, most of whom are socialized in the paradigm of the discrete, bounded individual.

The Petersen/Garcia article is a multivocal account by an ethnographer, his wife, and daughter that compares field experiences in Pohnpei over about twenty years. Glenn, the ethnographer, contrasts his lone fieldwork, characterized by a valued freedom of mobility but an unhealthy loss of sense of self, with accompanied fieldwork, characterized by a richer sense of self but less control over the research process. Even though Victoria, Glenn's wife, at first had to grapple with a sense of humiliation in not knowing the rules of everyday life, she gained access to information that is less available when actively pursuing research. On a subsequent trip, she felt less need to behave as a Pohnpeian, which resulted in experiences enriched by a genuine sharing of two different behavioral systems. She had a stronger sense of self, assisted by the presence of her daughter, who adds her own comments to the chapter. Victoria's experiences with Pohnpeian families led her to re-create aspects of its communality in her neighborhood back home.

My article compares fieldwork alone, with a nonethnographer husband, with a child, and with both husband and child in three related Micronesian sites. The sense of self and identity was most stressed during the lone fieldwork. Connections with Micronesian families in each site affected relationships in subsequent sites and helped establish the ethnographer's social identity. The differences between my family background (educated, middle class) and my husband's (working class) shaped our differing attitudes toward and relationships with our Micronesian families.

Karen Sinclair began fieldwork among the indigenous Maori in New Zealand alone but soon married a white New Zealander and has returned several times with their daughter, Emily. Since Emily's loyalty in New Zealand is to the Maori, she is appalled by the racism and intolerance of her father's family. It has also been painful for her to recognize the differences between her own privileged life and the relative poverty of the Maori population Sinclair has studied. Reacting to her daughter's emotions has forced Sinclair to reexamine her own work, especially her neglect of class issues.

The next four chapters analyze cases of acquiring and being incorporated into families in the field, and the ethnographers examine the extent to which local people interpret and negotiate the positions of fieldworkers. Tamar Gordon arrived in Tonga single but left married to a Tongan man, with Tongan relatives and a new social identity; she therefore had to bridge two different models of intimacy and family relations. She uses the concept of "border-crossing" to challenge the traditionally conceived role of an anthropologist in which there is no blurring or merging of the self without endangering the authority of the anthropological discourse.

David and Dorothy Counts, with separate research projects, have spent five periods of fieldwork in Papua New Guinea since 1966 together as a married couple and with some or all of their four children. Since unconnected people are anomalous in Kaliai society where they have worked, they were given relatives. The Counts also helped their hosts attribute kin status to a graduate student, Bil Thurston, making him a classificatory brother of Dorothy's, to facilitate field relationships. The Counts underestimated the extent to which the local people considered these relationships to be real and serious, however. When their daughter was honored with gifts marking her status as a firstborn, David was obligated to reciprocate with gifts of shell money and a pig to the oldest of Dorothy's brothers—Bil Thurston. They all became real participants, not just observers; David certainly felt the responsibility and worry about appropriate reciprocation, which he had previously understood only intellectually.

The kin-ordered society in Papua New Guinea with which Bil Thurston worked incorporated unattached people within that framework. It was determined through behavior and other cues how such a stranger fit into the kin network. Thurston acquired a local family, and some people even believed he was a woman's dead husband. He was also the brother-in-law of his field supervisor, David Counts, and a matrilateral cousin of a fellow student in the field. When he later returned to the field with a partner, however, he noticed that instead of incorporating yet another fieldworker into a kinship scheme, local people, because of cultural change in the area, were using a modern urban (wantok) scheme to explain their relationships.

Larry Carucci analyzes shifts in his incorporation into a Marshallese kinship system over several periods of fieldwork. The local people ideally hoped to incorporate him as a son-in-law but settled for adoption, a less effective strategy for manipulating the metaphor of family unity for controlling foreigners and gaining access to their potentials for power. When his future (American) wife joined him on a later trip, local people interpreted them as married. Carucci and his companion experienced conflicts, however, between an egalitarian personal relationship and an unequal work relationship as project director and assistant, a situation exacerbated by Carucci's greater knowledge of the local language and culture.

Notes

1. All of the contributors and editors participated in the symposium with the exception of Anne Marie Tietjen (who attended the previous year's session). This group acted in effect as a focus group, with ideas emerging through an interactive process. It was therefore not appropriate in most cases to attribute particular ideas to specific individuals.

2. This is not intended to deny the existence of cultural variation among

Canadian and U.S. families. In fact, at least two of the contributors explicitly discuss some class and ethnic differences. Nonetheless, all the contributors are of European heritage and recognized a commonality in the notion of family, especially the role of a mother.

3. Collections edited by Carroll (1970) and Brady (1976) provide a number of examples and analyses.

4. It is also clear from Goodenough's chapter that a volume such as this one would have enabled them to consider a variety of options, including one that allowed their daughter to spend some time with them in the field.

5. The Goodenoughs provide a counterexample; because of Ward's prior experience, he felt it inappropriate for their nineteen-year-old daughter to accompany them because of potential problems for a young woman of her age, especially given local courting customs.

1   Fieldwork and a Family
Perspectives over Time

RUTH GALLAGHER GOODENOUGH

For a variety of personal reasons I have found it difficult to write this account, and rather predictably its form reflects the false starts and the shifting focus of the effort. Emotions that were buried in the experience continue to pervade this particular piece of family history, along with issues of privacy and confidentiality. I found that to get started I had to limit the piece to something emotionally neutral, and so I took as my initial focus the subject of the schooling we provided our two sons who accompanied us to the field.

Once underway, the narrowed approach I had settled for took on a life of its own as the physical memories of our year in the field flooded in. I found myself savoring them as I wrote them down, even as I encapsulated them away from the larger frame that I was avoiding—the one that included all six members of our family. When I had finally written this least troublesome segment, I gave one more try at including the experiences and reactions of our two daughters, who had not accompanied us, but only after consulting at some length with them both. The larger frame was put in place around the somewhat extravagantly detailed central piece, and the result is the effort that follows. What emerged makes little pretense at being of ethnographic interest. Rather, it is an experiment of sorts in writing family history (and in dealing with the conflicts and guilts of parenthood) whose occasion happened to be an anthropological field trip. Perhaps, as one of my daughters said, it can be helpful to other families anticipating or managing the consequences of such a trip.

In the context of recent literature on the personal aspects of fieldwork, most of it by other women participants (e.g., Bell, Caplan, and Karim 1993; Golde 1986; Okely and Callaway 1992), this account is one of the few by an accompanying professionally trained but nonanthropologist wife/mother. It is also different in its incorporation of material and insights from all members of the family in question. (See Petersen, Garcia, and Petersen, chapter 6, for another such contribution to this volume.) The present account thus can also help advance the new literature's multivocality.

Planning the Trip: Division of the Family

When an anthropologist and his or her family go into the field for a year or more, one of the major concerns of the parents is for the well-being of their children. Fieldwork entails enormous changes that offer adventure as well as potential hardship. However lightheartedly we may undertake to deal with the insecurities of the unknown for ourselves, we take our children into it to some extent with our hearts in our mouths. For us personally the fieldwork in question meant dividing our family, with the older children staying behind and the younger ones going along—in a sense doubling the unknowns and adding separation from loved ones to the mix.

The events surrounding this fieldwork happened more than a quarter of a century ago—far enough in the past for memory to lack the sharpness of recall that more recent events enjoy, but with the advantages and corrective vision of long-term hindsight. Looked at from a perspective that includes the inputs of our now adult children, my husband, Ward Goodenough, and I see at times pain and difficulties that we did not foresee or even fully appreciate at the time, and it is enough to make us wince and to wonder at our blindness. From this same perspective we also became aware of hard-won gains or elements of growth that we had neither anticipated nor previously marked. In any event, things went as they did; perhaps this retrospective view is, among other things, a way of coming to terms with them.

In late 1963 when we began to plan for a year of fieldwork in Micronesia, we were a middle-class, white, American family with four children: two college-age daughters, a son in the sixth grade, and another not yet in kindergarten. Our girls were both at Cornell University, in Ithaca, New York, Hester in her junior year and Deborah a freshman. Oliver, at age eleven, was in his last year at a small progressive school where his brother Garrick was also enrolled as a four-year-old in the nursery program. Although I had no training or experiences as an elementary school teacher, I was working that year as a teacher's assistant in the first grade of the boys' school to help defray tuition costs.

For Ward, the projected trip would be a return after seventeen years to the small island of Romonum in what was then known as Truk (now Chuuk) Lagoon. As a Yale graduate student in 1947, just after World War II, he had been one of a group of four anthropologists and one linguist who conducted a seven-month field study in Truk as part of a U.S. Navy-sponsored project on the languages and cultures of the islands of Micronesia, then newly under

U.S. protection (W. Goodenough 1951). When the opportunity arose for a follow-up investigation in 1964, Ward's intention was to explore aspects of status and role and to work on an expanded Trukese dictionary. This time, however, he would be accompanied by family members, and he began early on to make the necessary arrangements for our stay.

When we talked with the children about the proposed trip, we assumed that our daughters would choose to continue at Cornell for their respective senior and sophomore years and that only the two boys would accompany us to the field. We were somewhat surprised to get objections to these prospective arrangements from two quarters. Debbie, not yet as thoroughly committed to college life as we had thought, and remembering the hardships of separation that we had all known from her father's previous field trips, said she would rather go along with us. Garrick, newly turned five, thought he would rather stay with Bibbsy, a favorite teacher in his nursery school. Since we would be leaving in June 1964 after school was out, Garrick was easily won over, particularly with accounts of the kind of adventures he might find on a Pacific island. Debbie's expressed preference posed more serious considerations.

From his previous experience on Romonum, Ward was dubious about the wisdom of her proposal. He felt that nineteen would be a particularly awkward age for an unmarried girl to appear on the island scene for a year's stay. For one thing, separated from American friends and classmates, she would be thrown back heavily upon parents and younger brothers for company—not her first choice of companions under ordinary circumstances, even at home. At a time when she was working hard to establish her independence as a young adult, the confined living conditions in the field would be a hermetic throwback to childhood. Moreover, language and culture barriers would complicate relationships with islanders in general, but with those in her own age group there would be the additional uncertainties and hazards of the local mating game. On Romonum, as in other societies, this game was a lively concern of late teens and young adults, and it was played with rules that were at considerable variance with prevailing Euro-American ways. Seeing much of this as a potential minefield, Ward argued with Debbie that her age raised the possibility of serious difficulties, not only for her but for the field project itself, and he urged her to continue on at college with her present friends and her older sister.

There was time yet to think it over and indeed an attractive alternative prospect for the summer months emerged: an opportunity for Debbie to work on a student-assisted archaeological excavation in England, being run by a family friend. Debbie responded with enthusiasm to the prospect of spending the summer in England and agreed to return to college in the fall. She was still not without some lingering (and, as it proved, realistic) misgivings about the eleven-month separation from family and was clearly not persuaded as to the seriousness of the difficulties her father foresaw. Hester, two years older and on the threshold of becoming engaged to a fellow Cornell student, had little problem with our projected arrangements. She went ahead on her own to set up a summer trip to Europe with an old friend, later to meet up with the friend's parents for a tour of England and Ireland.

We planned that the girls would return to college after their summer adventures and arranged for them to spend Christmas and spring holidays with their paternal grandmother in Massachusetts. The summer trips went very well for both of them. At the end of her archaeological stint Debbie went on a carefree jaunt of her own to Scotland, before returning to the United States to begin the new college year. Hester, whose major was in medieval history, found her travels in Italy and the British Isles to be of rewarding interest.

Providing for what we saw as the educational needs of the remaining two proved to be less complicated. We made no preparation for formal schooling for Garrick beyond packing a lot of books to read aloud to him. For Oliver, the counselor at his school simply gave us the seventh grade texts and workbooks they expected him to cover. We took reading books of his choice along, as well as a number of "good" books for ourselves. Thus equipped, we would soon be off to a place where whatever formal education these two young ones received would be in our hands. What we had no inkling of was how much informal education of all kinds was in store for both sets of children.

Family in the Field: Entry

Our trip to Truk included stopovers of several days in the state of Hawai'i and Guam. These stays put to rest any qualms the boys might have felt over leaving home. In both locations we availed ourselves of a car and toured the beaches and other tourist attractions. The crowning experience for both boys, however, was flying from Guam to Truk in the small amphibious plane that made the trip once a week. We were unprepared for the excitement of our first water landing in Pohnpei and, when airborne again, to see from the sky the great Truk Lagoon with its beautiful coral reef encircling the inner islands.

When we deplaned, it was on the flight strip of Moen, the administrative headquarters island of Truk. We stayed there for a week or more, waiting for our house on Romonum to be finished. We spent the time getting acquainted with both Trukese and American officials on Moen and equipping ourselves for the field. We found the Truk Trading Company reassuringly supplied with the things we would need, and we set to work with lists and checkbook. Fortunately the aluminum skiff and other things we had ordered from the United States had arrived, and on Sunday of that first week we made the eleven-mile trip by outboard motor to Romonum for our first visit.

The chief of Romonum's Chorong District, Boutau, knew of our coming, since it was on his land that the house was being built. We had made an agreement with Boutau to pay for its construction as our rent for the year. When we left, it would revert to him and his family, an arrangement that guaranteed a prime location and good workmanship. It was to be a not-quite traditional Trukese *wuut*: a large, enclosed living area with an adjoining roofed-over porch. Its supporting posts were of coconut logs, and it was thatched overall with fresh green ivory-nut palm fronds. On an islet only a mile long and a half mile wide, almost any location would be acceptable, but we were delighted both with the nearly finished house and its location, only twenty-five yards inland from the sea and the loveliest small beach imaginable.

Men were putting the last bundles of palm thatch on the roof as we watched that Sunday afternoon, and the boys were fascinated to see how each bundle was tied to the frame with the same stout coconut fiber twine that tied the large beams together. As we walked around it, admiring the work, Ward greeted people he had known so many years before and introduced us to them.

The boys were particularly pleased to learn that Boutau had three sons, the youngest, Mesian, only a few months older than Garrick and the two older ones, Pisentius and Serafin, roughly Oliver's age. Since they were living just down the path from us, it was clear we would be seeing much more of them and of their first cousins who lived upland in the interior. We had known that Boutau spoke some English, but it was a welcome surprise (particularly for me) to learn that his wife, Alexia, had studied English at the Catholic Mission Intermediate School on Moen and spoke it well. When we piled into the boat for the return trip to Moen, we felt that luck had smiled on us generously, and we looked forward with impatience to getting back to Romonum and settling in.

Aside from our own skiff, communication with the main island would depend on the biweekly round-trips of the *Koang*, the small interisland boat that circled the western islands of the lagoon picking up passengers and copra as it went. It was this boat (whose home port was Romonum) that brought the bulk of our supplies over in the next few days. Included were the small, kerosene-burning stove and refrigerator we had bought on Moen, as well as the foam mattresses and other bedding supplies we had shipped out from the United States. Knowing that these essentials were in place, we wasted no time getting our own boat over and ourselves moved in.

Family in the Field: At Home on Romonum

Except when we used it as a place to prepare and eat meals, the house worked well. The sand floor was a nuisance, however, and the kerosene refrigerator and stove raised the fear of fire in our minds. After a week or two Ward talked the problems over with Boutau and learned that our cooking in the house was of some concern to our neighbors, too. Cooking in Romonum was done on outdoor fires, usually tended by the men. Everyone knew how flammable thatch was, and our neighbors were understandably uneasy about the possibility of a fire in the house. The solution Ward and Boutau agreed upon accommodated all our concerns. They would bring the workers back to build a smaller, screened cookhouse, ten yards or so from the main house and equipped with built-in table and benches.

The cookhouse turned out to be a great success. It was screened above the thatching from waist-height up, putting us in visual touch with the outside world. More important, it provided air and light while keeping mosquitoes and the pestiferous little "no-seeums" out. We could see that it would be the solution to the schoolroom problem, too, because it gave us a well-lit worktable away from the usual bustle of visitors and activities under the porch roof. One further and final structural improvement to the main house, after a concrete floor was put under the living area, was to build in a palm-mat interior partition for half the length of the house. This afforded a welcome measure of privacy among ourselves. With these changes completed we settled comfortably into what would become the routines of our lives.

Family in the Field: Getting Down to Work

Within a few weeks, Ward, using one of the two sleeping areas of the house as an office, was already well into his work with informants, although the rest of us were still on a vacation schedule for a while longer. Our chief task was learning our way around in the language, but it was the sea and the beach that drew us in the beginning to spend hours of every day in the water. In this we were often alone. Curiously, the other children on the island rarely swam, and adults only went into the water when they had to for some practical reason: the women to gather shellfish and the men to recover or control a boat while fishing. (Indeed, in September, when I developed a persistent high fever and had to be hospitalized on Moen, our Trukese neighbors attributed it to "water spirits" and blamed it on our swimming too much.) As a woman I followed their native custom of going into the water fully dressed and learned to maneuver despite the billowing of my Hawaiian-style full skirts around me in the water.

Our younger son, Garrick, did not know how to swim when we arrived and was cautious about going in the water by himself. When he put on a snorkeling mask, though, he became a daredevil. Discovering the magic of the underwater world, he began pursuing small fish with his head under water, and it no longer seemed to matter where his feet were. When we pointed out that he was actually swimming, he was surprised. He tested himself without the mask and, sure enough, he *did* know how to swim! One day, well along in our stay, a large boat full of visitors from Moen came out and anchored some fifty yards off shore. With this unusual event going on, I went to find my five-year-old and was alarmed to see him, in the company of two young girls, swimming bravely out to the distant boat. When they returned to where I waited rather anxiously on the shore, he reported matter-of-factly that this was the second time he and his teenage companions had made the round-trip. It was clear that I need no longer worry overmuch about his safety in the water.

Garrick and Boutau's son Mesian spent their days wandering and playing about the island, never far from the watchful eye of some adult who might be on the paths or in the trees cutting coconuts or breadfruit. Usually the boys were within calling distance of the house. Their only responsibility, aside from keeping out of mischief, was running errands. When fishermen took our boat out to the reef, as they did once or twice a week, the little boys would be put to work distributing the catch on their return. Between them they would carry fish up the hill to various relatives who lived in the interior of the island. If it was a large fish, they carried it strung from a pole between them; smaller ones they carried, Trukese style, with thumb and finger through the eye sockets. More often than not the fish tails dragged along in the sand of the paths as the boys dawdled on their way, but whatever the state of the gift on arrival, the elder relatives up the hill would thank them appreciatively for their effort.

When the local school started in September, Garrick and Mesian would often follow the older children into the one-room schoolhouse where the male teacher, Masaichi, would include them as visiting scholars for as long as their interest lasted. Where the Trukese children might be asked to recite in English, Masaichi would ask Garrick to answer in Trukese, and he soon learned to count and to understand simple requests. When he was alone with me, we would occasionally practice writing numerals and letters of the alphabet in the sand with pointed sticks. This, along with the many books we read aloud to him, was as near as we came to matching American kindergarten expectations.

Garrick was treated with gentle regard by most of the adults on the island, but his special friend was Pio, the father of the "cousins" up the hill and the official boatman for our sixteen-foot skiff. Early on, when we made the weekly run to Moen for the mail and supplies, Garrick's favorite perch was on the pilot's seat in the stern with Pio. Oliver chose the bow and would sit astride it, facing forward and often with his feet in the water. While Garrick would at times nap on the trip with his head on Pio's lap, Oliver would pass the time singing into the wind, running through his repertoire of Trukese and English language songs.

As we settled into the routines of the weekly trip, we found that only one of us needed to go with Pio to do the errands, and Oliver, whose proficiency in the language was becoming apparent, usually took on the job. Running this lengthy errand with Pio gave Oliver more responsibility and autonomy than a boy his age might have encountered back home. Pio drove the boat, but Oliver acted as surrogate for his parents in decisions that had to be made. These were ordinarily routine, but one memorable trip back to Romonum confronted him with a new and troubling situation. Two of Pio's inebriated friends had requested a lift to their home island of Udot, some two miles out of the way. Oliver agreed, but only on condition that they discontinue their drinking on the boat. However, soon after they were under way the two passengers began to pass the bottle of whiskey around again in spite of Pio's and Oliver's reminders of their agreement. With things getting somewhat out of hand and Udot still a good way off, Oliver spied the *Koang* on its biweekly rounds and told Pio to head for it. Hailing Puruta, the master of the *Koang*, Oliver explained that his father did not allow drinking on our boat and asked if the rowdy passengers could be transferred to the *Koang*. Puruta agreed and the men climbed unsteadily and somewhat sheepishly aboard the larger vessel, leaving Pio and Oliver to enjoy a subdued but peaceful return trip to Romonum alone.

Formal Schooling

With our curriculum set by the schoolbooks we had brought, Oliver and I decided to get down to work soon after our combination cookhouse cum schoolroom was finished. It was still midsummer by our calendar, but by starting early we could build in the flexibility of time we might need or want later on. We agreed to work five mornings a week with Sundays off and Wednesdays available for the trip to Moen. For Oliver the afternoons would be free for play or swimming or reading; I would use them to work on my own project, which was to gather information on the practice of adoption on the island, using Alexia as my principal informant (R. Goodenough 1970). It soon became a settled and comfortable routine, and we began to make good progress in our three-hour school days.

We concentrated on the three R's, trusting our environment to provide other inputs as we went along. Although congenitally a bad speller, Oliver was otherwise an excellent student. The math materials we had were what was then known as "New Math," and the text materials were the provisional ones the school was still testing. With these I was at times as much a learner as he, and perhaps even more so. At one juncture I rejected his answer in the book. His quiet reply, "Well then, Mom, the book is wrong," struck me as preposterous: math books were never wrong. When it became obvious that my student was indeed correct, our relationship as teacher/learner underwent a subtle shift. From then on I was inclined to accept his understanding when the book was unclear or where there was a question of typographical error.

Reading took care of itself. For keeping up with the world we had *Newsweek* magazine—which Oliver often got to read first on his way back from the weekly trip to Moen. As time went on, we supplemented the books from our original store with others sent by friends back home or borrowed from fellow Americans on Moen. Oliver had plenty of time for reading and obviously enjoyed it.

With Ward, we formed the habit of reading aloud together after Garrick had gone to sleep, and we parents made no effort to scale the level down. I remember two books in particular that we all enjoyed, William H. McNeill's (1963) comprehensive history entitled *The Rise of the West* and an entertaining one called *The Pooh Perplex,* by Frederick C. Crews (1965), both sent by a colleague at the University of Pennsylvania. These would not have appeared on any seventh grade reading list, but they and others made for much family enjoyment by the harsh white light of the Coleman lantern. We would read until bedtime or until the burning mosquito coil at our feet gave out—a signal that it was time to retreat to our respective beds and the sanctuary of their mosquito nets.

Sometimes the dark tropical evenings would be taken up by visits from our Trukese friends. Boutau and Alexia and their boys might come over to play checkers or one of the other board games we had brought along. Boutau was a checkers man but Alexia's favorite was the French game about automobile racing called *Mille Bournes.* She became an engaging demon when she played, with no quarter asked or given. Her quick mind dealt effortlessly with the French terms and the alien setting of the game. She played with the utmost good humor and often won, taking time along the way to make bilingual puns across the two foreign languages of the game.

Occasionally a larger group might show up on our porch of an evening. Some would peel off to play cards or checkers; most of us would just talk or sing Trukese or American songs. If a good storyteller was in the group, we would be treated to an evening of Trukese folktales. Both of our sons took part in these gatherings and clearly enjoyed and learned from them, although Garrick might not last the evening if the company stayed too long.

An unanticipated educational resource was the visitors with professional agendas who came our way. Some of these, like the U.S. Army mapmaker who appeared for a day, seemed to come out of the blue, but others came with introductions from friends or colleagues and stayed longer. Whether their concern was mapmaking, anthropology, botany, or simple curiosity (like that of E. J. Kahn of *New Yorker* magazine, who showed up the day before Christmas with our Christmas mail), they made their rounds of the island with Oliver as one of their guides. Taking off from school for the day, he helped carry plant specimens for our botanist friend, Ben Stone, or toted the surveying tools of the mapmaker, and in the process learned more about the world's work than if he had stayed with his lessons.

Perhaps the high point from Oliver's perspective was afforded by Capt. Dewey Huffer, master of the *Militobi,* the station ship that made the rounds of the Trukese outer islands and that lay many miles beyond the lagoon. At Captain Huffer's invitation in January 1965, Oliver went with the ship on one of its shorter rounds, living with the Trukese crew and exploring each of the small islands they visited. He came back after a week with rolls of film to chronicle his adventures and a heightened feeling of independence. We knew that he had grown a notch when, in the returning bustle on the pier, he greeted us with a handshake rather than the hug we had looked for.

Family Left at Home: Problems Unforeseen

Through all of these months we and our daughters continued to correspond by weekly letters, but given the delay between writing and getting a response, real dialogue was difficult, if not impossible. At best we simply described how things were going in our respective halves of the world and sent our love. The accounts, it turned out, were edited on both sides to spare worry and anxiety. This was not by any predetermined design, but simply in recognition that there was nothing to be gained by heartlessly raking the other through troubling events that would be old, and perhaps inconsequential, by the time they were read about. We did learn through the letters that first Debbie and then Hester had to have dental surgery for impacted wisdom teeth, a painful business that put each in the infirmary for the better part of a week. But we did not appreciate then the actual extent of their suffering nor the sense of isolation each endured through the experience.

For Debbie, moreover, her sophomore year of college also presented several very painful emotional crises that were seriously exacerbated by the physical absence of her parents and the difficulties of communication over so great a distance. She was haunted by a sense of being orphaned and without a home (our family house had been rented for the year). The two sisters supported each other where they could, but there was no doubt that this was a year made more difficult by family separation for each of them—critically so for Debbie.

Toward the middle of the school year the Cornell University student health staff recommended psychological counseling for Debbie, and we made the arrangements for it by mail. With this help she was able to weather the immediate crises and carry on with her scholastic work, but the aftereffects of the experience were such as to require fairly prolonged psychiatric counseling later in her life. At the time, we followed along as best we could with the weekly letters, but the comfort they might bring was always late.

Hindsight tells us that we certainly should have given her expressed preference to accompany us more weight, but whether coming to the field with us would have been less difficult, or even if we should have undertaken the trip at that time at all, are still problematic might-have-beens for each of us. One possibility that we did not think of until reading some of the other accounts in this volume (e.g., Flinn, Sinclair) was that of having her accompany us for the summer months and then return to Cornell for the college year. Such an arrangement, although precluding her trip to England, would have alleviated some of the all-or-nothing aspects of the separation without ensnaring her in the difficulties we had envisaged from a longer stay.

In March 1965 we were sharply reminded that one's "other" life does not stand still during fieldwork. Ward was called back to Boston to attend the deathbed and the final services for his father. On his way back to Truk after these sad events, he made a stopover of a few days in Ithaca to visit with our girls. This allowed him to form his own judgment as to their well-being. From his talks with them he felt that, at least at that point, things were going along fairly well with each one. With less than two months to go before our scheduled return, they, as well as we, could begin to plan for our family's reunion.

This stopover was also an opportunity to help with some of the planning for Hester's wedding, which was to take place in mid-June, shortly after our return. Hester appeared to have everything well thought through, even down to designing and making her own wedding dress, but there were a few things to be done that only a parent could do. Ward made the necessary arrangements for the reception that would follow the ceremony and gave Hester access to the money she would need for things like invitations and announcements. When he left Ithaca to come back to Micronesia, he felt that things were fairly well in hand with both our daughters.

For the several weeks that Ward was back with our family at home, the boys and I stayed on Moen in one of the small apartments maintained by the U.S. government to house visitors. This brought us back into an English-speaking community with greater access to communication and medical resources. When Ward returned, bringing word of all our family members, we were delighted to have him back and more than ready to return to our friends on Romonum for the remaining uneventful weeks of our stay.

Recollections of the Whole Family

Before writing this account, I consulted, as I have said, with our four children, now grown and themselves parents. I am grateful to them for being forthright with me about relevant experiences that we had never discussed at length before. Their inputs are included in the narrative above, but their overall summation of that time in their lives follows.

The youngest, Garrick, looks back on it positively as a time in his early years that offered new and interesting experiences, but because he was so young at the time, much of it is lost to memory. Surprisingly, one of his unforgettable memories is that of being deliberately deceived by an adult—a new experience for him. He remembers clearly an episode in which his friend Mesian had gotten into mischief and was hiding from his father. Boutau cornered Garrick and cajoled him into telling where Mesian was, after reassuring him that he wouldn't punish his son. Boutau then went to the hiding place, pulled Mesian out, and beat him soundly. This was all quite within the acceptable bounds of Trukese behavior, but Garrick was utterly dismayed. Against our values, it was a shocking discovery that an adult would deliberately lie to a child and use his son's friend as an informer.

Oliver's memories are almost all positive. He points out that his age at the time was ideal for the enjoyment of new experiences, particularly the new and challenging adventures that he found in the islands. He had left elementary school and had not yet entered middle school; thus the year in the field was not taking him away from an ongoing peer group, nor, at ages eleven and twelve, had he yet moved into puberty with its hormonal and social stresses. He enjoyed the warm and close family atmosphere that we found easy to sustain in that simpler world without television and other distractions. He speaks of his at-home schooling in positive terms, and it was certainly clear in subsequent years that it had been no academic handicap to have spent the year the way he had.

Interestingly, he maintains that he had far more contact with the world of adults both on Romonum and on Moen than he would have had at home and that he found it both challenging and affirming. He recalls hiking up the mountain on Tol Island with his father and Peter Hill, the director of education—a hard but rewarding climb, for Pete was a great naturalist. He recalls the company of adults at the hotel dining room and bar on Moen, including his friend Captain Huffer of the *Militobi*. He remembers the Catholic priest, Father Hoek, who sometimes stayed with us when he made his pastoral rounds from one island to another. And he of course remembers the various people who came to do their work on the islands and whom he accompanied as guide and junior assistant. To hear him tell of it is to know that it was a very special place to be at that time of his life.

The input from our older two children has a more somber cast. Separation from their parents and younger siblings left them feeling very much on their own. This was bearable when things were going well: both girls speak of their growing sense of maturity in managing their own travels abroad, for instance. Moreover, both of them came through the academic year successfully. But their isolation from emotional support became a serious problem when the months dragged on and they encountered more traumatic events. As we have seen, this was particularly true of Debbie, the younger and thus more vulnerable one. As much as they tried to take care of one another, each has memories of times when she did not manage to rise adequately to the other's need.

Separation from loved ones is hard when need is high, and the separation that often used to accompany anthropological fieldwork (and occasionally still does) frequently carries a heavy freight of pain and loneliness. As a family we had on five earlier occasions undergone months-long absences when Ward was away. The first two were army assignments, and on the second of these Debbie was born: she was six months old when she and her father first met. The three anthropological field trips that followed in the next ten years made no more provision for family to accompany the husband/father fieldworker than did the army.

We managed to weather those three cumulative years of family separation and made our adjustments, the one as absent father and the rest as a single-parent family, but there is no pretending they were easy. More than once we found ourselves resorting to psychological counseling for insight and support, and at the end of the last field trip, one that had taken him to New Guinea for seven months, Ward and I vowed heartily not to submit ourselves to another.

Balancing the Alternatives

In writing this account, I have had to confront the knowledge that however clear we were on the effect of long separations on ourselves as a couple, we did not sufficiently understand the cumulative effect of family separations on our older children. The story of our 1964–1965 stay in the field and our retrospective judgments on it reveal that Debbie was better clued into the possible psychological hazards of that trip for herself than either of the adults, her parents, had been.

As for us parents on our first field trip together with family, we found it to be an indescribable improvement over the alternative, where each of us would be toughing it out alone. Ward summarizes the difference succinctly from the point of view of his own feelings as well as for the effect on his research by saying, "Not being alone allowed me to be a whole human being. Of course it made the work go better," as Flinn and Glenn Petersen (chapters 7 and 6) also observe. My own essential work in the field was not ethnographic, but I could echo Ward's statement. I, too, was a more whole human being for being along on the enterprise rather than at home alone, holding the fort. The sometimes painful lesson of our experience has to be that family work goes better too, when family members are together.

Acknowledgments

Fieldwork in Truk in 1964–1965 was made possible by a grant from the National Science Foundation (NSF-GS-340).

2 Both Ways through the Looking Glass

The Accompanied Ethnographer as Repositioned Other

SHEILA SEILER GILMORE

During my four visits to Tahaa, one of the Leeward Society Islands of French Polynesia, my daughter, Elaine, accompanied me twice and visited me once. Most of the time, however, Elaine stayed in the United States and I worked alone, without another member of my culture. Thus I have had some opportunity to compare the experience of fieldwork in Polynesia from two different perspectives—accompanied and alone. One of the most striking differences is the degree to which we as fieldworkers are more likely to be forced to focus on our own status as a culturally different other in the community when we are accompanied. Much ink has been spilled lately concerning the other, but concise definitions of the term are lacking. I intend the term to signify an individual who is a cultural stranger. When we work alone in a community, we focus on understanding a group of others, whom we typically assume to be similar to one another in culturally significant ways, yet different from us as well. When we bring along a family member, on the other hand, our hosts have the opportunity to watch us interacting as members of our own cultures with members of our own cultures. We are often called upon directly, and sometimes feel the obligation without a specific request, to offer accounts of these interactions. This experience highlights our appreciation of ourselves as others in the host community.

Thus when accompanied, we are simultaneously looking both ways through the looking glass. We undertake to understand the culture of the people among whom we have chosen to live and to find ways to represent that culture accurately to members of our own culture. At the same time, however, we are called upon to explain our own interactions with our same-cultured companions in terms that are comprehensible to members of our host community. Usually such requests appear to be motivated by simple curiosity.

Occasionally, however, we may sense that an adequate explanation is vital to the creation or maintenance of good field relations.

I found myself dealing with a critical need to provide an adequate explanation when my daughter and I faced a major problem during her second visit to Tahaa. As we attempted to resolve the problem, I became aware of how carefully and consciously I was selecting aspects of the situation to highlight and others to downplay, or even to omit, as I attempted to explain to our concerned hosts what was happening. I realized that my selection was guided by my knowledge of the local Tahitian culture. This understanding led me to focus on my position as other in the community and to reflect in new ways on my own status and obligations as such.

Tahaa: The Setting

The community in which I conducted my research is the port town on one of the more rural of the Leeward Islands, or *Iles Sous Le Vent,* of the Society Archipelago of French Polynesia. In 1988 476 people were living in the community; the island as a whole was home to 4,005 people (Institut Territorial de la Statistique n.d.), the vast majority of whom identify themselves as *Maohi,* or native Tahitian. Fifty percent of the island's working population is engaged in agricultural or fishing enterprises (Institut Territorial de la Statistique 1983). The island has a number of small shops and two gas stations. A bank opened in 1991. A few families have television sets, and there is at least one video rental shop on the island. The island has no supermarket or movie theater, although rented films are occasionally screened in the warehouse at the dock or at the gymnasium in another town. The most popular form of entertainment is participating in or watching dance rehearsals for some upcoming festival. Telephone service was introduced in the early 1980s, but few homes are connected.

The island is not isolated, however. Cargo ships call at the port several times a week, carrying visiting relatives, the occasional tourist, and goods for the small shops. Launches to a nearby island leave nearly every day from the port, calling at small "backyard" docks along the way to pick up paying passengers with business or shopping plans.

I first visited alone in 1989, staying in the community approximately two weeks on a site-selection trip. When I returned in 1990, my daughter accompanied me for the first three weeks of my three-month stay so that she could have a short-term introduction to the community, and the community to her, before our anticipated long stay the following year. I also wanted an opportunity to assess her ability to adjust to life on Tahaa before bringing her back for a year. She claimed—and appeared—to enjoy this brief visit.

including changing definitions of "reason" and "culture." This skepticism typified thought at the turn of the last century.[4] Hatch's solution to the moral debates that confronted the early cultural relativists was to segment relativism into different types: methodological, ethical, and the relativism of knowledge.

Despite its philosophical plausibility, Hatch's solution has not been incorporated into anthropology's practice. Those same disputes that arose earlier in the century (Sapir 1924; see also Hatch 1983) when Benedict (1934), Boas (1901), Herskovits (1947), and others promoted a "moral theory of tolerance" (Hatch 1983, 68) continue today. They appear in formal spheres of communication (e.g., Skomal 1993; Kavapalu 1993; Gordon 1991; Scheper-Hughes 1987b) and in informal communiqués. Many issues of the *Anthropology Newsletter* and postings to the General Anthropology Bulletin Board (1993–1994) on the Internet seem to indicate a similar change in mood as we approach the turn of this century. In these forums, cultural relativism has generated considerable debate on the ethico-moral and methodological fronts. For example, Bartholemew's (1993) letter to the editor of the *Anthropology Newsletter* discusses the problem of instituting any particular moral code in the ethics guidelines for the American Anthropological Association, since such value systems tend to be culturally and subjectively constituted. The main difference between these recent debates and those at the turn of the last century is that female infibulation (the surgical excision and suturing of all or part of the female external genitalia) has updated Nazi Germany as the conundrum that sparks discussion of ethnocentrism and relativism.

Thus while Hatch recognized the untenability of a strict relativist stance and the temporal mood that allowed for the popularization of relativism, he did not account for the social, cultural, and political precursors that make relativism possible, and the similarity of those precursors to the basis of ethnocentrism. When it comes to being ethnocentric or being culturally relative, both require a degree of confidence, the kind of confidence inherent in relations of power or domination, such as being a member of a social majority. In other words, *being culturally relative or doing cultural relativism is relative in itself to the position of an individual in a society*. My point is echoed from a slightly different perspective by Hammel, who asks if "the utility of cultural relativism [is] established by its political convenience" (1994, 48).

Being culturally relative in Canada's multicultural society requires individual tolerance and reflection but also the politically secured confidence that one's own cultural practices and core symbols remain inviolate—challenged or criticized perhaps (Marcus and Fisher 1986), but never intimately, systematically threatened. When it comes to our professional relationships, we can always leave the field, quit the interview, or change topics of research if our own personal epistemologies are jeopardized. Furthermore, our concept of cultural relativism is usually applied to an "us" and "others" dyad, most frequently categorized as Anglo/Euro/Western/Judeo-Christian heritage groups and emigrant/indigenous/marginalized encapsulated groups; nothing I had read prior to fieldwork in Tonga ever prepared me for what would happen if another culture invaded and threatened one of my own core symbols such as the relation of mother and child. Yet this is, I suspect, something frequently experienced by immigrant parents, wherever they have emigrated.

The more Ceilidh behaved like a Tongan, the more frustrated, angry, guilty, amused, proud, and confused I felt. Many times, I did not like it. When she turned her eyes away from me and whispered, following normal polite requesting behavior for a Tongan, I tried to make her look at me and speak up. When she ran to some other woman and settled cozily into a large comfy lap, I felt betrayed. When she joked in Tongan with our neighbors, I was jealous. When she was naughty, especially by Tongan standards, I pleaded with my neighbors to admonish her, even punish her as they would their own children, not to give her preferential "favorite's" treatment. In vain did I try to explain the concept of spoiling a child, especially one I thought of as intelligent and mentally acute. They countered that I should not hit her or be angry with her. At almost three, Ceilidh was not yet *poto* 'capable'; she was *kei iiki* 'still little' and therefore not responsible for her actions nor ready to be controlled. No one else felt frustrated on these occasions when my daughter taunted me, *"Sio? Oku sai pe"* ("See? It's okay").

Anthropologist/Mother: Advantages and Disadvantages for Research

Certainly, true to all expectations, having a young child at the field site enabled people to accord me a meaningful social category of adult, good/virtuous mother, which was beneficial to my research. My daughter was probably a major factor in my achieving the level of fluency in spoken commoner's Tongan[5] that I did. However, it also meant that I had less flexibility of time, spontaneity of action, and control over impression management, as Linnekin also discusses (chapter 5). There was always Ceilidh to be concerned about, and this put me in several ambiguous positions. On the one hand, I had tried to encourage women to talk to me about and show me their mothering practices, fears, successes, and frustrations. I was consciously cautious not to tell them what I thought was right, for I learned quickly that most people would be too polite to contradict me, at least at first. On the other hand, I struggled to prevent those same women from teaching my own daughter things I thought would do her harm, like eating handfuls of sugar or playing hitting games. Thus some days my actions implied "your methods are valued," and on others I denied their value.

At the end of our first year in the village, Ceilidh spent so little time with us that she became almost as much informant as daughter. I cannot always separate in my mind things I learned from Keli and things I learned from other Tongan children. This raises the question of contamination of my research data, both by my own and my daughter's interactions in the village.

My Tongan culture teachers watched me just as carefully as I watched them. Just as I was concerned not to offend them and consciously controlled my behavior, so were they concerned about showing their best sides to my family and me. In Tonga it is embarrassing not to know an answer to a question, especially if the question comes from someone who should be treated as if higher in rank, as most foreigners are, at least at first. In those situations, it is acceptable to either make up an answer (Evans and Young Leslie 1993; Korn and Decktor Korn 1983) or give the answer you think the questioner wants to hear. Since most of the women I interviewed did not really understand why I would want to know about what they did with their children, my questions in the early months of our stay seemed nonsensical. Women would often try to find out what answer I wanted to hear to a question or watch what I did with my child, and then claim that as their own practice. This was a major problem early on in the research term that resolved itself as Ceilidh became Keli. It is one analytic dilemma I might not have had to consider if I had not had a young child with me.

The personal angst I put myself through, juggling my relationships with my daughter and my Tongan friends, was a waste of energy that marred aspects of the experience. For instance, I felt myself forced to adopt a more disciplinary role than I otherwise would have simply because in my (ethnocentric) estimation, Keli was not getting any structure anywhere else. Also, even while I empathized with their motives, I resented my friends' attempts to lure my daughter from me and the insecurity I felt when she seemed willing to stay in Tonga. Despite the insights that I have gained, I would have preferred not to have had that particular aspect of the experience.

As if to gainsay most of that emotional pain, within less than a year after our return to Canada, just before her fourth birthday, Ceilidh switched completely to English and, after a rocky initial period, now relates well with her grandparents, cousins, and peers. She appears to be a typical child. Most of her Tongan behavior faded with her memories of her first language, friends, and fictive kin.

As I write and revise this chapter in 1996, I can reflect and say that by the end of our eighteen months in the field, I had adopted Tongan beliefs about North American society and was due for disengagement. At the time, though, I felt myself trapped between my desires to conduct good research, my concern to do what was best for my daughter, my belief that I had the good sense to be the best mother possible, and my unquestioned acceptance of cultural relativism. My maternal good sense was threatening to convince me that I was not the best mother for my daughter, that for her own good, I should give her up and let her stay a Tongan. That it was even a possibility terrifies me still. I can empathize now with immigrant parents who try to keep their children from adopting the cultural practices of the new society.

As adults, we go to the field as researchers, consenting and armed with as much information as possible. With a young child, consent is rarely considered, and informed consent is impossible. How do you inform an eighteen-month-old toddler, who uses sentences of three words, about living in a different cultural milieu? How do you explain that it is temporary, when the time span is the same as that child's life? How do you explain "going home," when the only home known is the home in the field?

Consenting to enter into a new and different cultural milieu is not the only problem we create when we take a young child to the field. When I went to Tonga, I planned to behave as if I accepted certain local practices, even if I did not (see Goffman 1959; Linnekin, chapter 5). The young child does not know that "as if" is in force; those local behaviors are viewed, experienced, and cognitively processed as acceptable and endorsed. The young child receives those social markers of the host culture with no sense of alternatives, little reflexivity, no insight. For the very young child, the dominant culture is the only culture. When I took my daughter to the field, she did not realize it was "the field," and she knew nothing about cultural relativism. Ceilidh went to Tonga as an immigrant. She returned to Canada the same way.

Despite my assumption that other forms of practice and systems of organization and prioritization would be just as valid when we were living there, in the field, and despite my experience with living outside of my own society in the past, I never anticipated how being a *mother* would escalate my preference for my own culture and potentiate my distress at seeing my daughter behaving in ways which were strange, even alien. It gave me a renewed appreciation for the power of my own culture and one of our core symbols, the mother-child dyad. The experience led me to reconsider cultural relativism as an action, rather than just an ideology, to examine the similarities rather than differences between cultural relativism and ethnocentrism, and to recognize the precursors that make cultural relativism possible. I learned just how *relative* cultural relativity really is.

Acknowledgments

The research upon which this paper is based was funded by the International Development and Research Centre, and the Social Sciences and Humanities Research Council of Canada. I am indebted to the people of Kauvai, especially the village of the *Maka Fele'unga,* for their ongoing generosity. My thanks to

Sheila Seiler Gilmore, Elaine Szupello, Leslie Marshall, Barbara Burns McGrath, William and Channing Rodman, and Margaret Critchlow Rodman for their constructive comments, and to Jocelyn Armstrong and Juliana Flinn for their careful attention to detail.

Notes

1. Ha'apai is at the geographical center, but economic periphery, of the kingdom. It consists of parallel chains of coral atolls and occasional volcanic islands. The only town in Ha'apai is the administrative center, Pangai, on the island of Lifuka.

2. Personal names are pseudonyms.

3. I found myself wanting to wear the formal waist mats when singing in public, but also when delivering a paper at 'Atenisi Institute, even though as a foreign researcher I was not expected to follow Tongan custom.

4. I often wonder if cultural relativism would have made the same impact on North American society if Boas had stayed in Germany and done research among Siberian Aleuts or Japanese Ainu.

5. The Tongan language perpetuates and marks the social hierarchy. I learned to speak with commoners but never mastered the terminology appropriate for either nobles or the royals.

4 Through the Eyes of a Child
A Gaze More Pure?

BARBARA BURNS MCGRATH

Within the ranks of cultural anthropology, conducting ethnographic fieldwork is considered an initiation rite. One is not a member of the club until able to tell war stories with the best of them. A dominant image of the ideal ethnographer is a solitary male distant from all that is familiar, living for an extended period of time in conditions of physical discomfort. Obviously this is a simplistic and outdated picture, but one that endures nonetheless. The notion of a woman heading out alone fits in well enough, but a woman with a husband and offspring strains the image. Male ethnographers, of course, have been accompanied to the field by their spouses and children for years, but this fact is noted only in dedications, such as, "and thanks to my wife for her unending support, and to our children for their tolerance and good humor." There is no doubt that the presence of family greatly affected the project, but the details are left unstated. I offer possible reasons for these omissions along with stories from the field relating the impact of my family on my ethnographic research.

Ethnography as a research tool has its share of methodological pitfalls and ethical dilemmas, and these have been examined from a variety of perspectives (Clifford and Marcus 1986; Fabian 1983; Gordon 1988; Wolf 1992). Critique of the manner in which ethnography as a product is created and presented is ongoing. It is unlikely that the discussion over the complexities inherent in this manner of knowledge construction will ever be put to rest. As John and Joan Comaroff (1992) affirm, cultural anthropology is best distinguished by its method. We are what we do. As long as we continue to have confidence that ethnography is able to contribute to partial understanding of knowledge and practice of human experience, then we must recognize the need continuously to improve both the doing and writing up of ethnography.

Benefiting from the ongoing debate among scholars of the social sciences and the humanities, but also within the sciences, novice ethnographers such as myself are well equipped with directives to be reflexive and to attend to matters of authority, control, and subjectivity. However, this new theoretical orientation has not significantly influenced the commonly held beliefs within anthropology about the practice of fieldwork. The method and the way it is taught are unchanged. "Go out there, take in everything, and write down as much as you can remember," was the advice given to me. Other reported examples of preparatory instructions are to "take plenty of marmalade and cheap tennis shoes" (Jackson 1990, 29), "take a big stick for the dogs" (attributed to Kroeber, cited in Jackson 1990, 29), and "you'll need more tables than you think" (from Elenore Smith Bowen, cited in Clifford 1986, 1). One of the goals of this sink-or-swim research process is to "get into the culture." What is less often verbalized, but understood by all who have done fieldwork, is that the much-desired total immersion is possible only if it is accompanied by a degree of loss of identity. Racial, class, and economic inequality are a source of embarrassment for the anthropologist, and every attempt is made to diminish the difference, short of "going native." Being alone allows this process to occur more easily than if one is accompanied by friends and lovers. We all can relate to experiences of going somewhere new, where no one knows us. There is a tremendous sense of freedom. Children recognize this and often change their names and rewrite their personal histories to make themselves seem more interesting when they start a new school. It seems logical that having a spouse, and especially children, accompany one to the field jeopardizes the process of becoming an unattached, supposedly value-free observer of culture.

If assimilation into another culture is a necessary prerequisite for good ethnography (in itself an interesting question), then one must sacrifice aspects of the original culture (often referred to as baggage). Typically the first things to change are matters of personal identity. New kinship ties are formed, and a sense of belonging is established. The new home becomes "my village," and relationships such as adopted son or daughter, quasi-brother or sister, are welcomed as steps toward making the community "my people." In writing ethnography, these kinship terms are applied judiciously. A description of the researcher becoming incorporated into a kin relationship leads the reader to a comfortable acceptance that the written report is valid. In other words, being part of the group is evidence of having acquired an insider's understanding. This strategy for documenting reliability of data by conveying a sense of belonging is particularly critical in anthropology, where a qualitative research design is central. The standard measurement techniques for reliability, such as statistical tests, that are available in other types of research are not appropriate for data obtained from participant observation.

Returning to the ideal fieldworker, he is alone and quite free to take on any number of social roles within the community; he is a tabula rasa. The motivation to assume this position is the logical outcome of a number of unstated assumptions: (1) immersion is required for rigorous ethnographic research; (2) immersion is more easily attained with few personally identifying characteristics; and (3) results of research will be evaluated in part upon the reader's confidence in the writer's connectedness. These assumptions lead to the conclusion that anything that can be interpreted as a barrier to immersion is a negative force in the research endeavor. It is no wonder that the role accompanying family members play in ethnography is a well-kept secret.

The pressure on female researchers to conform to this model is even greater because of their need, given American culture, to prove themselves to be "objective" professionals. It is easy to see a double standard in operation. There is a sense that a man who takes his wife and children along will not be unduly distracted by their needs. His situation may not be ideal, but he will be able to focus on the question at hand. In contrast, there is an implicit contention that a woman who is with her family would never be able to put aside her role as wife or mother to allow for the clear thinking necessary for good research. Therefore, over the years women have followed the lead of their male colleagues and tended to downplay the impact of family on their research. Important exceptions to this are Crandon-Malamud (1991) in her report of research on social change in Bolivia and Dettwyler (1994) in an ethnography on life and death in West Africa.

One result of the new consciousness toward ethnographic practice is an appreciation for the context within which knowledge generation occurs. It is in this spirit of self-reflexivity that the part my family played in my own attempts at representing cultural beliefs of Tongans is presented.

Hidden Agendas

Fieldwork, however one defines it, is a continual shifting between the personal and the professional. As mentioned at the beginning of this chapter, it is a *rite de passage* for admittance into the academy. Writers also tell of the personal growth that results from time spent in the field (e.g., DeVita 1990; Sanjek 1990). The promise of an intense experience leading to greater self-knowledge is alluring, but these experiences rarely come without costs. An adult is able to choose to proceed, despite potential problems, but the children who go along for the ride are not in positions to make informed decisions. One of the many roles of American parents is to be an advocate for their children and act in their best interest. We believe parents should introduce their children to learning experiences and protect them from harm. The potential both for learning and for harm is probably higher in the field than at home. It is difficult to imagine a better education than one that includes an increased understanding of the differing lifestyles and ways of thinking that exist in the world. Countering this belief are the stories quietly shared among anthropologists about children who have died in the field. Parents do not take their children with them unaware of these potential benefits and risks. Part of the research agenda, then, becomes promoting a positive impact of the field experience on all members of the family.

My husband, Peter, and I did not formally prepare our children for fieldwork as much as they were witness to our discussions and the decisions made as to when and where to go. This talking phase began a year and a half before we eventually left Seattle for the Kingdom of Tonga. My initial plan had been to go to Australia, where Peter and I had lived ten years before. This possibility pleased everyone, particularly our son, Patrick, who was nine years old at the time, but also our daughters, Kate, six, and Allison, three. Their image of life in Australia was formed by Crocodile Dundee movies. As we started talking of Tonga, the enthusiasm cooled. No one had heard of it, and Polynesia did not seem a place where people actually lived; it did not seem real. We searched the library for books with photographs, but all we found were outdated travel guides recommending that travelers avoid the Tongan islands while on a holiday. According to the books, the lack of tourist amenities and general state of underdevelopment make it a poor choice. There were some facts the children could share with their friends: a king rules the country, there are beaches and coral reefs, and it is a poor place. We tried to explain in everyday language that Tonga is a developing country. We went on to discuss the political implications of the globe being divided into the "haves" and the "have nots." The children listened politely, but it is unlikely that much of what we said made sense to them; they had spent their entire lives enjoying the comforts of middle-class America.

The planning and packing soon took over and consumed all our energy. Patrick began a journal around this time. This is one of the earliest entries:

> *All last year we have been planning to go to Tonga. It seems that whenever I want a toy, the money has to be used on Tonga. Whenever people come over all they say is "How do you think you are going to like Tonga?" I hate it when people say that. And whatever my mom or dad says, I still don't want to go to Tonga. I don't want to go because I love Seattle and I think no one will speak English. And we will have a straw hut. The only thing I am anxious about is the plane ride. I love planes!*

The first four months of our time in Tonga were spent in a village on the main island about twelve kilometers from the capital. We lived on the outskirts of the village, an easy bicycle ride to the ocean, near the bush, and across from the village cemetery. It was a beautiful spot; however, the practice of avoiding cemeteries, especially at night, meant we did not have many visitors to our home. Later, as planned, we moved to one of the northern, more isolated islands, and this time lived in the center of the community. In retrospect, this worked out well. Our early days with more privacy allowed a gradual acclimation to the social scene. The intensity of our second home may have overwhelmed us had we faced it just off the plane. Adjustment to new daily routines was not a problem for the children at either site. It was like an extended camping trip, but one with lots of dogs and pigs around. One difficult hurdle that was different from camping in the Pacific Northwest, however, was the insects. This was a common subject in Kate and Allison's drawings, and a recurring theme in Patrick's journal. He often started with "These are the bug happenings of today" and then would chronicle his and his sisters' adventures with geckos, millipedes, spiders, and unnamed critters. Also included is a running count of bites and stings suffered.

All three children had many adventures, saw fantastic sights, made some friends, and came out of the experience knowing something of a way of life different from that in America. My husband's time away from his career in medicine allowed him to focus on other interests that had been left behind during years of training. There were also occasions when his medical background was helpful to others, including the time I developed a serious complication from dengue fever, and he had to juggle the roles of husband, father, and physician. Our hidden research agenda of a positive experience for us as a family had been achieved. Looking back, my own thoughts about research had always included the entire family. I was certainly aware of the professional standards regarding serious fieldwork, but anthropology is a second career for me, and I was not willing to make such a personal sacrifice based on a questionable assumption about only one way to conduct a rigorous study. I am now convinced that the presence of my family aided my research in very important ways.

Shared Knowledge

In terms of research goals, the positive or negative influence of family depends on many factors, not the least of which is the research topic itself. I was in Tonga to do research for my doctoral dissertation and planned to study the decision-making process regarding illness and dying. In Tonga, these decisions occur in the context of the family and the local community. Since I hoped to learn about common, everyday experiences that informed the decisions, the household was the setting for my study. Throughout Tonga, the way people get to know each other is with family talk, and that is how conversations with me always began. Rather than making note of the great differences that existed between us, the women talked of things we shared in common. We talked, for example, about the qualities of a good husband.

Before my family and I left Seattle, the most frequent reaction from friends to our plans had been astonishment that Peter would put his career on hold to help me achieve one of my goals. We could not understand why he was getting such respect for taking an eight-month holiday in the South Seas. People in Tonga, on the other hand, did not find this nearly so odd. His identity as a physician was subordinate to his personal characteristics, which included a good sense of humor, a talent for fixing things, and a commitment to being a loving father. These are qualities any woman would look for in a husband.

A favorite pastime of the women was to sit outside watching the children run around, talking about what was going on in their families or in the village. It is easy to see how a fieldworker's children are helpful in providing access or useful in establishing rapport. But more significantly, being part of a natural social group—not as an adopted daughter or an almost sister but as one mother among others—contributed to my field experience in ways I had not anticipated. There is something deeper available, closer to empathy, that emerges as a result of sharing similar roles.

One of my early acquaintances was Mele. She and her husband, Soane, have three young children, close in ages to our own. For several months Mele and Soane had been teaching me about traditional healing. We also had all gone on a number of family picnics together on one of the outer islands. We had become friends. One afternoon, after having one of those days where it seemed my children could not say anything to each other without causing a fight, I lost my temper and screamed at them, "Can't you just get along?" I had launched into a loud lecture on cooperation and sibling love when I noticed everyone looking over my shoulder at the kitchen door. I reeled around to see what was distracting them, and there stood Mele, with a basket of food to leave as a gift. She looked embarrassed and hurriedly dropped off the basket and ran down the path. I was devastated and felt certain I had jeopardized a relationship I had come to value. People are very restrained in Tonga, and showing strong emotion is frowned upon.

The next day I gathered up my courage and went to see Mele. It was a little awkward at first; then I told her that I was very sorry she had seen me like that and apologized for putting her in that position. Her reaction was not what I expected. She took my hand and said, "You know, it is very hard being a mother. We are the only ones who know what it's like." She admitted that sometimes she yelled at her children and felt bad afterward. Her eyes filled with tears, and then so did mine. There was a power we felt in sharing something intimate about ourselves. The personal rewards for me are obvious, but there were research benefits to come later. On our next picnic, as she and I prepared the yams, she talked for three hours about the time she had been possessed by a spirit. I am convinced that it was only after she had learned something personal about me that she was willing to disclose more of herself.

We had established a special link between two women who shared knowledge of being a mother.

Making Meaning

Despite the diversity among cultural anthropologists with differing styles and goals of research, we share a common concern with the method. The accepted moral position to take when studying cultures with beliefs and values different from our own is one of suspended judgment. Historically, ethnographic research has depended on what MacIntyre, a philosopher, refers to as practical relativism (1993). He suggests that it is not a relativism held intellectually as a theory; it is a set of attitudes informing practice. These attitudes prevent utterances of moral judgment and involve suspending moral judgment concerning the activities of those who are the objects of inquiry. The problem with this position, according to MacIntyre, is that it corrupts us morally by lessening our commitment to our own moral principles. Expressing that commitment is not always necessary or good, but his point is that "being self-consciously at odds with others is an important condition for genuine understanding of those others" (1993, 5).

For the anthropologist trying to understand the culture of another, a relativist position is the most comfortable place to be. Avoiding personal judgments about the actions of others allows us to take everything in, record it all, and put off until later any thoughts of our own response or its significance. Careful observation is hard work, and pesky thoughts about moral right or wrong can be very distracting during note taking. The notion of bias-free research has seen its day, but the image of the detached observer, although unattainable, still remains a guiding principle of participant observation.

Children cannot live as detached observers. When they see something, they immediately have an opinion as to its goodness or badness. In her account of families and fieldwork, Scheper-Hughes (1987a) discusses the idea of children and moral judgment. She points out that their developmental task is to gain a sense of right from wrong, and during this process there is no room for "grays." Children, out of necessity, are very dogmatic in their beliefs. Moderation comes later, with adulthood, as the complexity of life leads to a questioning of many previously held truths. I am certain this makes the experiences of the anthropologists' children more intense than those of their parents. The adults are busily maintaining a detached presence, careful to avoid any private moralizing about a particular custom or way of acting; all the while this posture is serving to distance them from their subjects. Children, on the other hand, are in the thick of it. From their perspective other children are different. The games they play are not the same; their way of playing is not the same. They either like the change, or they do not. The difference between the children and their parents is that the children are allowing themselves to feel the difference, rather than analyze it (see also Young Leslie, chapter 3).

For example, Patrick had become friends with a family on the other side of the cemetery. Their two sons had been to New Zealand and so spoke some English. One day the father asked if our son would like to stay for dinner at their home. I warned Patrick that he would be treated like an honored guest, presented with some things he might not want to eat, and watched by everyone. This did not bother him, so off he went. I will never forget the look on his face as he returned that evening. It was a mixture of anger, hurt, and just plain misery. Yes, the food had been weird, although not bad, but what bothered him was the way the mother had treated his friends. On other days the boys played in the bush or at the father's garden. That day they stayed around the house, and the little sister was there. She was a toddler, maybe two years old, and the boys were seven and ten. She kept bothering and pestering the brothers, but they never said anything to her. At one point the three boys were kneeling on the ground playing marbles, and she came up from behind and whacked the youngest on the head with a big stick. He started to cry. The mother came out, and to Patrick's amazement, she smacked the boy for making such a racket. The girl ran off and never got in trouble. Incredulous, Patrick asked the brothers why they did not just hit her back. They simply shrugged their shoulders. I listened to this story and then explained the pattern of brother-sister taboo in Polynesia, with the higher status of the girl in the family and the prohibition against physical contact. Having this cultural knowledge did not change his opinion of the practice, however. Patrick admitted that if we did things this way, he would hate his sisters for always getting away with stuff. This response startled me. I realized that I had never really thought about what it feels like to function under this social structure. I liked the deference shown to women in Tonga but had not thought through what the costs are to relations between the sexes.

My children's perceptions also provided me with new insights concerning Tongans' relations with their spirits. Every evening at dinner I would tell what I did that day. Since I was interested in knowledge of the supernatural, I often came home with stories of a spirit causing mischief or harm to someone I interviewed. Some of the incidents occurred right across the road from us, in the cemetery. Everyone looked forward to hearing what I had learned, and I was careful to repeat the narratives just as I had been told them earlier in the day. The first ones were met with amazement; the stories were mysterious and sometimes frightening. After awhile the children started to ask, "Mom, do you believe that happened?" My quick response was, "I don't know, but 'so and so' believes it, and that's good enough for me." Obviously, this response did not go far. We then got into discussions of whether one had to be Tongan to believe in Tongan spirits. Maybe we have Seattle spirits floating around, but no one recognizes that they are there. We tried to imagine what it feels like to live surrounded by different beings who protect us or others we might offend at any time. The children pursued the topic beyond its theoretical construct and into the realm of experience. In this, and in many cases, the inability of a child to assume a position of relativism pushes the adult to decrease the distance between observer and observed.

Going Home

Sharing membership in the natural unit of the village, which in the Tongan case is the family, was beneficial in establishing rapport, helped in gaining access to events, and pushed the research in new directions. Having family members present provided me with a different perspective on the emotional tone of everyday life. All three children experienced Tonga without the moral injunction to suspend judgment about what they felt. Their reactions, both positive and negative, encouraged me to look more closely at social relationships and describe them in a manner that attempts to capture their complexity.

Certainly being accompanied by others while trying to accomplish some goal is not without drawbacks. Factors such as the physical environment, type of research, age of children, age and gender of researcher, presence of another adult, and so forth are critical. The presence of others does influence the product, and as anthropologists are experimenting with ways to open up the process of ethnography, acknowledging the conditions under which data were gathered is one step toward this end. This of course introduces other questions and areas of analysis, for example, issues of gender differences and family influence, confidentiality when one's child is providing information about others, and the proper forum for writing ethnography that includes such information.

One of the agendas of this research concerned the benefits to the children. The effect on them is slowly unfolding. I think they know by experience that there are many different ways to live, and they have a greater understanding of the concept of the global village they keep hearing about in school. For their part, they simply had fun. During our last month we talked about returning to Seattle. Each of the children had mixed feelings. Kate drew a scale with Seattle on one side and Tonga on the other. Every day the scale tilted back and forth. I asked Kate and Patrick to think back to the time before they saw Tonga and see if it had turned out as they had expected. Patrick imagined we would be living in a grass hut with no running water, electricity, or cars. No one would speak English, and there would be no one with whom to talk or play. Kate said she pictured it as very poor. Everywhere we went, we would see poor people living on the streets, carrying their things in bags, like the homeless in our city. And now, what was the best thing about Tonga? The response of all three was unanimous: "the gentleness of the people."

Leaving Tonga was very difficult for all of us. I am not the first anthropologist to choose a field site based on more than research criteria. The best of the place captured a lifestyle longed for. I found an emphasis on human relations, an ethic of sharing, a commitment to care for family and community, and a slower pace of life. Day-to-day priorities relate more to people than tasks, and so there is a different rhythm to life. That was a welcome change. I wondered how returning to life in urban America would feel after my family and I had become so comfortable living on a Pacific island. My last journal note describes reentry.

> *Coming back was stranger than any of us had anticipated. We arrived at the airport in the middle of the night, met by a crowd of relatives. At home, Allison kept running from sink to sink in the bathrooms and kitchen, turning on the faucets, "Look, there's hot water in every one." Patrick and Kate acted as if their rooms were toy stores. Peter and I were a bit more dazed as we wandered around, noticing all of our "stuff." We wondered why we had three spatulas, isn't one enough? Going to the grocery store the next day left all of us laughing giddily at the rows and rows of things to choose. This initial culture shock is gradually lessening. Of course the children have more quickly jumped right back into things than Peter or me.*

Postscripts

The connectedness our family has with Tonga is enduring. Kate and I returned two years later for a long visit. It was very interesting to see that she remembered very different things from me. Landmarks in the landscape, such as a particularly large guava tree or a curve in the road, were welcome sights. She had great fun seeing her friends, but I did not realize that she had never had it straight which kids belonged to which families. The other two children are also eager to go back. Patrick is hoping one of his friends will be able to visit us in Seattle, and he wants to go to Tonga when he is in high school. Allison does not have as many memories because she was only four years old at the time and feels she missed out on many experiences. She recently described an image that captures what she does remember: we are walking through the village—not hurrying to get somewhere, just walking—and lots of people call out to us and say hello or invite us over to sit and talk. As Allison put it, "Everyone always had time to talk in Tonga." At the time of this writing I have been working with Tongans who live in the Pacific Northwest of the

United States, some of whom are relatives of friends we knew on the islands. This is certainly a less intense experience; however, doing research within one's own country presents a whole new set of challenges.

I completed the writing of my doctoral dissertation (McGrath 1993). I did not, however, discover a reasonable way to include in it the influence of my family on the project beyond the dedication page and mention in the methodology section. In terms of presenting a corrective to the dominant image of how fieldwork is conducted, I am offering nothing new. As long as fieldwork accounts such as this and the other contributions to this volume remain separate accounts and not an integrated part of data analysis, they will always be afterthoughts comprising what James Clifford (1986, 14) treats as a "subgenre of ethnographic writing."

Acknowledgments

The research was supported in part by the Wenner-Gren Foundation and by the National Institutes of Health (5 F31 NR06525-02), which I gratefully acknowledge.

5 Family and Other Uncontrollables
Impression Management in Accompanied Fieldwork

JOCELYN LINNEKIN

In a classic work aptly titled *Behind Many Masks,* Berreman (1962), influenced by Goffman (1959), argued that the presentation of self is an ever-present issue during fieldwork. Both ethnographer and informants, Berreman wrote, seek to control the impressions that the other party will receive. Although Berreman acknowledged that he as the ethnographer engaged in impression management, most of his analysis was devoted to his Himalayan informants' attempts to shape, launder, and conceal information. In keeping with the reflexive gaze of contemporary anthropology, I invert that proportion in this chapter, addressing primarily the anthropologist's efforts at impression management and the complications associated with the presence of close companions in the field. If the ethnographer's behavior is viewed as a would-be controlled performance, then the presence of relatives, and particularly of children, renders impression management difficult, if not impossible. In part this is because interaction with family members is likely to bring into public gaze precisely those aspects of self that we would most like to "manage," even conceal, while in the field.

The notion of impression management implies that the anthropologist in the field is, like Sartre's famous waiter, engaged in playing *at* being something.

> His movement is quick and forward, a little too precise, a little too rapid. He comes toward the patrons with a step a little too quick. He bends forward a little too eagerly; his voice, his eyes express an interest a little too solicitous for the order of the customer. (1956, 59)

Such self-conscious role playing aims at constructing an impression of self for public consumption, "a 'representation' for others and for myself" (Sartre 1956, 60). Depending on the ethnographer's personal and theoretical vision, that role may be empirical researcher, empathetic listener, objective analyst, or self-conscious poet. The anthropologist may even alternate in assuming different roles at different times. As Cheater (1987, 169) points out, the possibility of thus existing in "bad faith" with oneself is equally present for anthropologists working in their own societies. Goffman and Sartre, however, were describing self-presentation in *everyday life*. In day-to-day professional settings, the anthropologist may similarly play the role of professor or social scientist. But I would argue that fieldwork is not everyday life, and impression management in the field differs at least in degree from these more routinized performances. In the field, the strain of impression management is not so much existential, a dilemma of individual authenticity and consistency, as it is a tension in relationships.

Role playing and impression management are common tactics among fieldworkers, whether they style themselves as "humanists" or "scientists." The important point is not the specific content of the ethnographer's performance so much as the fact of performance itself. In the current era of "reflexive" ethnography and concern with ethics, Berreman's candid talk about deception on the ethnographer's part becomes discomfiting.

> If the researcher feels morally constrained to avoid any form of dissimulation or secrecy he will have to forego most of the insights that can be acquired through knowledge of those parts of his informants' lives that they attempt to conceal from him. (1962, 12)

But even the obsessively honest fieldworker strives to fulfill the role of conscientious ethnographer, attempts to construct an acceptable public image of self, and thereby engages in impression management. A methodological handbook on ethnography candidly advises: "Impressions of the researcher that pose an obstacle to access must be avoided or countered as far as possible, while those that facilitate it must be encouraged; within the limits set by ethical considerations" (Hammersley and Atkinson 1983, 78). In these ethically conscious times anthropologists may tell few outright lies, but intentionally or not, they convey many polite fictions (see Cheater 1987, 168–169). Family members in the field may significantly threaten the maintenance of those fictions.

Berreman cites Goffman's notion of "performance risks"—persons who have the potential to reveal too much about the "back region" that informants seek to conceal from the ethnographer. Particularly significant for the issue of families in the field is Goffman's identification of "children, drunks, and the indiscreet as performance risks" (Berreman 1962, 22–23). For Berreman, low-caste people, children, and women were the most uninhibited and honest informants, those most likely to provide material on the "back region" of social life. Ethnographers, too, of course, have a "back region." This includes, in general, everything that we attempt to conceal from our informants, although I suspect fieldworkers see these issues as personal rather than social. By showing us in an intimate context, family members challenge some of the myths that comprise the mystique of fieldwork (see Freilich 1970), notably the fictions that the ethnographer is (a) without intimate connections and (b) more rational and objective than the people under study.

I was single when I did my doctoral fieldwork in a rural Hawaiian community on Maui in the mid-1970s. I was married with two children when I made several short research trips to Western Samoa in the 1980s and 1990s. Based on these experiences I offer a comparison of accompanied and unaccompanied fieldwork, focusing on the issue of impression management. I will address the advantages and drawbacks of field companions, and the impact that family members have on the ethnographer's social standing, constructed personhood, and self-presentation. My experiences and those of other fieldworkers raise compelling questions that I cannot fully answer. Why are ethnographers so concerned with managing their informants' impressions of themselves? Why does fieldwork amplify our need to control others' perceptions of us? Some would answer that a degree of deception or "management" is necessary to persuade informants to associate and speak with us, if the truth about our lives would violate local cultural norms and thus alienate our would-be subjects. But this is not always the case; impression management in the field seems more profoundly motivated by a sense of vulnerability and a perceived need to protect the boundaries of self. Such a need, I hasten to add, may well be culturally specific to Western fieldworkers, most of whom are socialized in the paradigm of the discrete, bounded individual.

Unaccompanied Fieldwork

Fieldwork has been typically presented to anthropology students as a solitary undertaking. Indeed, loneliness has been an essential element in normative representations of fieldwork as a *rite de passage* wherein the student experiences culture shock. In the making of an anthropologist, fieldwork is analogous to an initiation rite in which "radical resocialization" is achieved through emotional trauma (see Herdt 1981b). In the classic scenario the ethnographer is separated from family and friends, thrown into an unfamiliar setting, and unable at first even to communicate with those in the immediate social environment. Moreover, he or she is supposed to spend at least a year in self-imposed exile, braving the rigors of exotic diet, severe weather, health problems, and novel sanitation arrangements. Again, social isolation is expected to have a coercive function, intensifying the experience by forcing the ethnographer to rely on and interact with the local people.

I call the paradigm of the unaccompanied fieldworker the "normative" view because of its prevalence and evident power in our disciplinary discourse. It would be revealing to do a survey of anthropology Ph.D.s to determine how many of them actually lived the model. This volume and the Butler and Turner (1987b) and Cassell (1987b) collections suggest that deviance is more frequent than has been commonly acknowledged in the teaching of ethnographic methods. Nevertheless, I sense that in anthropology's disciplinary semiotics, prestige and perceived seriousness are diminished to the extent that a field experience departs from the solitary, angst-ridden ideal (see Butler and Turner 1987a, 15). In practice, details about family and other close relationships are still inadmissible in "straight" scholarly writing; discussions of personal dramas and entanglements are acceptable, if they are compartmentalized in volumes specifically dedicated to the theme. The dominant paradigm is profoundly gendered, for it presumes that the fieldworker either is unaccompanied or brings along a nonworking spouse to manage domestic matters and care for the children, if they are present. In the past, the accompanying spouse was presumed to be a wife who insulated the male researcher from household duties while in the field; she and the children were then invisible in the resultant ethnographic accounts. The dominant paradigm is perpetuated when junior scholars perceive that writing about personal field experiences should be postponed until one has first established the seriousness of one's work with objectivist accounts.

The normative representation of the fieldworker's status has a parallel in contemporary theories of personhood. In kin-based societies such as the Pacific featured in this volume, personhood is "consocial" (Schutz 1962; Geertz 1973, 364–367; Howard 1990, 262). Persons are defined by and through their relationships with others. The Western individual, in contrast, is alienated and atomized, an existential hero or anti-hero. This variant on the us-them distinction renders fieldwork by Americans and other Westerners in Pacific settings even more poignant because the ethnographer is portrayed as lacking intimate attachments while living amid people who by definition enjoy a wealth of social connections. In time, we were reassured as students, the anthropologist forges connections in the field. Such relationships are always imperfect, ambivalent, even tortured, however, because the ethnographer is always—in Powdermaker's (1966) felicitous phrase—"stranger and friend."

I took these understandings of fieldwork with me when I began my doctoral research on the island of Maui in the mid-1970s, and the reality proved somewhat more severe (Linnekin 1985). Though hardly an exotic locale in comparison to most of the other field sites described in this volume, the rural Hawaiian community where I lived was isolated by contemporary standards. Ke'anae was certainly culturally different, and the heavy pidgin spoken by most residents was not, at first, easily understandable. The villagers did not exactly welcome the prospect of a resident researcher, and I had difficulty finding a long-term living arrangement. After staying two weeks with a local woman who (I later discovered) was a notoriously difficult personality, I spent two months living in the Catholic church hall, which was drafty, infested with rats, and plagued with a badly leaking roof. The area is one of the rainiest places in the Islands. It began raining shortly after I arrived and rained daily and continually for about six months (at least that was my perception). Visiting informants meant considerable trudging in the wet, and "hanging out"—that most indispensable of ethnographic methods (Bernard 1994, 151–152)—was usually impractical. Because the nearest Laundromat was over an hour away by car, I hung laundry inside the hall, but the humidity was so high that even lightweight items took a week and cotton clothes tended to mildew before they would dry.

At night I lay in bed listening to the rats play football in the ceiling. Several plastic buckets were set around the room to catch the rain or, more accurately, the rain mixed with rat urine that dripped through the ceiling. The leaky roof was a source of stress not just because of concern over my belongings. Someone had warned me about Weil's disease, a potentially fatal illness transmitted through rat urine. I considered myself remarkably fortunate because the leaks somehow missed the bed. I began poisoning the rats with warfarin, but they did not always have the grace to go outside to die. On one memorable cold and rain-drenched evening I went into the kitchen and found one in its death throes, stuck in a knothole next to the counter where I prepared food. My room in the church hall was actually the traveling priest's bedroom. On Sunday night I had to vacate it and sleep in the corridor on a chaise lounge, which was pushed against a closet full of statues wrapped in newspaper. Unfortunately, the bedroom was the only part of the hall not overrun with rats at night. The closet door did not close securely, and all night I listened to the rats rustling in the newspaper a few inches away.

I eventually found a room for the duration in an old YMCA camp that overlooked the village, in exchange for serving as a resident caretaker. The camp building, too, was badly infested with rats that would jump on the bed at night or on one's head in the shower, but it was at least dry inside, and I eventually trapped and poisoned the rats. The point of this account is that the normative ingredients of solitude, loneliness, and hardship were acutely present during my doctoral fieldwork even though it took place in that delightful tourist destination, Hawai'i. In turn, this lack of comfort served to legitimize my fieldwork in my own eyes.

The loneliness of my first fieldwork was intensified by the demands of impression management. Maui in the 1970s was overrun by footloose young *haoles* (whites) from California and other parts of the mainland United States. As hippies became increasingly passé in those areas, they seemed to move west, many of them ending up in Hawai'i. Many fit the local stereotype perfectly: they were indeed dirty, unkempt, unshaven, and shiftless. Antipathy toward the newcomers was particularly intense on Maui. Local working people resented the fact that many of the hippies, though apparently able-bodied, paid for their groceries with food stamps. Hawai'i's welfare policy was reputed to be so generous that the hippies could step off the plane and immediately get food stamps. In some communities there had been violent confrontations over public nudity and the construction of shantytowns on beaches frequented by local fishermen and families.

Rural Hawaiians particularly hated the "heepies." In an old pasture up the mountainside from Ke'anae, some young *haoles* were living in houses made of plastic sheets and, I was told, dumping their offal in the stream that irrigated Ke'anae's taro patches. But hippie identity seemed to be a taint that went far deeper than appearance and overt behavior. I had no apparent hippie characteristics other than youth and long hair, which I usually wore in a bun, but as a single young *haole* without an understandable job I automatically came under suspicion. I presented myself as honestly as I could, as a student on "scholarship" doing research for a degree (I first tried "fellowship," but found that no one could relate to that term). But this explanation—and particularly the word "research"—only exacerbated my potential informants' skepticism.

In the local theory the proof of your character lay with your associates. Even when I went "outside" (to the town), people in the village had an uncanny way of knowing where I had been and what I had done. Extended family members whom I might not even know would nevertheless recognize me and report back. An informant cautioned me about consorting with hippie types: "They find you out. They see you outside with one heepie, they know you one." The implication was clear: if they did see me in the company of hippies, no one would have anything to do with me. In this atmosphere of suspicion my unattached and incomprehensible social status could have been my undoing. In order to remain even marginally acceptable in the community, I avoided public contact with peers who might look "hippie" in local eyes. Given American hair and dress styles in the 1970s, this was not easy. Achieving social isolation became yet another worry. A well-off young *haole* woman who had bought a house in the community was particularly difficult to avoid. She attempted to strike up a conversation with me on a few occasions, but I knew that the local people considered her "one heepie, that." I feared that merely talking to her in public would have been the "kiss of death," and in one instance literally hid from her behind a house.

Fieldwork in this community was never easy or comfortable, but I was eventually able to redeem my social standing somewhat by doing research in the land tax office for a few families. Dressed in a skirt and carrying a briefcase, I could not credibly be tarred with the label "hippie." Moreover, I brought back information that the elderly Hawaiians had been unable to obtain from the local clerks. I also shared with my informants some of the title chains and genealogies I had reconstructed from nineteenth-century land records and archives during research in Honolulu. This assistance and other incidents where I had helped people became part of my local biography and eventually were enough to prove to most residents that my "character" was sound.

Predictably enough, this level of rapport and trust came quite late in my fieldwork. I do not know whether having children in Keʻanae would have made a difference in those strained early interactions; hippies, too, of course, had children. Presumably I would have had to bring along a husband—and a clean-cut one at that—to prove that I was indeed married. In 1970s rural Maui being single, young, and *haole* amounted to grounds for suspicion.

My social standing was in itself a major liability that could only be overcome with time and performance. In retrospect I am convinced that "married with children" would have been a much easier status to present and manage than that of single student. This opinion was confirmed when I returned to Keʻanae for a brief visit in 1981, accompanied by my husband and infant son. We stopped to see the woman who had initially housed me, and I showed the baby to her; with perfect timing, his face lit up with an enormous smile. The woman—with whom my relations in the field had been somewhat strained—seemed to melt, and I was instantly convinced that children must be the most effective ethnographic tool available.

Accompanied Fieldwork

The opportunity to test this conviction came several years later. In the course of a project on economic transformation and ceremonial exchange I made three trips to Western Samoa between 1985 and 1989, staying with a family on the island of Manono. Lying off the west end of Upolu, Manono is considered—and considers itself—a bastion of the *faʻaSamoa,* Samoan 'tradition' in the sense of a self-conscious, normative model of past customs (Linnekin 1983; Handler and Linnekin 1984). There are no automobiles, no paved roads, and, until 1995, there was no electricity. By a legendary stricture there are also no dogs, a fact that makes Manono somewhat safer for small children than the major islands. During the 1980s Manono's erratic supply of fresh water came from Upolu via a pipeline. The several scattered communal taps usually flowed at night but were dry during the day. The pipeline was destroyed in the cyclones of 1990 and 1991, and the local member of parliament initiated a project to install concrete water catchment tanks on the island. Most dwelling houses on Manono are open-sided, Samoan style. Although remittances have funded many tin roofs and Western-style walled houses made of concrete, even the latter retain an open-sided feeling with floor-to-ceiling jalousies. As a number of other ethnographers have noted, family life in Samoa is ever open to public gaze.

Although I was certainly doing participant observation during these trips, I do not characterize the visits as systematic fieldwork, and my longest stay was only five weeks. I view the trips as accomplishing cultural familiarization, language study, and background research. Nevertheless, my host Samoan family has very much become "my" family. I continue to correspond with them and send them remittances and gift packages as a dutiful daughter should, and while on a library research trip to New Zealand in 1989 I stayed briefly with my Samoan 'sister' and her family in Auckland. On my first trip to Manono I took my twenty-month-old daughter, who was still nursing. On the other two visits I was accompanied by both children. In 1986 my daughter was nearly three, and my son celebrated his sixth birthday in Manono. On a short visit in 1989 the children were six and nine, and we were joined by my twenty-five-year-old sister, whose previous experience of the Pacific Islands was limited to Hawai'i.

In Samoa as in any field location, people judge you by watching your interactions and your public behavior. But in Samoa, as in much of Polynesia, the ethnographer is under almost constant scrutiny because guests are typically assigned space "in front," the most public precincts of the family compound, nearest the common pathway and the sea. To walk inland in Samoa is to chart a gradient from public to private, high status to low status. On Manono chiefs' meeting houses and residences are generally located closer to the sea and the public pathway. The households of untitled and lower-status individuals occupy smaller, more run-down houses in the rear of the family compound, closer to the smoke and soot of the cookhouse. The pigs are fed behind these houses. The bush, where the bats cry at night and trysts between the unmarried sometimes take place, lies beyond. Since houses are open sided and foreign visitors stay in a chief's residence, the ethnographer has little privacy; essentially, all behavioral settings are public.

Berreman (1962) noted that impression management is the most stressful aspect of fieldwork, and this would seem to be especially true for fieldworkers with families. Briggs (1970) vividly describes the interpersonal conflicts she encountered because her emotionalism violated Eskimo interpersonal etiquette. The accompanied ethnographer, less isolated and dependent, may be less stressed and therefore better able to maintain self-control. The problem is that family members, and particularly children, are essentially uncontrollable. They do not have the same stake in impression management, which after all is a way for the ethnographer to feel in control of the research, and they may not be willing or able to exercise self-restraint when uncomfortable.

I outlined above the normative scenario of solo ethnography that I was taught as an American undergraduate and graduate student in the early

1970s. Fieldwork with young children radically alters this model (see Butler and Turner 1987a, 14–15). Can one really experience alienation and culture shock to the fullest when one has diapers to change and toddlers' clothes to organize, much less cuts and scrapes to examine, clean, and disinfect every evening? At the very least, the parent-fieldworker—much like any other working parent—has little empty time or energy left to dwell on existential matters. The presence of children also significantly affects the kinds of data that become available. Though my ethnographic focus in Samoa was exchange, I learned much about Samoan opinions on child rearing and child health care. For example, my preconceived Edenic notions about child nurturing in more-or-less "traditional" settings were shattered when the women in my family chided me repeatedly for nursing my daughter so long. They weaned their babies much earlier, they told me. While respectful of their views, I had no intention of stopping; in my observation and judgment the Samoan toddlers, no longer nursing but unable to fend for themselves as the older children did, were by and large an unhappy and undernourished lot.

In Samoa as in Hawai'i, I found the status of "married with children," that is, an adult with visible social connections, infinitely superior to that of single student (see Butler and Turner 1987a, 25). Though the Samoans did not understand or agree with my modes of child rearing, at least we had a common ground of parental problems and experiences, and in time were even able to discuss our differences in good comparative fashion. I believe the presence of my children helped to create a degree of intimacy with our Samoan host family within a relatively short period of time. For one thing, I sensed the family was flattered that I did not hesitate to bring the children along. With no dogs or cars on the island, I was comfortable letting them roam around with their Samoan peers or, when my daughter was a toddler, with older girls. My children were quite blond and very visible in Manono, and I felt confident that at any one moment several pairs of eyes were watching them. My daughter, with her blond ringlets, was everyone's favorite, and girls loved to style her hair in braids or ponytails. Fundamentally, I entrusted my children to the people and the environment on Manono, and perhaps I won some of their trust in return.

Shore (1982) and other ethnographers have noted that Samoans place a high value on self-control, restraint, and formalism in public settings. My son was a particular problem in Samoa because his behavioral style was antithetical to Samoan norms. He was verbally precocious, impulsive, and expressive, while his Samoan peers learn to be quiet, stoical, and restrained. Lively and impulsive Samoan boys are called *ulavale* 'mischievous' or 'naughty,' but the word is often used with affection and warmth. My Samoan mother and I would refer to my son as *ulavale,* but we both knew that his behavior went well beyond 'mischievous' to an extreme that was intolerable and empirically absent among Samoan children. Attempting to manage him was the most stressful aspect of living in Samoa. He was never physically aggressive, but he was active and verbally expressive at inappropriate times. I particularly came to dread Sundays because we were supposed to attend two church services. I did not mind church and wanted to observe the proceedings, but my son's fidgeting was torture. To my relief I discovered that there is an established etiquette for babies and fidgety children. After a reasonable length of time, mothers simply take them outside and stand behind the church chatting for the rest of the service. It would be unseemly to go home, and their attendance counts even though they may have been inside for only a fraction of the service. I missed the public enumeration of contributions from *matai* 'titled persons/chiefs' but had productive contacts with the mothers and children who comprised the outside contingent.

I began this chapter with Berreman's statement, following Goffman, that children are "performance risks" for the ethnographer. This is not simply because they are honest and spontaneous, and do not share our mission of impression management. The anthropologist-parent is "humbled" (DeVita 1990) by the presence of children not least because they shatter the ethnographer's facade of rationality, whether by provoking anxiety or anger. It is not always possible to be gracious and culturally sensitive while worrying about the health of a child. As safe as I felt Manono to be, there were many small hazards to concern an American parent. Pigs and chickens run free, and their droppings are everywhere. Broken glass and discarded tin cans lie about and are particularly thick at the beach, while children go barefoot. People do not always wash their hands before preparing food, and Samoans as well as visiting *papalagi* 'foreigners' suffer periodic intestinal upsets. There is a medical clinic on Manono, but the nurse is not always on the island. In a serious medical emergency one would have to take the family boat to Upolu—perhaps after waiting for the tide to rise sufficiently—and then catch a bus or hitch a ride to Apia. The trip takes two to three hours under the best of circumstances.

For better and for worse, children in the field seem to intensify the moments of intimacy that one shares with informants. Worries about children's health and mishaps are grounds for empathy, and I am dubious that an anxious parent can successfully carry out impression management. On our first visit to Samoa my toddler daughter had recurring diarrhea. I was both concerned and embarrassed, but the women in the family were wonderfully kind, quickly and matter-of-factly cleaning up after her. On our last trip my son came down with a serious case of chicken pox. He was clearly miserable but did not complain overly much, and the entire family took turns covering his inflamed back with wet cloths.

As every parent knows, there are occasions when one overreacts or "goes ballistic" because a child has done something very wrong or very dangerous. At these points in the field, or at home, one becomes quite simply a public spectacle. Sometimes I sought privacy at the back of the house or the beach when I wanted to discipline the children. Perhaps my worst moment in Samoa occurred while we were staying in our family high chief's residence in Apia, the capital city. An open-sided *fale* 'house' had recently been constructed next to the chief's Western-style house. This was the boys' house, where the untitled young men stayed when they were in town. The *fale*'s wooden floor was about three feet off the ground, a sensible design given the marshy land and the roaming pigs and dogs. The young men also prepared food in the *fale* and threw the rubbish behind. My son found the goings-on fascinating and, appropriately by Samoan standards, liked to "hang out" with the boys—until the evening he fell off the back of the house platform.

I heard his bloodcurdling screams, and one of the boys carried him into the chief's house. He had a large bump on his head and was cut and scraped in numerous places. Moreover, soot and unidentifiable bits of grime were ground into the cuts and had to be removed with tweezers. Frantic and angry, I proceeded to lecture him as I tended to his wounds, enumerating the varieties of unspeakable rubbish that were thrown behind the *fale*. Even as I spoke, I knew that I must be insulting the family, but I was too upset to behave otherwise. At the height of the drama our chief arrived with a distinguished guest, the Methodist pastor. My son was still wailing, and I was carrying on about the infections that were sure to result. Painful in my own memory, the incident probably embarrassed our chief; rationalizing, I hope that in some way it also brought us closer together. (See Turner 1987 for other "distressing incidents" involving the ethnographer's children in the field.)

Children—and Others—in the Field

A common justification for solo fieldwork is that the ethnographer, forced to depend on "the other" for company, solace, and subsistence, thereby learns the language faster and collects more and better data. While having children in the field tends to facilitate interaction with informants (see Counts and Counts [chapter 10], Goodenough [chapter 1], and McGrath [chapter 4] for additional rich examples), the presence of coevals may detract from that communication. The temptation is too great to spend time talking with another English speaker, and an established intimate at that. My sister who came to Samoa was a wonderful companion and guest in that she was relaxed, adventurous, and interested in Samoan ways. However, I inevitably interacted more with her than with the Samoans. I had to translate for her, linguistically and culturally. Ironically, because she was a good guest, inquisitive and willing to learn the local courtesies, I became an eager teacher. I acknowledge the hazard of basing a comparison on relatively short stays, but I suspect that the presence of a "nonworking spouse"—that is, one not directly involved in the research—could prove detrimental during long-term fieldwork. This observation is profoundly gendered, however. A married male ethnographer might find it a great convenience to have a wife to look after the children and keep them out of the research. (See Petersen [chapter 6] and Carucci [chapter 12] for two married male viewpoints.)

Still, a visiting relative in the field has undeniable advantages for the ethnographer's impression management. On every trip to Manono, I seem to meet more members of the *'aiga* 'extended family,' siblings and nieces and nephews who live abroad and visit only occasionally. Introducing my sister to the village showed that I, too, have an extended family. Moreover, I believe that my Samoan host family was flattered that I did so, just as when I brought along my children. Even though several years have passed since my sister's visit, they continue to ask about her and were pleased when I showed them her wedding pictures.

Bringing along relatives can impose an undue burden on the host family, however. During my sister's visit the family felt even more compelled to put on their best, but perhaps less so than if she had been a man. Samoan public authority is very much male dominated, at least in numerical terms. I have seen the ceremonious way in which foreign men and their visitors are treated, in part perhaps because foreign men are seen as having, or having the potential for, chiefly status. As a foreign woman with the status of *porofesa* 'professor' I am an honored guest, but as a woman I am unlikely to be the subject of chiefly exchange presentations. The family tries to assign me to the "front of the house," but it is not as difficult or as eye-catching for me to roam around as it would be for a foreign man of status. For one thing, I can always take the children for a stroll.

The Broken Mask

Sartre used the example of the assiduous café waiter to argue that role-playing is part of the human condition. The existential dilemma is that such role-playing, like the ethnographer's impression management, is symptomatic of "bad faith" or personal inauthenticity.

> It is precisely this person *who I have to be* (if I am the waiter in question) and who I am not. . . . I can be he only in *representation*. But if I represent myself as him, I am not he . . . I can only play *at being* him; that is, imagine to myself that I am he. (1956, 60; italics in original)

In *Behind Many Masks,* Berreman (1962) was frank about deceiving his informants on several points, but impression management in the field consists equally if not in the main of controlling our emotions and monitoring our own behavior. Children, so inseparable from our personae, touch emotional territory that we would prefer to conceal and thereby reveal the cracks in the ethnographer's mask.

Dumont (1978, 8) points out that women anthropologists were the first to write openly about the ethnographer's human frailties, while male scholars tended to cling to the rational, scientistic ideal in presenting their work. Women scholars such as Bowen (1954) and Powdermaker (1966) pioneered the realistic discussion of fieldwork with all its "impurities . . . feelings and sentiments included" (Dumont 1978, 8). Perhaps women could take this risk because they are accustomed to having their narrative authority questioned. For anthropologists today, the most thorny issue is whether—and why—impression management is so necessary to ethnography, as Berreman and other researchers have claimed. As I suggested above, the perceived necessity goes well beyond respect for local sensitivities. Why must we become "control freaks" in the field? Why do we need to construct public fictions when we conduct fieldwork? Is it necessary for anthropologists to live thus in "bad faith?" Fieldwork with families, because it forces us to be more honest about ourselves, may point to a different research paradigm—one that challenges the inevitability and necessity of the ethnographer's impression management.

Acknowledgments

Fieldwork in Hawai'i from 1974 to 1975 was funded by the National Science Foundation and the National Institute of Mental Health. Research in Western Samoa in 1986 was funded by a grant from the University of Hawai'i; several other trips to Western Samoa were funded by myself. For hospitality and insights into Samoan culture, and for their patience, I thank Vaisagote Isaako, Lemalie Vaisagote, Leiataua Iosefa, and the members of their *'aiga* in Manono, Western Samoa. For instruction in Samoan language and culture I am grateful to John Mayer and Aumua Mata'itusi.

6 Field and Family on Pohnpei, Micronesia

GLENN PETERSEN, VICTORIA GARCIA, AND
GRACE PETERSEN

The following essays by our family members were composed independently. None of us saw what the others were writing until the work was essentially completed, and we opted not to alter our contributions after reading one another's work. Each piece presents an individual perspective upon what has, during the past decade, become a shared experience, and the whole reflects the intersection of quite distinct outlooks.

Glenn

Ethnographic fieldwork has long been characterized by the stereotype, perhaps even archetype, of the solitary—usually male—fieldworker, so much so that a number of our fellow contributors to this volume (including Linnekin, McGrath, and Sinclair) have commented upon this supposed convention. Whatever the stereotype's relation to reality might actually be, there is in fact little in this volume that describes the norm of the lone male fieldworker, and there is not much agreement about what typifies it. McGrath, for instance, writes of a shared sense that an accompanied man in the field is not likely to be distracted by family needs, while a woman fieldworker may well be. Sinclair, on the other hand, demonstrates that women can experience companionship in the field as compromising the limited time available to get the job done. In this section of our chapter, I chronicle some of the personal and professional changes a male fieldworker experiences as he makes the transition from solitary sojourner to married ethnographer, and on to full family accompaniment, thus fleshing out the stereotypical portrait of the solitary male in the field and, I hope, adding some depth to it.

When I first began working on Pohnpei, largest of the Eastern Caroline Islands, in what was then the United States Trust Territory of the Pacific

Islands and is now the Federated States of Micronesia (FSM), in 1974, I was a single man in my mid-twenties doing research for my doctoral dissertation. My only responsibility, as I experienced it then, was to my work. I was free to join in whatever activities loomed in front of me, and I made a virtue of this: I vowed never to let my sense of what I *should* be doing, which usually meant, in my own mind, writing up field notes, keep me from seizing every opportunity to join my Pohnpeian friends in what *they* were doing. My work, as I conceived it, was first to experience Pohnpeian social life, then to describe it, and finally to analyze it. I often did all three at the same time, of course, but for the most part—despite my many worries about whether I would have enough data for my dissertation—I went where chance dictated, when it dictated.

I would later learn that it was not so much chance that was dictating these opportunities as it was my Pohnpeian hosts. Whatever forces actually conditioned this behavior, my own rationale for it was mostly rooted in the material facts of Pohnpeian social life—Pohnpeians tend to live in highly dispersed communities, and the island's dense vegetation cuts off any vistas of more than a dozen meters or so. It is difficult—if not impossible—for an outsider either to see what is going on or to learn much about what will be going on without actually being present. A great deal of the social interaction that goes on beyond the precincts of individual homesteads takes place at daily, informal kava sessions. Kava, a mild, tranquilizing drink prepared fresh from roots, is consumed in casually constituted gatherings of five to twenty people, as well as at all feasts (see Petersen 1995 for a full account of Pohnpeian kava). As a consequence, I made sure not only to seek out kava sessions, but to be prepared to join anyone who invited me along. Sometimes I would be led to something that turned out to be far more elaborate or significant than an informal kava session, a *tohmw* 'apology ceremony' or marriage proposal, for example. It seemed to me that the only way I would be sure to learn much about Pohnpeian life was consistently to put myself in places where Pohnpeians could instruct me.

I pursued my work with great intensity and a fair measure of success, but in spite of the immense pleasure I derived both from work and from Pohnpeian friends, it was a painful time for me. Living in a household and community full of people whose patterns of social action were so different from mine left me quite without a clear sense of who I was. I felt as if I were without guideposts; I had nothing to mark my progress through daily life but a slowly accumulating pile of field notebooks. As I recall phrasing it in my own mind at the time, my sense of myself derived from the images reflected in the mirrors that were those with whom I interacted. Because so many facets of Pohnpeian interpersonal relations differed from those I had grown accustomed to in the military and graduate school years immediately preceding my first trip to Pohnpei, I experienced myself as deprived of the mirrors I needed in order to know myself. As a consequence I felt—to put it in the simplest of terms—crazy.

It was not the sort of exultant wild and crazy feeling that had led me into anthropology in the first place, but a distressing kind of crazy, the sort that comes from having lost one's moorings. It seemed at times that the only thing defining me to myself was my work, and I think that part of the reason I am so thoroughly enslaved to my work now is because of that experience: on Pohnpei, work was salvation for me. But I did not like the feeling, and I felt sure that it was dangerous to my well-being. For all my sense that this freedom to come and go as I chose stood me in good stead as a fieldworker, I was also convinced that living as a single man in the field was not healthy for me. As I departed Pohnpei at the end of a year and a half, I told myself that I would not return alone. It was too painful. There was no doubt in my mind that I would be coming back, and the intent to avoid coming back alone implied changes in my domestic arrangements, although I had no such plans at the time. These ideas remained implicit, but it is probably no coincidence that I, who had long shunned the possibility of ever marrying, began thinking seriously about the prospect shortly after I finished my Ph.D. in 1976, a year after returning from the field. I am conscious of this shift because I recall that when the head of the department I joined the following year asked me (*after* telling me I was hired) if I were married, I replied, "No, but now perhaps I can."

Two years later, in 1979, I was on my way back to Pohnpei—still a single man. And I know that I never seriously contemplated finding someone to go with me. In fact, I do not think I ever even entertained the idea of doing so. The notion passed through my mind a few times, but it was never more than a fleeting thought. By the time of that second visit I had been away from Pohnpei for four years, and whatever fears I had of going there alone had been more than offset by the value I continued to place upon freedom of mobility. Moreover (and I think this played a substantial role in my mind-set), I was going for only three months during the summer, and I fully expected that my old problems would never arise in so short a time period. Was I wrong! From the outset, I experienced almost exactly the same kinds of difficulties.

Despite this problem, my own drive pushed me to begin working on projects that might bring me back to Pohnpei for a longer stay. I was fully aware of the contradictions: I wanted to spend more time on the island, I did not want to be alone there, but I was unwilling to bring anyone along with me for fear that they would interfere with the freedom I felt I needed to conduct my work there. When I then returned for the summer of 1981, I once again encountered that original angst. No solution was in sight. It seemed that I was going to continue my stays on Pohnpei, alone. In retrospect, I suppose I thought it worth whatever inconvenience it brought me.

Victoria and I married in a civil ceremony in February 1983, and in June we had a formal wedding in New York City at Columbia University's St. Paul's Chapel. A few days later we were on our way to Pohnpei, where I was to observe the plebiscite on accepting the negotiated political status of Free Association with the United States. The two of us retain slightly different memories of the manner in which I informed Victoria of this trip, and my recollection is relevant here. Shortly after we had selected a date for our chapel ceremony, I read in the *New York Times* that the FSM would be holding its plebiscite in June. I knew that I had to be in Pohnpei to observe it, but I had no idea whether Victoria would want to travel there. We had never really talked much about travel to Micronesia, as I recall, and I did not know how she would view the prospect, especially since she had just begun working on her doctoral dissertation. She has long maintained that I simply announced one day that *I* was leaving for Micronesia immediately after the wedding, with the implication that I was planning to leave her behind, but my own recollection is that at the moment I read the news item, I shouted out, "I have to go to Micronesia." For me, the implication was that she would choose on her own whether or not to come along. By that time I had adjusted to the notion that I worked alone on Pohnpei, and I did not marry Victoria in order to have someone accompany me there, although I did marry her knowing she was the sort of person who would probably be interested in making such a trip.

I tell this story to make it clear that I was experiencing my characteristic ambivalence. I knew I had to go to Pohnpei, but I did not know whether to ask Victoria to come with me, fearing that I might be imposing a burden upon her. She immediately made it clear that she was planning to go to the ends of the earth with me, and that was that. I had by this time slipped into the habit of taking my field site so much for granted that it was difficult to think about it as a place that had to be discussed in advance. Although I began teaching Victoria Pohnpeian prior to our departure, I do not think I told her much of what to expect; in retrospect this was probably not such a bad idea.

When we reached Pohnpei, I had to confront all of the issues I had worried about. My mobility *was* reduced. I was no longer free to do whatever presented itself to me, whenever it presented itself. Although the impact of this change spread throughout all the facets of our life there, I am most conscious of it in the context of kava. Finding a kava session on Pohnpei is an inherently uncertain task. More often than not, it finds me, a fortunate consequence of living with a large, relatively prosperous lineage with extensive kava plantings. But there are still many evenings when no kava is being pounded in the immediate vicinity of our farmstead, and none of my coresidents or close friends admits to knowing where to find it. This means a search, carried out in an apparently casual manner, along the main trails that link the community together. Ordinarily, anyone out searching for kava eventually encounters someone who, after asking the rhetorical question, *"Sohte sakau?"* ("No kava?"), admits to knowing where some is being prepared (and toward which he is headed), and then extends an invitation to come along. By the time this happens, however, one may be quite some distance from home.

Although Victoria expressed an eagerness to attend kava sessions, it struck me as disruptive to the spontaneity of these encounters to have to return and collect her, then set off through the gathering darkness across Pohnpei's generally intractable trails. Moreover, Victoria had no particular desire to join in kava night after night, whereas in those days kava sessions were for me still the primary source of my education in Pohnpeian life, and I sought to attend them every day. Although it was fully clear to me that I needed to stay at home and spend some evenings with Victoria, I was confronted with one of the key stumbling blocks that mark our joint travels to Pohnpei: these trips are relatively short, and I am desperate to gather as much material as possible. This means, in my own cognitive calculus, attending as many kava sessions as possible. Quite frankly, then, I began to find myself dealing with a new sort of strain, even as the older one began dissipating.

Traveling in the company of my wife did much to dispel the old stresses of identity and integration that had troubled me on my solo trips to Pohnpei. Not only was I with someone to whom my knowledge of Pohnpei meant something, but I was with someone who shared a full set of unspoken cultural assumptions. There is no doubt in my mind that I am far calmer when I am on Pohnpei with her. (See Goodenough, chapter 1, for another husband's sense of being "a whole human being" when his wife was able to accompany him to the field. See Flinn, chapter 7, for a related account of a loss of sense of identity when moving from accompanied to lone fieldwork.) On the other hand, the very process of not cutting myself off from the flow of normal interpersonal interaction with Victoria seems, as I experience it while it is happening, to cut me off from some of what I have come to Pohnpei to accomplish.

In 1990, while I was studying the FSM's Constitutional Convention (ConCon), I was particularly conscious of this dilemma. We were now parents. It was our daughter Grace's first trip to Pohnpei, and I felt an even stronger sense of responsibility to keep the family company. At the same time, however, I was trying to gather some quantitative data on participation at kava sessions for presentation to a symposium on kava at an upcoming Pacific Science Congress. I had to leave Awak, our home village on Pohnpei, at six-thirty or so each morning in order to ensure a ride to the FSM capital in Palikir, on the far side of the island, in time for the early morning committee meetings at which the bulk of the ConCon's business was transacted. By the time the afternoon committee meetings were concluded and I had managed to find rides back into town and then on to Awak, it was usually time for evening kava. So there I was, returning home approximately twelve hours after I had left and feeling that I should be heading straight out the door again.

This sense of having to work ceaselessly is linked to another recurring strain. Living conditions on Pohnpei can at times be rugged and intense. Victoria and Grace reasonably expect that we will take breaks for pure recreation: they look to do a bit of tourism on this lovely island. I, on the other hand, cannot imagine stopping for a moment. I want only to do my work. Not surprisingly, this results in sporadic tension and discord. There is little doubt in my mind, from the perspective of the desk in Lawrenceville, New Jersey, at which I am now writing, that my work on Pohnpei would proceed more successfully if I relaxed, and that to the extent that I cultivated more reasonable interpersonal relations within my American family, I would learn more about Pohnpeians, those masters of the interpersonal realm. But I also know that patterns that have shaped themselves over the course of two decades are not likely to dissipate easily or rapidly.

Victoria

I went with my husband, Glenn Petersen, to Pohnpei, Micronesia, for three field trips over the course of ten years. My aim here is to recount that experience, with an emphasis on a comparison of my first experience with the most recent one.

A few months before our wedding, my husband said, "I thought you should know that I will be going to Micronesia for two months. I'll be leaving the day after the wedding." After my surprise wore off and the usual "he said/she said" type of miscommunication had occurred, it emerged that he thought it inconceivable that I should want to be subjected to the rigors of fieldwork on a remote Pacific island. I reassured him, and plans for the trip nearly overshadowed those for the wedding.

I was no stranger to travel. Since early childhood, I had traveled in Latin America and lived in Europe. The year before our wedding, I had spent two months in Nicaragua, including the then war-torn Nicaraguan/Honduran border area, doing fieldwork for my doctoral dissertation for the Princeton University Department of Politics. I felt that any potential difficulties I faced in Micronesia would pale by comparison. I was psychologically prepared.

On Pohnpei, I was quickly cured of that self-assurance. Dorotea, a large middle-aged Pohnpeian woman who later became a 'sister' in my extended host family, provided my first strong impression of the island of Pohnpei itself. My husband and I had packed a large suitcase so full of books and papers that we could barely lift it onto the luggage conveyor belt at the airport. When we cleared customs and prepared to leave the airport for our village home, Dorotea asked us where our bags were and without expression flung that suitcase into the back of the pickup truck. This was where I started to take measure—of Pohnpei and of myself.

We drove to the house. I recall a landscape of staggering beauty, a misty mountain, flowers, rusted cars and pickups overgrown by the green everywhere, friendly faces, some lovely painted houses, and finally rest on a mattress on a clean floor. That first night, however, will be etched in my mind forever. Glenn said to me, "We are going to drink kava up the mountain, want to come?" The "hurry up" was tacit in his voice, and I scrambled for my pull-on sneakers, a choice that proved important. We walked along a coral road, then into the forest, and up, following a small river, over mud, large roots, slippery rocks, wobbly rocks, jagged rocks, rocks of all descriptions. When we arrived at a clearing with a thatched meeting house, the men were already beginning to pound the sacred root. I do not recall any women—just men, bare chested, many oiled, passing the cup of kava to me. With some coaching from Glenn, I took it and drank. I did not dislike the taste, as other first-time kava drinkers have reported. The scene that night had a sacred quality—the palms silhouetted against the dusk, and then the rising moon, the beautiful sound of stone pounding on stone, then the singing voices of the men that rose one by one into the night. I slept throughout the following day, but soon thereafter word got back to me that I was considered a good sport and swift climber.

Although I had traveled extensively and intensively, that first night was my first experience with culture shock, a realization in my gut of how different a culture could be. Preoccupied with my own dissertation work, I had taken the uncharacteristic step of deliberately not reading anything about Pohnpei before going there. The impressions of that night were therefore not affected by others' interpretation. I saw those men sitting in the moonlight and felt that I had slipped into a secret microcosm somewhere between time and space. The night had a quality that subjectively appeared primeval. I also experienced a deep kindness in the words that were addressed to me and an easy communalism in the silences that were shared that left an indelible impression on me. This quiet essence of Pohnpei I have felt again and again since, very openly at kava sessions but also running quietly under the cacophony of feasting and the uneven rhythms of daily life.

What sustained me through the "culture shock" of that first trip was the inclusivity of that communal feeling—the fact that I was always made to feel included in whatever it was that was Pohnpei. Over the next few weeks, I made my way over many more rocks, physical and cultural, stumbling much of the way. The language, the activities of daily life, and formal rituals felt totally foreign to me. In previous travels, I had always had familiar reference points to hold on to. On Pohnpei I had only my sneakers and Glenn.

Like a fool, I shed my sneakers. I wore rubber zoris on my feet and the Pohnpeian skirts I had been given, and otherwise dedicated much of my energy to trying to "go native." I pored over the manuals given to Peace Corps volunteers and took Pohnpeian language lessons, torturing myself practicing with giggling children. I tried to wash my clothes in the stream. I ineptly helped with the cooking and struggled with Pohnpei technology. I attended feasts and always attempted to speak Pohnpeian instead of concealing my ignorance (as any self-respecting Pohnpeian would have done). Painful blunder appended to painful blunder. My clothes never came out clean, I slipped and fell in the mud, I used too much kerosene on slow-cooking stews, and I tired quickly of coconut grating. I was always running into people when I went to the outhouse, and my own upbringing created the spectacle of making polite conversation while clutching toilet paper in my hand and trying not to fall into the lagoon. At my first feast, I addressed all of the proper high-language greetings to the wrong person, while fifty Pohnpeians watched, smiling. The worst part was not knowing the attitude reflected in their smiles.

I needed a vacation. Glenn did not believe in vacations at home, much less in the field, where every minute had to be consciously dedicated to getting the fieldwork done. I tried to persuade him that serendipity often yielded unexpected knowledge more valuable than what the charted course provided. No dice. I finally fell back on what my daughter, Grace, has learned to call "plan B": crying and yelling. It was an effective tactic. We visited Pohnpeian friends inland and also took a canoe to a tiny island in the surrounding lagoon. Despite a detached outrigger and other minor mishaps, this time off proved relaxing, and Glenn indeed had a chance conversation that proved important to his research.

I rarely allowed myself to relax in a non-Pohnpei context, feeling that this would be both cowardly and a slight to my hosts. One evening, however, we did have a dinner conversation with a group of expatriates who were voicing complaints about Pohnpeians. Although I felt their comments were unreasonable and wrong, I could understand why these views had emerged. This provided me with some insight regarding my first trip to Pohnpei. It was terribly hard to be so out of control. I did not know the rules of everyday life. I had to learn everything again, without the indulgence provided to infants. The constant self-imposed humiliation of my awkwardness was wearing. I could understand how this might give rise to anger and frustration. We are used to knowing the rules of the game and, indeed, controlling them. After several weeks, I myself was ready to leave, from sheer cultural exhaustion even though our host family ensured that I felt no sense of physical deprivation while on Pohnpei.

I was sustained by the unfailing kindness of the Pohnpeian people. Over the course of subsequent trips to Pohnpei, I realized it was my own judgment of myself that was exhausting me, not any Pohnpeian reaction to me. My own bumbling attempts to understand and live this new culture caused me discomfort, but I never felt the trauma of rudeness or meanness or resentment or tacit violence that I had experienced at varying levels of frequency and intensity elsewhere in my travels. Indeed, I discovered that on Pohnpei people had gone out of their way to spare me embarrassment, concealing even their kindness from me. It was this delicacy of spirit and the friendliness of my Pohnpei hosts that took me back to Pohnpei for subsequent visits.

During the days on all of our visits to Pohnpei, Glenn and I functioned independently of each other, except for unscheduled projects, like driving to the FSM capital, Kolonia, or attending special events. Although I had traveled throughout Latin America alone, I was more keenly aware on Pohnpei than ever before of a sensation of having to sink or swim, culturally speaking. I was alone in the deep water of a new culture. I was unwilling to ask for the lifesaving float of association with expatriates, so the only options were to learn the local culture or perish.

In the evenings, I greeted Glenn with a barrage of questions, which he often answered with good humor. I wanted to interpret Pohnpei, to understand whatever I saw. In retrospect I was very lucky that Glenn refused every attempt of mine to fit Pohnpei into a familiar reference pattern. It forced me to suspend my own interpretation and live through the discomforts of *not* understanding until I could begin to intuit the Pohnpeian perspective—or retain the perspective of myself living there, rather than myself being there while remaining cognitively safe on the East Coast of the United States.

At the time, however, my observations and his resistance made for some uncomfortable moments. At times I felt that he discounted completely the value of the interpretations one can have only at the first observation. We agree in retrospect that as our first trip progressed, we both benefited intellectually from some of my observations and analyses. They hit the mark some of the time.

My complete fascination with Pohnpei was also, I suspect, something to be reckoned with. Since I was hampered by the language barrier and eager to be culturally correct, I frequently tagged along with Glenn whenever anything interesting might occur. He was usually gracious about this, but I know it was also a source of strain for him.

My initial language limitations were occasionally also enlightening for Glenn. He was under the impression that his male friends did not speak much English at all. They had never spoken English to him, preferring to subject him to the rigors of learning the Pohnpei language. They still recount hilarious stories relating to his language lessons during his first fieldwork period. When they greeted me, however, many spoke perfect, articulate English. But none of the English speakers indulged me for long. As one friend, a local chief, warned, "Victoria, you and I will speak in English for two weeks. Then it will be Pohnpeian."

Glenn and I had differing approaches to Pohnpei during our first trip. Glenn was in a research mode, and there was intentionality in nearly everything he did there. I was deliberately not in research mode, although I was passionately interested in understanding Pohnpei and in experiencing it. In some ways, I believe that my stance freed me to gain access to information that is less available to me when I am in research mode, as in my own fieldwork in Nicaragua in 1982 and 1984. Thus, for instance, I felt little inhibition about asking friends and acquaintances questions because I was unencumbered by any feeling that I might be using them or mining them for information. I was limited only by my concern to maintain a relationship characterized by common courtesy.

When I felt personal awkwardness during that first trip, Glenn helped me to understand the Zen of field experience, how to remain flexible and calm despite uncertainty, instead of giving in to frustration. I also relied on him to retain my sense of humor. On subsequent trips, I felt far less need for that support. Glenn went off to work in Palikir every day, and I went where I wanted. I often opted to remain at the house and experience the ever-changing patterns of unexpected visits, feasting, visits to other households and villages, and household life itself.

Compared with my first visit, my most recent trip to Pohnpei in 1990 was quite different. I see at least four reasons for the difference and share them in kind with the experiences of most of the anthropologist contributors to this volume, female and male, whose "family fieldwork" has involved multiple visits to the same place (see, e.g., Flinn, Sinclair, and Thurston). First, I spoke the Pohnpeian language. This made me feel more comfortable on my own in every context—at home, in stores, with strangers, and at feasts. Second, I knew my hosts and had a network of friends and others with whom I had a history of shared experiences. Third, I was now more adept at necessary chores and familiar with both the routines of daily life and the more formal rituals. Fourth, I felt comfortable with myself and with my relationship with Pohnpei, which I expect will always be evolving. These objective and subjective differences led to important changes in my experience on Pohnpei. On the first trip, I craved the familiar cultural referents I had left at home while trying to emulate Pohnpeian behavior. On the most recent trip, on the other hand, I seldom craved anything from the United States. I was very comfortable in my Pohnpeian village, and I made little attempt to be a Pohnpeian.

While attending feasts and participating in daily life more intensively than I had in the past, I also allowed myself the time to do things that were alien to traditional Pohnpei culture. I felt less hesitation about taking time for myself. I went out with snorkeling expeditions run by a local hotel every two weeks. I exercised to aerobic audiotapes. I occasionally went to dinner at restaurants in Kolonia. My more Western behavior made me more interesting to the women in my household. I engaged my hosts in a new reciprocity, which they seemed to appreciate. I allowed them greater access to the "real me" and the combination of U.S. and Spanish Celtic cultures that are my ethnic heritage than I had on earlier visits. (This reciprocity of cultural exchange in the course of fieldwork is treated with sensitivity by Flinn and McGrath, chapters 7 and 4.) My ever-adventurous Pohnpei friends often enjoyed participating in the new experiences I offered, like snorkeling and aerobics dancing, which yielded such intense laughter that it still echoes in my mind.

My ease in being myself on Pohnpei during our most recent visit was assisted by the presence of our three-year-old daughter, Grace. She loved Pohnpei right away. With no language in common, she immediately joined the gang of ten or twelve children who played together in our household, as did the young children described by other contributors to this volume (e.g., Flinn, McGrath, Young Leslie). She was oblivious to cultural differences. Now and then, however, I felt she could use an excursion into the natural wonders of the lagoon, and her presence made it easier for me to go off on those boating expeditions. The only mishaps were physical, as when she dispensed vitamins as candy in large doses to her new friends, and when she fell out of a guava tree and incurred minor bruising. The hazards that attend older children in the field are amply discussed in other chapters, and I have noted the possibilities for our future trips to Pohnpei. I also experienced the delicious freedom of permanent childcare in an environment extremely hospitable to children. Grace ran off each morning with a group of children of varying ages, under the loose supervision of a teenage girl. The extended family household was always populated by women attending to chores of laundry and household management, so children were never left alone, although they roamed freely around the household compound.

Pohnpei is no longer foreign to me. I expect to prolong, rather than shorten, the duration of my stays there. For me it is a fascinating and beautiful place where I feel a calm sense of belonging and the warmth of long-standing friendships. As I continue to write about Pohnpei, an important aim will be to ensure that the demands of accurate and sensitive observation will not overshadow the pleasures of participation in Pohnpei's richly rewarding culture.

On Pohnpei we lived in daily intimacy with an "extended family" of friends. Our behavior with each other was characterized by a mixture of control and spontaneity. Living in such close quarters, we could not "manage our impression" (Berreman 1962; see Linnekin, chapter 5). Our hosts saw the messier aspects of our behavior, and we saw theirs. The discomfort of this was more than balanced by the intimacy of feeling accepted despite one's failings.

I felt the lack of this intimacy poignantly upon our return to a chillier (in all senses) New Jersey. Our contact with neighbors and friends was mediated by the custom of "calling first" and cleaning house before the arrival of "company." What we gained in impression management from these practices, we lost in spontaneous interaction. Furthermore, these relationships proved inconvenient from the standpoint of childcare. With a neighborhood full of children, we had to pay a stranger to care for our child. I no longer found this acceptable or even reasonable. (See Flinn, chapter 7, for a related set of responses.)

I worked over the ensuing years to create community where we live. I had to persuade resistant parents that children could play together despite gender and age differences. I adopted an open-door policy for neighborhood children, and other parents soon followed. This did gradually loosen the bonds of convention and achieved some of the more communal ways of interaction with my neighbors that we had enjoyed in our extended family on Pohnpei.

Grace

Going to Pohnpei was fun. I got to learn about a new place. I learned a different language. I wore interesting clothes. I remember that some of the children were not wearing any clothing. I didn't like seeing the pigs being killed. When I grow up, I am going to go back there.

I remember that it was green and beautiful. I remember there were huge turtles that were kept in a pool next to a restaurant for the local people in our community. I remember playing hula hoop in front of our house with the other children. I remember the river by our house. I remember the crickets on the ceiling when we went to sleep and the women making baskets out of the big leaves. I *also* remember that we ate rice and fish and drank juices. I remember that we ate breadfruit and that they had videos on television and places to rent movies. I remember that we watched "Puff, the Magic Dragon." I remember that I liked to wear the Pohnpeian skirts and necklaces. I remember walking in the sunshine on a tiny grass field to church. I remember Irene used to baby-sit me sometimes and I remember hiding in the fish nets with Georgie. I remember Mom giving me a bath in the river with a bucket and I remember visiting *Nohno* [grandmother] Victoria.

I'm glad that my parents are anthropologists because I get to go to so many different places that other kids in my class haven't been to. I want to go back and I don't want to go back. I want to go back because I like to watch the turtles and it's nice and warm and I like seeing how they live. But I really don't remember anybody there and I haven't been there in a long time so I forget a lot of things that I did.

7 Single Woman, Married Woman, Mother, or Me?

Defining Family and Identity in the Field

JULIANA FLINN

When we as anthropologists make decisions about taking—or not taking—family members with us to the field, we are inevitably influenced by our own cultural understandings of family. Regardless of our recognition, understanding, and acceptance of other constructions of family, and even in the face of some dissatisfaction with our own, we rarely want to completely abandon our own beliefs. Schneider (1980) has characterized American cultural notions of the family as rooted in biology and shared biogenetic substance, derived from sexual intercourse. Even though the family is "an ideological construct associated with the modern state" (Collier, Rosaldo, and Yanagisako 1993, 151), we view it as a natural, inevitable form: it consists of mother, father, and children who live together. Gender and kinship are both believed to originate in biology, even though often treated as separate domains (Yanagisako and Collier 1987), and thus the roles of mother and father are conflated with the gender roles of woman and man. This is not to deny variation according to class and ethnicity, however (e.g., Dickinson and Leming 1990; Eshleman 1991), or the changing roles of mother/wife and father/husband.

As American anthropologists we take these notions with us when we take our families to the field, and we carry them to places where notions of family and kinship are quite different. For the most part, whereas blood kinship is acquired in our society, it can be achieved in others; kinship and family relations may be as much demonstrated as simply given. Shared biogenetic substance is not a universally accepted concomitant of kinship (Marshall 1977; Schneider 1984). Especially when we have family in the field, we continue to grapple with alternative constructions. They may present problems when they impinge on our own (Turner 1987; Young Leslie, chapter 3); they may broaden or reshape what we want for ourselves. In this chapter I analyze my shifting views of family as I experienced fieldwork in Micronesia in a variety of family configurations, and I examine the impact on my sense of identity.

I was first in Micronesia as a married Peace Corps volunteer on Onoun, Namonuito Atoll, in Chuuk (formerly Truk) State, from 1974–1976. My husband, Jim, and I returned to Micronesia with our son, Colin, for my dissertation fieldwork in 1980, and we lived on Pollap (formerly spelled Pulap), an atoll to the south of Onoun. Then in 1986 I continued fieldwork with Pollapese on Weno, the capital of Chuuk State; I was divorced and had my son, eight at the time, with me. I returned to Weno once more in 1989, alone, but only for a few weeks. I began unaccompanied fieldwork on Saipan, in the Northern Marianas, in the summer of 1992 and returned in 1993.

Each time I grappled with the notion of what a family is. In fact, we all did—my husband, the Micronesians with whom we lived, and I. The diaries, journals, and letters my husband, son, and I wrote shed light on developing definitions of a family. We clearly had to contend with contrasts between American and Micronesian definitions, but at the same time, my husband and I struggled with our own differing visions. As younger Americans (at least when we first went to Micronesia), we were striving for egalitarian relationships in contrast to our perceptions of older patterns, with gender-segregated roles of husband and wife, father and mother, prevalent in American culture. In addition, we had our own personal expectations and perceptions based on the families in which we grew up. Many of the differences in our visions were connected with my upbringing in an educated, middle-class family, versus Jim's in a working-class family.

Married and Childless

My exposure to Micronesian notions of family and a growing awareness of my own values and beliefs while we were in Micronesia as Peace Corps volunteers shaped my notions of family such that I decided to have a child while still a graduate student and to conduct fieldwork as a family. To a certain extent, this followed a pattern of rejecting aspects of what we viewed as a traditional American family. Even our choosing to apply for the Peace Corps reflected in our minds a progressive notion of a family. We saw ourselves as a "couple family," and we opted not to be bound by traditional American expectations of finding steady jobs and settling down when we married, and we idealistically planned to define and pursue an egalitarian relationship.

We viewed the decision to join the Peace Corps as a joint one and—at the time—a sign of a relatively mature relationship. We worried very little about the warnings we received of the stresses that Peace Corps service could bring to a marriage. We felt that ours was a "liberated" relationship and an unconventional marriage. Not only were we deliberately trying to avoid the unequal family relationships with which we had grown up, but we also viewed ourselves as avoiding standard American materialist goals. Instead of pursuing money and careers, we were embarking on a selfless adventure.

This adventure was more my dream than Jim's, however, and that difference eventually contributed to strain. He and I requested—and were assigned—the most traditional of the sites available to us, the island of Onoun in the Namonuito Atoll of Chuuk. As an anthropology major in college with a long-standing interest in the Pacific, it was my preference. With no preference of his own, Jim accepted mine. Furthermore, I discovered I enjoyed our assigned job of teaching English as a second language at the junior high school, but Jim disliked the work and felt discontented, especially during the first year. Materials both of us wrote at the time suggest that much of our discontent and stress were related to family issues. In particular, our upbringing in different kinds of families affected our goals in life and thus our interpretation of our lives in the Peace Corps and our future. The differences also contributed to divergent expectations of our Micronesian host family, to my satisfaction with our time on Onoun, and to Jim's dissatisfaction.

Jim's family of orientation fits textbook descriptions of the working-class family (e.g., Dickinson and Leming 1990; Eshleman 1991). His father held a series of wage-labor jobs, and his mother worked as a housekeeper and nanny to help support the family. Their income was never sufficient to alleviate their sense of economic insecurity. Furthermore, his father was the authority in the family, his mother the nurturer. He had a temper; she was accommodating. Both had minimal schooling but worked in the traditional ways, following the expected gender roles, to improve the lives of their children, hoping to move them into the middle class. Thrilled to see their children simply finish high school, they were even prouder to see both son and daughter attend college.

My family of orientation also had clear distinctions between father/husband and mother/wife, with my father the provider and my mother the homemaker. Except for a brief period teaching, however, my mother did not work outside the home, and my father worked either in industrial research or as a university professor. Both took it for granted that all of their children would pursue a college education, if not even higher degrees.

Differences in a sense of financial security were part of the family differences that eventually affected our experiences in Micronesia. I noticed them in our discussions of family customs such as Christmas gifts. In Jim's family, gifts filled needs, whereas in mine, they were extras and centered on special interests and hobbies. The pattern continued during our marriage: we bought his mother household goods she needed, and she did the same for us. Yet we bought my mother an "extra" chair and an ice cream maker. Gifts were also more of an obligation in his family than in mine. Missing a birthday gift in my family did not endanger the relationship, especially considering our isolation on Onoun; in contrast, Jim's letters to his mother often refer to her getting a present for someone "from us," even though we were sending no suggestions or ideas. The fact of a gift—at a certain value—mattered.

These differences also contributed to conflicting attitudes about the Micronesian family that sponsored us as Peace Corps volunteers. Although these attitudes related in part to personality and perhaps gender differences, they can also be traced to our expectations of family based on our backgrounds. Jim's letters are sprinkled with complaints about our sponsoring family's lack of economic and social support in his eyes. He worried they were not giving us food as often as he would like, yet they wanted money, food, and other goods from us. He worried they might ask us for "too much," and he regretted not participating in many activities with the men in the family. On the other hand, my journals make frequent references to interaction with a young man and an older woman in the family. I wrote of conversations, especially ones where I gained insight into the local culture. Jim's comments focus on the possibility that a visit by members of our host family "really" concerned wanting something from us. In a typical example, he wrote, "Teresa came over this morning with a shopping list for me to buy for them on the ship with the rent money." In another letter he was "displeased with our family—the food has stopped coming and we have minimal contact with them." For some reason I was not concerned, and for the same days I wrote such things as "had a talk with Teresa." I was more comfortable with sharing what we had without looking for balanced reciprocity. At the time I attributed this to a background in anthropology, but my family background allowed me to focus on the emotional aspects of family, whereas Jim's had a heavier economic component. He counted on economic support in ways I did not.

Jim worried constantly about this perceived neglect, however, and his relationship with our Onoun family was a source of stress for him. Eventually it put a strain on the two of us because I did not want to keep track of the give and take. I wanted to believe that some sort of generalized reciprocity was in operation. In hindsight I do not know whose perception was closer to the truth; I may simply have wanted to believe we had a good and close relationship with our Micronesian family.

My own tensions about our Onoun family were of a different sort. The Peace Corps had arranged for us to have our own house, but I felt ambivalent about the arrangement. To an extent I had hoped to live in the same house as our hosts so that we could more easily become a part of daily activities; at the same time I felt some relief at being given a separate house so that Jim and I could form a semblance of an American family. During the two years we had been married thus far, for example, a common activity we enjoyed was cooking and preparing meals together, experimenting with recipes. We wanted to continue that and have a sense of being our own little family while still enjoying the benefits of attachment to a Micronesian one. Work at school kept us busy, but we also wanted to spend time getting to know local people and assumed the best way was through our sponsoring family. I was comfortable with the relationships that grew, but Jim remained suspicious about the family's motives.

Not only was Jim unhappy with relations with our Micronesian family, but he was also frustrated with teaching and worried about his future, especially his financial prospects. The assumption in my family was that my brothers, sister, and I would all attend college and pursue professional careers of some sort. Thus even after I finished college, I never questioned my ability to pursue a higher degree or profession. For Jim, however, the issue was uncertain. With a bachelor's degree from an Ivy League university, he was presumably on his way to a secure, middle-class life-style—as was I—but without having grown up with the unquestioned security and assumptions I had. Furthermore, he is an American male, for whom identity, work, and salary are more connected than they are for women. It was galling for him, for example, to receive letters from friends who were studying in graduate school, finding good jobs, or beginning promising careers. It made him feel trapped, out of circulation, and permanently two years behind. Those years were perhaps irretrievably lost. In one letter to his mother he wrote:

> *If the unemployment rate keeps up, we may have to reenlist in the Peace Corps [P.C.]! It seems bleak! . . . A lot of times I wonder about my life so far and in the future. Have I wasted it since I graduated from college? And what will I do after P.C.? . . . But now with the economy as it is I have no desire to leave Truk and try my hand in that uncertainty now.*

Jim's dislike of teaching and his lack of contentment with our Micronesian life in general presented us with a problem: should we remain? And what about our belief that our relationship would be egalitarian? Jim knew I liked living on Onoun, enjoyed teaching English, and had no desire to leave early. In fact, he never asked me to leave, in part because he felt he had made a two-year commitment to the Peace Corps, in part because of a commitment to me. It was central to his definition of our relationship and existence as a family. He wrote his mother:

> *I look "towards" and not really "forward" to another year out here on Ulul. I have not been very, very happy here. There just hasn't been enough that has satisfied me, and therefore, there just isn't enough for me to look forward to next year. Perhaps next year I will be looking forward to returning to America. You may wonder why I am staying here. Well the*

> biggest reason I guess is my commitment both to Peace Corps and Julie to stick it out for two years. And then the job market in America is not very inviting right now. From what we have heard from other volunteers, whom we trained with, we have a really good, if not the best, site. But that is because there is very little "negative" about Ulul, but on the other hand, there isn't anything "positive" either. And I guess this is what I am looking for: something positive. I have been here, but so what? The place hasn't excited me, nor has my work. So I have made it through the first year, and hopefully, I will make it through the second year. Perhaps things will improve next year given our better command of the language.

The second year on Onoun was better primarily because Jim anticipated leaving at the end of the year with a commitment fulfilled, able to start building his future in the United States. We both applied for graduate school and formulated some concrete plans. Our two-person family unit was no longer endangered.

My own experience and responses continued to differ from his, and living in association with the Micronesian family had me reevaluating my definitions of family in yet other ways. Certainly the contrasts between American and Micronesian families intrigued me. After one talk with Teresa, the grandmother of the family, I wrote the following:

> We were talking about "taking care" of other people's children.... It's very common here, children living with people other than their parents. Here it's seen as being generous and a kind of sharing. Teresa mentioned how her brother had 10 children and she had only two. This wasn't "enough"—so her brother "gave" her some of his. She was really surprised to find out how uncommon that is for us. She kept asking questions like if I had five kids and my sister didn't have any, wouldn't I give her one of mine? Funny that what is generous in one culture is heartless in another.

Living where kinship pervaded so much of daily life, especially when I was so distant from my American kin, clarified and probably even shaped what I wanted in a family. In particular, for the first time I knew I wanted a child. Previously I had been at best ambivalent and assumed I should wait until my career plans "allowed it." I grew to resent and reject some standard American beliefs about women, work, and children as I saw local definitions of womanhood seamlessly combine kin and productive activities. Even though I realized the cultural settings were different, I wanted that notion of womanhood for myself, and Jim and I decided to have a child while still in graduate school. The other major impact for me was wanting strong relationships with my own family in its extended sense, and we nurtured those attachments with our parents and siblings. Our letters and diaries are full of comments about receiving their letters and valuing that contact above all others, including college friends we assumed we had been closest to.

In addition, we cultivated our own sense of family (see Petersen, Garcia, and Petersen, chapter 6), taking care in particular to celebrate holidays. Having a kitten for a stretch of time was probably another effort to contribute to a sense of family. In addition to island festivities, we celebrated American holidays, pleased with our creativity in using resources at hand. I wrote in my diary:

> *Our Thanksgiving menu is tentatively spam as ham with cloves, brown sugar and pineapple; sweet potatoes, string beans, and either pineapple upside down cake or a pumpkin pie—we have to see if we can get a pumpkin from our family.*

We celebrated personal anniversaries with as much "tradition" as possible. A letter of Jim's describes one such special occasion:

> *Today is the 5th anniversary of Julie and I meeting each other! We made a variation of (corned) beef stroganoff, taro, and pineapple (canned) fritters. We usually go to a German restaurant for this occasion, therefore, the stroganoff.*

We even incorporated extended family traditions. At Christmas we baked cookies from recipes handed down from my great-grandmother. To do so, we had to plan ahead and buy the necessary ingredients in the port town and bring them out on the ship with us. We prided ourselves on some necessary innovations, including a ship biscuit tin as an oven and an alternative to "chilling" dough in the absence of refrigeration. Jim wrote:

> *We baked a half a recipe of Mrs. Flinn's Christmas sand tarts. We baked half a recipe of her ginger snaps last night. We even have colored sprinkles and walnuts for the sand tarts! But our "dozen-at-a-time-oven" really slowed us up! They taste good though.*

We took walks together, played games, planned picnics as ways of cementing our view of what we, as an American couple, wanted to be. Shared activities and shared problem solving were two ingredients we had agreed we wanted in a family.

Married with Child

Even though Jim had not been content during our two years on Onoun, he nonetheless expressed a willingness to return to Micronesia for my doctoral fieldwork in 1980. Meanwhile, we decided to have a child. Unlike some other fieldworker wives and mothers (e.g., Goodenough, chapter 1; Turner 1987), I was less concerned about our son being part of fieldwork than I was about Jim because of his dissatisfaction with Onoun. Furthermore, he operated best with structure and activities that kept him busy, both of which I assumed would be problematic for him in the field. At least in the Peace Corps he had had a structured job that occupied him for much of the day.

We saw our decision to return to Micronesia as a family as further evidence of how progressive we were by American middle-class standards. Our choice involved an American husband taking leave from work to accompany his wife on her research tour. The decision did not come easily, and a critical part of it was a unilateral decision on Jim's part—the first in our seven years of marriage. Throughout the first years of graduate school Jim assured me he had no problem with the idea of accompanying me—especially if we had a child—but he was speaking as a graduate student with no firm career plans or options in place. When the time came to make the specific fieldwork arrangements, Jim was working in a job that he liked and valued, and he worried about risking it. Without consulting me, he requested a nine-month leave. He informed me only after the leave had been approved and after we had agreed that I would probably need at least a year for my research. These developments were a sign of strain in our family. My notion of us as a family involved joint decision making; Jim placed a high priority on avoiding confrontation. I believe he wanted to keep the peace and avoid an argument that he saw as potentially disruptive—so disruptive in fact, that it might tear the family apart.

What appeared to others as unconventional was less the idea of Jim accompanying me than the thought of taking a small child to the field. Descriptions of other anthropologists' experiences (see, e.g., Butler and Turner 1987b; Cassell 1987b; Young Leslie, chapter 3) often touch on worries about socializing children to be Americans, but for some reason that did not concern us. If it concerned friends and relatives, I missed it. Health was what I heard as the primary concern others had, although we worried very little even about that. Perhaps we ought to have been anxious, yet we believed we knew clearly the situation we were about to encounter because of our experience in the Peace Corps. We assumed taking care to boil drinking water and to give Colin local foods prepared in safe ways would take care of the major dangers. We also knew children were susceptible to dangers at home in the United States.

Having read other accounts of taking children to the field, I wonder now why I had so little concern about Colin learning American values and behavior. Certainly I believed that the field experience could have a positive effect on his acceptance and appreciation of differences. Young as he was, I assumed the lack of creature comforts would not pose a problem. Schooling was not an issue either because he was still a preschooler. In addition, much of the way of life I had seen on Onoun I interpreted as beneficial for a small child. Children his age received considerable attention, lived relatively unstructured lives, ran around naked, and could remain at least at the periphery of island activities rather than be secluded at home. I also assumed that a year or so in the field might even be better for us as a family because we could more readily combine work and our personal lives, all without excluding Colin from life around him. We would have considerable time with him, and he would not be sent off to day care for most of the day and much of the week. He would have other children readily available around him and adults watching to keep him from harm.

In hindsight I believe an experience comparable to anthropological fieldwork with my parents and siblings contributed to my lack of concern about Colin learning to become an American. When I was seventeen, my father accepted a visiting professor position in France, and we all accompanied him. My parents believed that for us to reap the most from the experience, we should live like the French people, residing in the local community, attending French schools, worshiping at the local church, and learning to speak French with our friends. They operated under the assumption that the experience could only enrich us and probably helped ensure that it did. In the end, we all learned French, made friends, succeeded in school, and enjoyed our year abroad. I am sure that contributed to my sense that in taking my son to Micronesia for fieldwork I was providing him with a special opportunity, not placing him in jeopardy.

If anything, I saw a year in another culture as a way of avoiding problems I had with typical American childhood socialization patterns, especially practices and beliefs contributing to prejudice, close-mindedness about cultural differences, and assumptions that American ways are inherently superior. I assumed I would be contributing to the development of a sensitive and adaptable child. I also saw conducting fieldwork with my family as a way of growing as a family, sharing such an unusual experience (see McGrath, chapter 4).

In large measure my expectations were borne out. Of the three of us, Colin adjusted most completely and quickly. I do not believe he was even aware that the place, people, or way of life were unusual. One photograph is telling: Colin is standing amid Pollapese children, his body stance and facial expression reflecting those of the other children, unaware of the stark contrast of his white skin and yellow hair with the brown skin and hair of the other children. One evening in the communal cookhouse he rejected roasted fish pieces I had carefully rid of scales and bones; instead he insisted on pulling the scales off the fish—just as everyone else was—and picking out the flesh with his fingers—just as everyone else was. He tended to ignore a plate of food set aside for him; he preferred squatting around the communal bowl with the others. He learned to comb our hair and, following local practice, go through the motions of looking for head lice. In fact, some American ways, such as warm baths, he found odd and bordering on child abuse. I wrote in my diary:

Jim wanted to give Colin a warm bath before his nap, but Colin would have nothing to do with it. He put his foot in and promptly took it out, complaining it was "hot" and wouldn't go in until Jim made it as cool as he was used to.

We were as careful as possible about his health. To prevent illness, we boiled all our drinking water and avoided giving him food contaminated after being cooked. To prevent the possibility of a nutritional deficiency, I had brought along a prescription vitamin/fluoride solution and enough boxes of powdered milk to last the entire stay. None of us had problems with dysentery, a common health problem for visitors, but several times Colin acquired ascaris worms. We had medication to kill them but really no effective preventive measures because he constantly stuck his fingers in his mouth. My early diary entries are sprinkled with occasional anxious comments about his health and diet, but they are gradually replaced with comments about his growing social connections with islanders.

As anticipated, I saw advantages in our family life there. Colin had lots of attention and time with both of his parents. I could easily take him with me when I went visiting, or I could leave him with his father or with women in our host family. Adults and children were eager to be around him. They readily accepted him, even though he was more independent than Pollapese children his age. As a result he tended to run around with older children. The only concern I recall about values was the possibility that he was learning what to me was cruelty to animals. The local children taunted animals, prodding them with sticks, for example, or throwing stones, and I discouraged Colin from acting this way.

We kept him on a more structured schedule than Pollapese parents expected of their young ones, especially for naps and bedtime. However, this was probably more for our sakes than for his, especially since we wanted to continue such a pattern on our return. The local people seemed readily to accept our few "oddities"—primarily boiling water and keeping to a sleeping schedule. In fact, they were delighted at the extent to which he showed a propensity to follow their ways. We did not experience the problems Turner (1987) and Young Leslie (chapter 3) describe of feeling their children being almost socialized away from them. Part of the explanation probably lies in the fact that our hosts did not overtly attempt to change Colin's behavior or laud the superiority of their ways over ours. They appreciated the extent to which he behaved like a local child but accepted his different qualities and characteristics, such as his greater sense of independence.

Jim spent most of his time either teaching English at the elementary school or spending time with Colin. Our roles in the Peace Corps had been parallel, with both of us teaching and having about the same amount of contact with community people. The fieldwork year was harder for Jim, in part because he had less to do, but also because I was the one involved with the community, getting to know people, participating in more activities, and learning to speak the local dialect. He was often bored, but he had made a commitment he intended to keep. The months he was with us gave him more time with his son than would have been possible at home. Unlike the years in the Peace Corps, at least this time he knew he had a job back home, and regardless of how long I stayed, he was away for only nine months.

I deliberately tried to help frame in Jim's mind a relationship with our Pollap family that would avoid his resenting them the way he had resented the Onoun family. I pointed out that, unlike the Peace Corps situation, we paid no rent and that aside from his teaching, we were otherwise giving nothing back to the community. We were receiving hospitality, food, friendship, and a fund of information.

Even though we ended up divorced several years later, I do not believe the years in Micronesia were a cause; if anything, they delayed the divorce by giving us enough to share to maintain a sense of family. We eventually realized that we had little in common. Interestingly, about the only time I tell Jim much about my life now is when I return to Chuuk. I find myself writing him a letter to catch him up on events and news about the people with whom we shared those years.

Divorced with Child

I returned to Chuuk during the summer Colin turned eight. I was divorced, so now what was a family? Jim had recently remarried and was intent on creating a sense of family that involved both Colin and his new wife; for my part I wanted Colin and me to retain a sense of family ourselves. I discovered that my experiences on Onoun and Pollap had loosened my grip somewhat on American biological notions of family and our focus on the importance of a single caregiver, and this revised perspective helped my adjustment to this situation. I found I was able to watch a stepmother and other adults care for Colin without the expected threat to my relationship with him. In fact, I had come to see value in Colin having a number of nurturing adults to whom he could turn. I also realized there did not have to be inherent contradictions, at least for me, between the family Jim wanted with Colin and the one I wanted. The only problem was that I was not content with biological motherhood alone. I had to have the opportunity to behave as a mother. Furthermore, with mother and woman conflated in our culture, I felt inadequate as both, since I had so far failed in my attempts to have Colin move with me when I took a university teaching job. Accordingly, I found summers to be critical for building a sense of family with Colin; I felt as though they were all I had.

Before that summer in Chuuk began, I had more reservations about Colin's adjustment. For one, we were on Weno, the island with the port town, which was much larger and had more potential dangers than Pollap. Colin was also clearly an American boy at eight, one who took for granted much of his way of life and who was unlikely to consider local people and behavior as natural, the way he had as a toddler. In addition, I was worried about the impact on our relationship should he have a miserable time.

I arrived well before Colin finished school in the United States and stayed with members of the family we had lived with on Pollap. It was ideal for my fieldwork, and I felt myself slipping comfortably back into observing the local activities, listening, and socializing, in addition to the interviewing I had planned with returned college students. But as the time for Colin's arrival approached, I worried about how he would adjust. I doubted that he would readily become a part of the Micronesian family as he had before; he had no memories of his year with them. Most of all I worried that if he were miserable, it would hinder our sense of being a family. During most of Colin's elementary school years, my only prolonged time with him was during the summer, so I was afraid to take many risks. On Weno, he would have no privacy, which he valued, and I felt sure he would reject Micronesian food and probably refuse to eat with them. I desperately wanted the months we had together to be as good as I could make them, so with the help of one of the women in the family, I made arrangements to live in a small apartment in a separate building in the village.

The remaining months turned out to be good ones for us. I probably spent less time on fieldwork than I would have otherwise as I balanced my work needs and Colin's interests. He was reluctant to stay with Pollapese—essentially strangers to him—so at times I delayed or put aside my plans. He enjoyed playing with the children, however, and like the sons of other female contributors to this volume (e.g., Goodenough, McGrath), shared his own ethnographic observations with me—everything from how the men took showers to how they played Crazy-Eights. We made an event of regular trips to the post office for mail from home, and he wrote letters to his father. We played games together, and he enjoyed telling me about the books he was reading. We worked together on a book preparing him for first communion in the Catholic church, an event we celebrated at the end of the summer.

Alone

In 1992 I began fieldwork on Saipan, alone. Custody arrangements had changed so that Colin now lived with me and spent summers with his father. Even though I was alone, both my American family connections and those with Micronesian families shaped my experiences. I began my work on Saipan by looking for a Carolinian family I had briefly met while there twelve years earlier. Since this family traces its ancestry from Pollap, I had visited them for a few hours in 1980 at the end of my dissertation research, taking Colin along. After spending the year on Pollap, he managed during that brief visit on Saipan to impress our hosts. Twelve years later no one in the Carolinian family was quite sure they remembered me, but they clearly remembered Colin. I was the mother of that charming two-year-old.

I soon met some young Pollapese attending the community college on Saipan who had been elementary school children during my dissertation fieldwork. They politely attempted to figure out who I was from among the various Americans, primarily Peace Corps volunteers, who had lived on their island. It took mentioning Colin, however, for them to remember. Again, I was the mother of that child, and I was also then connected with a Pollapese family and a woman who played an active role in caring for Colin. One student recalled my husband teaching him English in the elementary school, so for a few I was the wife of that teacher. In other words, I was someone connected with an American family and with a Micronesian family, and only as an aside was I "that woman who asked questions about our customs." I was remembered through my attachments or connections to others.

Initially I was somewhat disconcerted at being so invisible or forgettable, but I soon came to interpret it as a measure of a certain type of success. Although I seemed merely to blend into an array of Americans coming to the islands, I decided that perhaps I had been appropriately unobtrusive. At least I did not stand out for having committed some major faux pas. I also realized that I was probably hearing less about my being quiet than I was about who a person is. Here was the "consocial person" (Geertz 1973, 365). Certainly one method used for determining who I was concerned who my family was—how I was connected with others. Often a Carolinian learning that I had lived on Onoun and Pollap asked about what family I had lived with in either place. Who was my sponsoring family? Who was I connected with? It is proper to deal with all newcomers in this manner, asking not so much "Who are you?" but "How are you connected with us? What clan are you from? Who are you related to?" I was connected both to local families as well as an American family.

Thus even though I came alone to Saipan and had to forge new connections, my previous connections with local families and my having trusted the outer island way of life enough to bring my child eased my entrance into this new community. I had some existing connections, and I repeatedly discovered that having lived in their ancestral home area, with a local family and with my son, gave me credibility.

Yet at the end of a second summer in the Carolinian community, I began to realize how much I had unconsciously used the visible connections with an American family to contribute to my sense of identity and my conviction that others perceived me as a person with needs, feelings, interests, and a history of my own. My unobtrusive style probably contributed to my feeling effaced, because I focused so much of my attention on listening to others. As I befriended people, they more and more readily talked about themselves and personal issues. I could easily sit for an hour or so barely saying a few words myself. I rarely volunteered information about myself, and even those to whom I have become closest rarely asked. I felt almost disembodied. In the company of a son or a husband, people could observe our interaction, comment on it, participate in it. I could more readily talk of myself against the backdrop of visible evidence of my identity as someone more complex than "person who listens" or "woman who asks questions."

Epilogue

In the wake of lone fieldwork, I have also missed the sense of sharing the experience with someone else—and bringing back common memories of the experience. I have no one at home in the United States with whom to share memories of Saipan, making that field experience much more distant, almost unreal. France, Onoun, and Pollap I can all share with various family members, but not Saipan. A piece now feels missing at home. The feeling is coupled with the sense of having expressed little of myself, even though being alone in the field relieved me of an enormous sense of responsibility and gave me more time with Carolinians. I feel quite close to two in particular—more so than I remember feeling with any Pollapese—but that sense of closeness and friendship comes from what I know of their feelings, thoughts, and concerns, not the reverse. Family in the field made me visibly a more complex person as I played out a variety of roles under close observation.

Acknowledgments

My fieldwork has been supported by grants from the National Science Foundation (1980–1981 and 1986) and the University of Arkansas at Little Rock (1989 and 1992). I gratefully acknowledge this support.

8 Dancing to the Music of Time
Fieldwork with a Husband, a Daughter, and a Cello[1]

KAREN SINCLAIR

Since 1972, I have been conducting fieldwork among an extended family of New Zealand Maori, involving several subtribal groupings, many of whom are members of a religious movement, *Maramatanga,* whose prophet was Mareikura (1877?–1946). Located in several cities and towns in the North Island, the members have monitored my activities since the early days of my research. Originally working in Levin (on the southwest coast of New Zealand's North Island) from 1971–1973, I moved to Ohakune (on the North Island's central plateau) in 1982. All of my subsequent field trips (1987, 1990, 1991, 1993, 1995) have been based in Ohakune. Collectively, these field trips have yielded close to four years of daily contact.

In the course of the more than two decades in which I have known this family, I have married, had a child, and watched her grow to adulthood. Since I married a Pakeha (a New Zealander of European ancestry), both he and my daughter are New Zealand citizens, and both are Pakehas. Doing fieldwork in New Zealand has become much more complex in the intervening decades, perhaps especially for an American woman who is attached to a Pakeha family. This chapter addresses issues raised by others in this volume, namely the importance of gender and family participation as integral aspects of how the fieldworker understands the lives of the people she (or he) has come to study and how she (or he) in turn is understood.

Twenty-four years is a long time for fieldwork. Such a duration has blurred distinctions, forcing us all to reevaluate what is meant by "family." To be sure, my husband, daughter, and I are defined differentially in this domain. But it has become clear that the mutual construction of our relations as those of family was inevitable, for in both cultures—Maori and American—family is the metaphor most conducive to the expression of closeness and intimacy. Our closeness is not a pretense; we have all watched and judged one another over the decades. We have argued and been embarrassed on each other's account. We have ceased to fool one another. Many Maori individuals have become very important in my life and in the lives of my husband and daughter. Juggling loyalties and allegiances has not always been easy.

With the exception of a few months in the initial stages and an occasional month in the intervening years, I have always been accompanied during fieldwork. Before I was married, I lived in the home of a Maori elder, a woman who generously opened her household to me. From 1982 on, my daughter, Emily, has accompanied me on all but part of two of these occasions and on all of those that lasted several months. She has attended primary and intermediate school and college (high school) in Ohakune; she has been cared for by the local doctor. In short, she has grown up with a new generation, which means that she both counts her closest friends amongst its members, and like them, has been disciplined by the elders. Indeed, at the time of this writing, when Emily is twenty, she feels closer to many Maori individuals than she probably ever will to anyone with whom she is connected by blood or origin. She is now a university student. She is not always able to leave her responsibilities—to academic work, to music, to her job—in order to accompany me. Yet there are additional reasons for her reluctance, indeed her embarrassment, that go to the heart of what accompanied fieldwork means on both sides of any cultural divide.

First Fieldwork

When I began fieldwork in 1972, families, at least as they related to me, were far from my mind. In my early twenties and single, I had gone to New Zealand to complete my Ph.D. research. I had no intention of transforming my status during my projected two-year stay. As is the case with so much of my fieldwork, events overtook my anticipations. Within three months of starting my fieldwork, I returned to the United States and reemerged in New Zealand a married woman. I had met my husband, Mike, also a graduate student, while doing preparatory work at Victoria University of Wellington, learning the Maori language, and auditing anthropology seminars.

I had arrived in New Zealand in September 1971. By late March 1972, I had moved from Wellington to Levin, a rural center of twelve thousand people, forty-five miles up the west coast of New Zealand, to begin the study of the *Maramatanga,* a religious movement. I moved in with a Maori elder, who shared her house on the local *marae* 'ritual space' with her grandson and her daughter. This was a very propitious turn of events. The elder's mother had been an important and early participant in the movement's beginnings. In addition, the *marae* where I was then living had gone through a resurrection twenty years earlier, as members of the movement were inspired to settle and to build in this area. Thus the history of the *marae* was clearly tied to the history of the movement. This history was recounted by the local residents on many occasions. Moreover, I was well positioned to observe the ceremonial organization of the community; such activities were focused on the meeting house that was just three hundred yards from the elder's house.

At this point, Mike was in Wellington, tutoring and writing his thesis. I was immersed in fieldwork, and since I understood next to nothing about what was going on in the Maori world around me, it was just as well that we were separated. In my naïveté, I did not recognize how puzzling and potentially threatening I must have appeared to the people with whom I hoped to work. In March, shortly before I became a resident in the community, there was a *ra*, a day in which the members of *Maramatanga* celebrate both a specific event and at the same time commemorate the history of the movement. Overwhelmed and confused, barely able to understand the discussions taking place around me in Maori, I consulted a kindly looking gentleman placed next to me in the meeting house. He was the *kaimahi* 'worker,' but should also be understood as "leader" of the movement. He was also one of the prophet's sons, but I was too ignorant to know this. Also, unbeknownst to me, he had placed himself beside me quite deliberately; only years later did I realize this was the beginning of a relationship in which he oversaw the information I was given. Members of his family were more than a little nervous that an anthropologist was in their midst, and he had vouched for me. I was, unwittingly, his awesome responsibility.

It soon became obvious that Mike and I would scarcely see one another unless he moved to where I was working. Marriage seemed the most pragmatic way to allow us to be together and to avoid offending the community's sensibilities. By the time I started fieldwork, and by the first *ra* then, my status was changing. I was not a single American woman, but someone about to be married. People were only slightly interested in my husband-to-be, since he was not there. Nevertheless, my impending marriage legitimated me in Maori terms. I have no doubt that my fieldwork would have been more difficult had I remained single. Once married, however, I faced other problems.

Mike and I were married in May in the United States and returned to New Zealand in the middle of the winter (May–July). As the winter wore on, there were a number of movement events that I attended, but frequently Mike was unable (he had work that required his attention) or unwilling (he did not want to be defined by his wife's career and the demands of her work) to accompany me. The latter would have made sense to most Maori I knew, but the former was incomprehensible. In fact, for the next eighteen months no one could figure out what my husband did. They would say to one another, "He is writing a book" and nod sagely, which translated into "She is supporting him. He is a slacker. Poor Karen."

As time went on, and I was given kinship terminology to explain my singular position, Mike was not so included. Although he remained my husband, he was not treated as kin. On my own, I found that discussions centered on events and history specific to the movement. When Mike did accompany me, our conversation would shift into arenas that were more inclusive and less personal.

We settled into a fairly regular routine. We lived on the edge of town at the beach, and I would leave for the day in our car, drive to the *marae* nearby, and then go shopping with whoever wanted to go into town. I took life histories and learned about the movement. The members of the movement who lived on the *marae* were especially knowledgeable. The elder with whom I lived had grown up in the movement; in an adjoining house was another son of the prophet and his wife, a woman gifted in both knowledge and songwriting abilities. Their presence justified the frequent visits of the leader I had met in March. In addition, there was another house, built by a relative—a middle-aged man who had had a rather late life conversion. It was he who had refurbished the *marae* and whose zeal often led him to reveal much about the movement.

The movement had begun in Ohakune, in the center of the North Island. The prophet and his children had lived there, and most of the early events that had marked the movement as important had taken place there. The prophet's grandchildren continued to reside in Ohakune. My presence made some of them uncomfortable on general grounds. But they were especially concerned that my information might come from one of my neighbors in Levin, whose knowledge they had reason to question.

The prophet's immediate family—his son resident on the Levin *marae*, his brother, the leader discussed earlier, and their two well-informed wives—assumed responsibility for my education. They monitored my conversations with others and then retold me their versions of stories I was likely to have heard. When I think back on it, this was, in fact, an amazing commitment, expressing faith in me that I am not sure I warranted. The four of them spent hours relating narratives of the movement's early days, explaining complex kin relationships, and then going over it all again to assure themselves that my understanding was sufficient to meet the standards set by the family at Ohakune.

Their problem was getting me aside for long enough periods of time. As a result of their efforts, I repeatedly missed dinner. I would tell Mike that I would be home at five o'clock and not get away until nine, ten, or even later. Since food is always part of Maori hospitality, I would have already eaten (many times) by the time I returned. But Mike would remain hungry until he gave up on me, finally sitting down to a solitary meal.

Another time-consuming task involved writing out *waiata* 'songs' that had emerged in the early days of the movement in the 1930s and 1940s. But because copy machines were not readily available, hundreds of songs had to be copied in longhand. Mike helped me, but only after I asked the family's permission and only after they were reasonably satisfied that he would not understand what the songs meant.

As the people in Levin got to know Mike, mostly through evenings in which we watched television together or played cards, they liked him, but he remained an enigma. I was certainly problematic myself, but at least I had a purpose in life: I was trying to learn about them. Mike's purpose was unclear to them, and accompanying me was typically uncomfortable for him. Occasionally, he did accompany me to the *ra* that punctuate the year.

However, once we were there, he found he had nothing to do. While I was in the meeting house listening, Mike had to try to figure out where he should be and to whom he should talk. Although everyone was very friendly, this was exceedingly awkward for Mike. My repeated forays had given me allies and buffers, but Mike had neither. It is not hard to understand why he would choose not to place himself in this position.

Mike had certainly known Maori individuals during the times in his youth when his parents had lived in rural areas. He knew several young men with whom he played rugby. Perhaps most important, he had boarded and become very close friends with a Maori woman, who had taught him the Maori language. Indeed, he had chosen the Maori language to meet the requirements for his bachelor's degree. It was this woman, whose family lived in a town near Levin, who facilitated my first contacts with *Maramatanga*.

Nevertheless, Mike had grown up in a family with many prejudices, some conscious, others less overt but no less insidious. He had attended a Pakeha-dominated university. He was unfamiliar with the protocol that is so critical in the conduct of Maori life, especially in rural areas. While he clearly liked the people and enjoyed being on the *marae*, he was also shy and more than a little uncomfortable.

While this quasi-standoff might have gone on indefinitely, a major turning point occurred in March 1973, when the Maori queen came onto the *marae* in Ohakune. There had been ties between her father, King Koroki, and Mareikura, the prophet of the movement. King Tawhiao, one of the first Maori kings, is intimately tied to the Maori prophetic tradition. The queen's appearance on the *marae* would solidify ties that linked two tribal areas. In all parts of New Zealand where movement members resided elaborate plans for the day were made. Everyone was coming—everyone, that is, except Mike; he was going sailing over that weekend. Repeatedly people asked me if he was coming, and repeatedly I had to say, "No, he's going sailing," knowing that any attempts to hide the truth would only backfire, since the community was far too small to allow for any secrets. I attended this most important event alone, as I had been attending other things alone all through that first year of fieldwork. Everyone asked me if Mike was there, and I always answered the same way, "No, he's not here; he's gone sailing." This was the nadir of Mike's relationship with the Ohakune people. They have never forgotten it. And while I know that Mike has come to be seen in a much more favorable light, people still say to me, "Remember when the queen came and Mike went sailing?"

Interestingly, this turning point had a positive aspect, although I persisted for at least a decade in seeing it as thoroughly mortifying. It was clear to everyone (and everyone was either present or heard about it) that I could not control my husband's actions; he stubbornly retained his independence in the face of my wishes. The point is that by this apparent lapse, I had placed myself in the company of Maori women whose own inability to influence their husband's behavior was all too familiar.

By the time Mike and I left in 1973, my relationships with the people belonging to the *Maramatanga* had grown quite strong. Those who lived near us in Levin had learned to appreciate Mike as a person, although it is not clear if they ever fully understood his work. For other members who lived farther afield, the threat of my presence was in what I would write; it had little to do with my husband. My impression is that they gave him little or no thought.

We returned together to the United States, and there followed a nine-year hiatus. During this time we had Emily. Not insignificant in our choice of her name was its importance within the history of *Maramatanga*. The members readily appreciated the name's significance and our choice in giving it to our first child. While I think they were flattered, they also knew—and hoped we were aware—that names carried meaning and significance. And while we received only infrequent communications, and those generally to announce bad news, Emily's birth was an occasion for presents and letters from them. However, I sent telegrams at the time of each *ra* and in this way kept intruding into their lives at regular intervals during each year.

Fieldwork with Family: 1982

In 1982, for three months of the northern summer (southern winter), I returned to New Zealand, accompanied by Mike, now a gainfully employed professor of law, and six-year-old Emily, whose name attracted much attention. All that most people remembered of me was that I sent telegrams.

I changed my field site for several reasons, one of which was the thriving nature of the *marae* at Ohakune, which had a considerable reputation for its commitment to Maori conventions. More important, this was the center of the movement. To continue my research, I had to overcome the reservations that certain individuals had about me and my work. If Mike's ambiguous employment situation was problematic before, it was now so impressive that it caused considerable social distance. While I was now a professor and had a Ph.D., I remained basically "Karen," the young American woman first known and nurtured as a student. Mike still was an enigma. Emily, however, was a child and our hosts readily understood her as such (see Counts and Counts, chapter 10).

Emily thrived on the *marae*. She played with the other children, she enjoyed watching adult activities, she relished the hustle and bustle, and most of all she savored the constant company. Emily's experience on the *marae*, as one of the children, was a wonderful antidote to being an American only child. She did not always behave well by Maori standards (see Linnekin and McGrath, chapters 5 and 4, on other children in the field), frequently intruding in adult interactions, for example, while younger children were able to obey the rules of etiquette far more easily. Such lapses were never seen as her fault, however, but as mine. Just as I had failed years earlier to have any authority over Mike's behavior, it was now clear that I exerted an even more unacceptable lack of control over the actions of my offspring.

Emily was also unaware of her father's family's notions that we were jeopardizing her health and well-being by allowing her to live in a Maori community. They were, quite simply, appalled by our behavior. Mike and I, in turn, were appalled by the overt racism and intolerance that characterized their stance. Indeed, difficulties between Maori and Pakeha increased as New Zealand entered difficult economic times in the 1980s. Emily is now older and therefore much more aware of racism. She will not tolerate it. She is far more blunt than I when I am in the homes of Mike's relatives and makes it quite clear that she finds their prejudices unacceptable. She rants about this to our Maori family and refuses to spend more than minimal time with her New Zealand Pakeha relatives. Considering the importance of family to the Maori, our Maori family is both shocked and delighted that we arrive in New Zealand on Monday and quite often are in their living rooms on Tuesday, having traveled the better part of a day to get there from Auckland, our place of arrival and the home of Mike's relations.

Emily's obvious delight in the *marae* situation opened many doors for me. First, I was more natural as a mother than as an anthropologist. Moreover, my hosts responded to her obvious affection (in some cases adoration), her staunch loyalty, her delight in arriving, and her reluctance to leave. To this day, Emily has to be peeled off the *marae*. In part because of their feelings toward Emily, people decided to have another look at Mike.

His profession proved finally to be useful rather than puzzling. By 1982, most New Zealand Maori tribes had formulated grievances that would be heard and adjudicated by the Waitangi Tribunal, designed to honor the treaty the Crown signed with the Maori in 1840. Mike's skills as a lawyer were pressed into service, and he was asked to review documents. His protests that he was not admitted to the New Zealand bar were cavalierly waved aside. In fact, for the work he was called upon to do, this did not seem to matter.

Mike was willing to do all of this happily. He also picked Emily up from school, cooked dinner if I was doing interviews, shopped, and maintained the day-to-day details of our life. He balked, however, at being seen only as an extension of Emily and myself. Although he attended *ra* and birthday parties, he would not go to meetings when the agenda was essentially Maori in nature. Once again I was asked, "Where's Mike?" and although the answer was not "sailing," it did not go over well that he was back at our house. Maori culture tends to be inclusive whereas Mike tends to be reclusive, a difference that inevitably produced conflict. Ironically, my research, which in 1982 focused upon Maori women, provided a way of coping with this. From the women's point of view, I was a wife with a problem husband on my hands, a situation they could understand and empathize with. Furthermore, in the course of interviewing women, I learned many things about their marriages because mine was clearly so far from perfect. Husbands who insisted on doing what they wanted were laughed about and discussed. In other words, Mike had found his niche; he was a difficult husband and thereby occupied terrain that was all too familiar to many women. Mike was now cast in universal terms; to a large extent, he ceased to be a "Pakeha" and was seen as a doting father and difficult husband, both familiar categories for Maori men. Indeed, Mike did identify with the husbands of the women with whom I worked; he attended rugby matches with some of the men, went hunting with others, and worked in the kitchen during the *ra*. People readily revised their opinions of Mike. Our family came to believe that the problem was not with him but with my handling of him.

This stay also revealed the fact that I could not handle my daughter. At six years of age, most Maori children can dress themselves and, at the very least, prepare a breakfast and get off to school with little or no supervision. Emily was not yet competent in any of these domains. I was told quite bluntly that I spoiled her, that I stunted her growth by interfering with her independence, and that she would certainly benefit by the presence of siblings or cousins.

While these very public and direct commentaries on my shortcomings as a wife and mother were not exactly good for my ego, they helped to humanize me. My academic qualifications and university position ceased being important in the face of my obvious failures in domains in which the Maori themselves performed admirably. Boundaries fell away as I was directly criticized. My inadequacies were increasingly the subject of public commentary, making me ultimately appear less aloof and far more approachable.

Accompanied Fieldwork

My next four field trips to Ohakune were characterized by Emily's presence and Mike's absence except for a two-week visit. By and large, I was the one people had to adjust to—not Emily. She was treated as my child, and following Maori custom, she was relegated to an age group and expected to amuse and take care of herself.

In 1987 we were in New Zealand for five months. Emily, in the sixth grade at the time, entered intermediate school in February in Ohakune with children she had met in 1982 and others with whom she had been living on the *marae*. She also joined the junior song and dance group for the *Hui Aranga* (the Easter Feast of the Ascension) and attended practices.

The decision to take Emily was made far more by accident than design. Originally, we assumed she would remain in the United States with Mike, who was already used to being a single parent for much of the week because of our commuting arrangements. Mike and I had been teaching at universities in separate states—Indiana and Michigan, respectively—and I commuted for long weekends, while he and Emily remained in the family home in Indiana. Although accustomed to being alone with Emily, Mike was not enthusiastic about having full responsibility for a female adolescent for such a long period of time. Less than two months from my projected departure, however, circumstances fell into place so that Emily would accompany me. In fact, a decision was reached rapidly and with little conscious planning that Emily would come along.

Emily was delighted to return to New Zealand and happily anticipated being reunited with her friends, who were now four and a half years older. We arrived in Auckland shortly after the new year began, a time when New Zealand is largely on vacation. Emily demanded that we travel immediately to Ohakune. This was somewhat awkward because Mike's relatives had expected something more than a telephone call and an hour of casual conversation over a cup of tea. Nevertheless, within two days of our arrival in New Zealand, we made train reservations and arrived in Ohakune.

Several of the elders had gone to visit relatives over the Christmas/New Year holidays; thus only a few of them were in town when we arrived, but they were there to greet us at the train. One of the elders took us on a trip to visit his wide-ranging family resident throughout the town. Emily had arrived home.

Once again, even though Emily was older, it became apparent that she was incompetent by Maori standards in many of life's basic details. While Maori five-year-olds could and did direct themselves to school on occasion, such navigation was beyond my eleven-year-old—a genuine liability. This meant that every day I had to walk her to school and either pick her up or arrange for her to be transported back to the *marae*. This occasioned much negative commentary on my failure as a parent. As for Emily, her poor sense of direction and her inability to function properly in areas of life that far younger Maori children handle routinely continued to be seen as endearing deficits. In the face of these incapacities, her superior scholastic achievements were all the more surprising and celebrated. The combination of her skills and inabilities achieved a balance our hosts identified as hers. She was accepted for the person she was.

Of much more enduring consequence for Emily and for our hosts was Emily's perception of racism as endemic in the school she was attending, which was 75 percent Maori in its population. Emily would come home from school enraged about how classmates were selected as scapegoats; others were ignored by the Pakeha teachers or bullied. These negative reactions of teachers became self-fulfilling prophecies; as an eleven-year-old schoolgirl, Emily witnessed the development of negative behavior patterns she staunchly maintains were forced on the Maori children. It also bothered her that their parents appeared to reinforce the teachers' attitudes; children who were disciplined at school might be beaten at home for the same behaviors. If I knew the family well, I explained how it looked from Emily's point of view, but this was often futile.

By late March, with the Easter festival coming up and practices taking more time, Emily decided that she would no longer attend the school. She insisted that she would learn far more were she to work in the *kohanga reo*, the Maori language "nest" for preschoolers located on the *marae*. She was supported in this by a friend who found school equally uninspiring. I was sympathetic, and Mike, at home in the United States, concurred.

One of the more alarming experiences of all my fieldwork visits took place several weeks later. I had gone to a meeting with several of the elders, leaving the junior group practicing for the Easter festival in the communal dining room. Bored, Emily wandered up to the house of a family with whom we had stayed and with whom she was especially close. There, watching television, was the grandson of the family, a boy Emily regarded as a brother, and one of his cousins, a teenager unknown to Emily.

This cousin had recently been in disciplinary trouble in the local high school for unwanted sexual encounters with the female students. Emily, however, had no way of knowing this. In the meantime, my meeting had ended far earlier than anticipated, and we returned three hours before we were expected. As we arrived on the *marae,* the cousin had made advances and chased Emily into the deserted *kohanga reo* building. When I suddenly appeared and called Emily's name, he ran out. I do not know what he would have done had I not arrived, but I do know that over the years he has been in trouble because of sexual offenses. More important, I knew at the time that

Emily had been in jeopardy and that I had placed her there. This incident raised important questions: what kind of danger was my daughter in? What right did I have to put her in that danger? Could it possibly have been avoided? In short, would she have been better off staying home in Indiana?

One of my closest Ohakune friends, the eldest daughter of important elders and today a social worker, decided to handle the situation. She sought out the young man, suggested that the next time he was interested in a woman that he pick on her, and punched him in the nose, probably breaking it. For the duration of our stay, he was banned from the *marae,* and we never saw him again. Even though Emily was not hurt, this incident brought terrible emotions upon the family in question, who were ashamed, *whakamaa* ('made white,' drained of prestige, humiliated) because, as they saw it, I had entrusted Emily to their care, and she had not remained safe. No matter how much I explained that I did not hold them responsible, that this could have happened anywhere in the United States, and that indeed she was unhurt, each individual in the family felt compelled to explain their shame to me. I have realized only in retrospect that it is a testimony to the intimacy that existed among all of us that our relationships withstood the pressures of this event.

Indeed, Emily herself has no doubt that the experiences she has had with her extended Maori family have been overwhelmingly positive. She appreciates their sense of humor, their kindness, and the often awesome intelligence and articulateness of many of the elders. While the incident described above was difficult, it was probably no more difficult than dealing with the realities of prejudice, class differences, and her own privileged position.

She has been angered by any suggestions that Maori are not the social equals of Pakeha, an attitude she has encountered with her father's relatives and the Pakeha New Zealanders who have visited us in the United States from time to time. She is more than appalled by ignorance and racism; her own experiences deny facile characterizations.

Fieldwork and Adolescent Children

In 1988 Mike, Emily, and I moved from Indiana to New York, and Emily, then twelve, was forced to leave her friends and change schools. For an American adolescent, such a relocation occurred at a very bad time. In addition, she moved from a small-town public school to an urban private one. Ironically, when she accompanied me for three months in New Zealand, it meant returning to one of the few stable points in her life.

During our 1991 visit, Emily was my research assistant, working in the language nest and attending high school. Young people were learning to speak Maori, carve, weave, and be proficient in office skills and auto mechanics. Several of Emily's friends were now active in high school social life, and Emily looked forward to seeing local plays and attending school functions.

In addition, Emily took her cello with her this time. A fairly serious musician, she could not afford to spend three months without practicing. What did the family at the *marae* make of the cello? It is not an instrument with which people are ordinarily familiar. While our hosts were curious to hear her play, the sound produced was unknown to most of them and probably not pleasant. Musical considerations aside, the social class implications of Emily's affinity for this less popular and expensive stringed instrument were hard to miss. When Emily sat down to play for the first time, we were reassessed; our social position clearly provided privileges and opportunities that were not available to our closest friends.

For several weeks, Emily diligently wrote down the kinship relationships of all the children in the *kohanga reo* and the words to the songs they sang, and she helped document the subculture of adolescents. Abruptly, however, she stopped in disgust. This was too much for her: she had become an informant, with all the nasty connotations of surveillance and control through information. She treated me with a new contempt, a contempt directed at both my occupation and my methods. She received a second jolt a few days later when she attended the school play. Emily had known most of the players well for many years and eagerly looked forward to the performance. I was not well and stayed home. As soon as she returned, I knew something was wrong. With almost a dozen people in the house, however, I could not ask her. In due course I discovered that the problem was with Emily and her expectations. In New York, she had attended a private school with a reputation for high scholarship and artsy eclecticism, where it is not uncommon for their theater faculty to have professional associations and advantageous contacts. As a result, the school's productions often have sets and costumes made by professionals, with lighting and sound systems worthy of a Broadway production. The contrast between the two high schools' (her private high school in New York and a country high school in rural, small-town New Zealand) productions brought home to Emily the class differences between her experience and those of her Maori friends.

From then on, I never saw Emily for more than ten minutes. In her attempt to cope, she constantly kept active with friends, returning occasionally only to sleep. This running from group to group was uncharacteristic. Normally, Emily is by nature solitary; over the years, she has learned to entertain herself and has come to need and enjoy privacy. In the wake of the school play incident, she probably worked hard not to think about her new perceptions. She had come to realize that her horizons were different, her world and her future were different, but through no merit of hers, nor defect of theirs.

An accident of time and place of birth had led to radically divergent paths. This could not help but be painful. Emily had her first, piercing perception of class differences and their implications.

Emily's reactions to what I do and who she was forced me to reexamine what happens in anthropological fieldwork encounters. Having been an anthropologist for several decades, I no longer examine what I do. I rationalize my note taking by believing that I am so unsystematic and my handwriting so impossible to read that these notes are worthless to anyone but me. Furthermore, there is the ultimate excuse for what may be a very nasty enterprise: any notes that are valuable will be placed in archives and made accessible to others. But there can be no question that Emily's disdain was illuminating. Also enlightening was her recognition of class differences. When I concentrate on Maori, with my students or in papers aimed at professional audiences, I stress their personal characteristics or their ideological beliefs. While I certainly mention that most live below New Zealand's poverty level, I neglect the telling contrast with my own relative wealth. Emily's experience no longer allows me to sustain the comfortable fiction that class is irrelevant to my relationship with the Maori or that such differences have never erected a barrier between us.

What was most moving about this time in my fieldwork was the clear evidence of the community's devotion and commitment to Emily, whom they regarded with a proprietary interest untainted by external considerations. There was no doubt in anyone's mind—ours or theirs—that Emily has privileges unavailable to Ohakune Maori children. Recognizing that she was depressed and alienated, the community closed ranks around her, inviting her into their homes, demonstrating in every way they could their protection and sympathy for her. In those months they, not I, were her family. This may have been the young adult extension of the experience reported by Young Leslie (chapter 3) for her toddler (see also Turner 1987). In a symbolic sense, in refusing to take any more fieldnotes, in sleeping in others' houses, in remaining oblivious to my whereabouts, Emily cast her lot, conclusively I think, with them.

Emily is appalled at racism, which is not an abstraction to her. In fact, she takes racist remarks personally and will not tolerate them, which has led to some uncomfortable moments, especially with Mike's family. I exempt my husband's relatives from judgment because of our emotional ties. Emily does not. When they say anything against Maori, she demands a full retraction or threatens a speedy exit. She acts on her beliefs, while Mike and I squirm, silently wondering if she is the only one in our family with principles. In New Zealand, Emily is a New Zealand citizen and a Pakeha, but her loyalty, her allegiance, is unquestionably with the Maori.

Mike's identity is not so easily resolved. For one, he is a Pakeha, and for another, he has resisted fitting in, but after more than twenty-five years of research, his distance has been cast as a rather admirable characteristic. When Emily and I are in Ohakune for several months, he comes for a few weeks. He stays with us on the *marae,* goes to football games, eats dinner with everyone, and genuinely enjoys the companionship. He is consulted on legal questions, and in 1991 he wrote a multipage document on the problems young people face with the legal system.

Nevertheless, while Mike is a guest, Emily and I are not. Instead, we are intimates of the local people: they know our secrets, as we know theirs; we have discussed problems, and we have opened ourselves up to criticism. The rewards of being part of this community, of knowing that when we come back each time they will be happy to see us, have long outweighed any discomfort over lack of privacy.

None of this is true for Mike. Emily can threaten to depart a house in which nasty words are said against Maori. She does not have divided loyalties. Nor, for that matter, do I. When in New Zealand, Mike has a foot in both camps. He is a Pakeha, with a clan of Pakeha relatives and a network of Pakeha friends. Remarks that send Emily and me fleeing (or into rages), Mike must endure. These individuals are his family and his childhood companions, but he is embarrassed by them, and my presence makes it worse, aggravating any sense of complicity he has as a Pakeha.

Recently Mike became an American citizen. He is comfortable in the United States. He is happy with his job, he enjoys New York, and his New Zealand accent permits him the luxury of separating himself from aspects of his adopted country that he finds unpleasant. Now, it is in New Zealand that he is uncomfortable. His discomfort derives from being both an expatriate and having affinities to two communities who generally erect barriers against one another. These conflicts are better off unwitnessed—at least for Mike. On his own, he can separate the two worlds that he must inevitably occupy when in New Zealand. It is easier for him to cope—to be an American, a Pakeha, and a close associate of Maori—by keeping his life somewhat compartmentalized.

Adult Children in the Field

Emily's ability to negotiate very difficult social terrain became evident again during short visits in 1993 and in 1995. In 1993, Emily anticipated a difficult stay. While she had recently been accepted for undergraduate study at Yale, several of her Maori friends were facing parenthood. By 1995, one of her closest friends, a young woman who had started university intent on a law degree, was pregnant but determined that having a child would not interrupt her study plans.

Emily had thought about the implications of much of this, but she was nonetheless unprepared for the reality. Boys with whom she had grown up were now men. Even though in earlier years she had seen them as family and had followed them on late-night fishing excursions, as young men they would do little more than nod at her. The separation of men and women that marks Maori social worlds was not, for her, an adequate explanation. The young women greeted her with a mixture of shyness and avoidance that effectively blocked casual conversation. For her part, Emily did not know what to say about their pregnancies nor what to make of their infants, despite her baby-sitting experience. After a few civilities, the discussion was over, leaving Emily unhappy and miserable.

There was, however, the rest of the community, which, sensing Emily's distress, quickly moved in to shield and divert her. We were staying with my contemporaries, who proved to be especially sensitive to Emily's discomfort. The concern for Emily was even more clear when, at the Easter gathering, she developed a sore throat and swollen glands. People stayed with us throughout the night to make sure she was all right, calling out inquiries across crowded billets about the state of her condition.

Moreover, everyone had heard of Yale and was enormously proud of her. The Yale sweatshirts and T-shirts we sent were coveted and worn by everybody. Her young friends, who were themselves university bound, introduced her, much to her amazement and embarrassment, as an American who was going to Yale. What was notable about their feelings was that they were proprietary: they recognized how much Emily belonged to them. Moreover, there was no envy, only pride. Perhaps that, too, bespoke a recognition of difference.

The community's feelings about Emily were made even more clear when she performed with a visiting New York–based youth orchestra in the main center of Taupo in July 1993. Twenty-five adults and children braved snow, fog, and horrible roads to drive up to three hours to hear her play. One male elder, very prominent on the larger New Zealand stage, shuttled between closed airports in an ultimately successful effort to see Emily's concert.

Emily knew in advance that members of the family were coming. As a result, she was delighted, flattered, and terrified. As principal cellist, she was already in a prominent position, but the conductor, knowing of Emily's affiliation with local people, organized a solo for her. Emily is a veteran performer, playing in public since her preschool days. Yet this was different; this was the first time that these very important people were going to see her in a public forum. She did play well and had read the situation correctly; one of the elders, a woman important in *Maramatanga*, told Emily knowingly that she had done them proud. Young children were silenced in their enthusiasm, instructed that people did not act thusly in this kind of auditorium, even though Emily would have liked nothing better than to have them uninhibitedly call out her name and wave enthusiastically from the audience.

It is significant of course that very important elders, with numerous responsibilities and places to be, traveled to see her under difficult conditions. But far more important, they knowingly placed themselves in a Pakeha environment, the Taupo Town Hall, and subjected themselves and their grandchildren to Pakeha standards of behavior. Emily saw this and understood what had taken place. What she was seeing was the intensity of her affection and commitment mirrored back at her.

Emily is now an autonomous adult. Like me, she will always go to New Zealand and, as always, will be in the country the minimal amount of time before she makes her way to Ohakune. In a world that has constantly shifted from Michigan, to Indiana, to New York, Emily maintains that she has two points of constancy: the *marae* and a summer music camp in upper Michigan that she has attended through all the other changes in her life. The elders are indeed correct when they express a proprietary interest in Emily; she does belong to that *marae*—in fact, in behavior, and in loyalty. But the new role of parenthood assumed by many of her friends there—and all that it implies in terms of employment and opportunities—has made Emily profoundly uncomfortable, raising the possibility that perhaps she does not belong there after all, and forcing upon her once again the extreme discomfort occasioned by class differences. Her last comment, after our 1995 visit, was that she would not return until she, too, was a mother. Inevitably, having raised a child and witnessed her transformation through the course of my research, I have been forced to reexamine my own fieldwork and the implications of Emily's participation.

Gendered and Accompanied Fieldwork

This is not a story with an ending or a neat moral. In our third decade of fieldwork, there will be differences in the constellation of people who visit the *marae*. Since 1982 Mike, Emily, and I have never done fieldwork as a family. Clearly the rigors of academic scheduling can account for this. But our inability and unwillingness to be in the same place for very much of the same time while we are in New Zealand is, ultimately, quite revealing. It is very likely that although each of us will continue to visit the *marae,* for different reasons and for different personal purposes, we will never be there together again.

Over the many years of fieldwork, I have grown especially close to several women my age, whose life experiences have paralleled mine: we have moved from being students to wives and mothers, and most of us work outside the home. We correspond in the intervals between my field trips, we talk on the telephone, and I almost always spend a few days in their homes when I return. There is little we do not discuss. We know one another's histories well.

While we are certainly sympathetic to one another and have grown closer over the years as the commonalities in our experience emerge, ultimately this group of women is unaffected by my academic concerns. It was their grandmothers, mothers, and aunts who were active in the religious movement, which has been the focus of so much of my academic research. Their role has come to be supervisory: it is they who ask questions about my intent and they who read most carefully what I have written. They probe my knowledge, checking that I am on the right track.

It is also their understanding of me and of my relations with Mike and Emily that is most complete. They have questioned me directly about how much money we make, where we stand in the American class system (at least as this can be gleaned through television and other media in New Zealand), and what our life-style is like. I answer truthfully and in as great a detail as fits the situation. In fact, Maori constraint and my personal reserve would prohibit such conversations except under extraordinary circumstances. My intimacy with these individuals counts as extraordinary.

These conversations take place only with women, however, and I am drawn to the realization that overall and from the very beginning my fieldwork has been profoundly gendered. Having my family with me—as companions and as subjects of discussion—has produced a situation that is biased in both production and analysis. This has forced me to recognize that knowledge is situated, a circumstance that applies equally to the Maori and to me. I learn different things when I talk to the daughter of the prophet, as opposed to his great-granddaughter; the leader and the led have vastly different stores of knowledge and different stories to relate. Along the same lines it is clear that over the course of my fieldwork, my position has changed, moving from young girl to middle-aged woman, while my knowledge of individuals no longer alive has, in keeping with Maori respect for knowledge, increased my standing in the community. Furthermore, depending on context and perspective, people respond to me as a woman, as a wife and a mother, and as a Pakeha.

Of late, there has been a tendency to recognize the gendered nature of fieldwork, to eschew disclaimers or cover-ups for violating the lone male model (see McGrath and Linnekin, chapters 4 and 5). As Bell (1993b, 29) has written in her discussion of women's fieldwork:

> It bears the stamp of the observing-participating self and hence is biased, interested and partial, all terms that are paired with woman in the gender-inflected dualism (partial/impartial, personal/detached, emotional/rational) of post-Enlightenment rationalist thought.

If, as Macintyre (1993), Dominy (this volume), and others (e.g., Bell, Caplan, and Karim 1993) claim, women's narrative authority is always questioned, there may well be virtues to what appears a very distinct liability: we can explore our questionable legitimacy with our counterparts—the women whose lives we are both observing and sharing.

Contributors to this volume and others (see Butler and Turner 1987b; Cassell 1987b), have written that the presence of families in the field may open up the possibilities of different paradigms, or at the very least cause us to question the managed aloofness of controlled masculinity that has served as our fieldwork model. These concerns have recently been echoed by Macintyre (1993) and Bell (1993b), both women, whose fieldwork has departed from published models precisely because they were not men. There are of course accounts of women's fieldwork experiences (notably Powdermaker 1966; Bowen 1954; Briggs 1970; and Golde 1986), but these have been treated as special cases. As Linnekin and Macintyre both point out, it is the likes of Berreman and Malinowski, despite all odds, who are held up as exemplars. Perhaps the most important aspect of this is that women possess "a gender inflected voice, which cannot masquerade as universal: they have a standpoint and cannot pretend otherwise" (Bell 1993a, 2). Women are more inclined (perhaps) to take heed of the situatedness of themselves as knower and to be more humbled by this fact.

As an unmarried woman in the early part of my first fieldwork, I was seen by my hosts as an anomaly: too old to be single, too old to be supervised as a minor, but too vulnerable not to need familial support. Marriage legitimated me. And while my husband's aloofness was at times problematic, it worked out much better—for me, for him, but perhaps most of all for the community in which I was working. Its people were free not to have to deal with a Pakeha male.

From 1982 until the present, I have always been accompanied by Emily. Emily has unmasked us: she has revealed my inadequacies (at least in Maori terms) with the effect of making me more human. My concerns whenever she was ill, my fretting over the limits of her autonomy (a constant issue), my disagreements with Mike—these have all made me recognizable, whatever other differences emerged. But most important, it was precisely in the ways that women *did* recognize me that revealed the gendered nature of my fieldwork.

Emily's cello playing, her failure to stand aloof, her unmitigated enthusiasm for the *marae,* for the people, for the culture have proved to be revelatory and certainly stand in opposition to what would have been my choice of relative reserve. In 1990, 1991, 1993, and 1995 we lived in Maori people's houses, where Emily is happy at the ready access that is mutually available but where

I have nowhere to hide. There are no literal or metaphorical walls to conceal my emotions, and Emily's reactions keep me honest. The clarity of her recognition of racism, of class, and of privilege has forced me to understand that these elements are integral parts of my research.

Emily's participation assured that my biography, my politics, and my relationships became part of "the fabric of the field" (Bell 1993b, 29), but there can be no doubt that however difficult this has been at times, my fieldwork has been enriched. As a mother and as a wife, I was validated as a woman. And as a woman, I learned about the specific cultural production of knowledge.

There are, to be sure, differences in class, privilege, and opportunity between my Maori friends and me. But the community's, especially the women's, understanding of the intensity of their bonds to Emily worked to undermine, or at least temporarily extinguish, these differences. What emerged instead was a shared womanhood, in which differently, differentially, and yet similarly we were somehow all engaged in the same process. Differences certainly remain and it is critical not to conflate these. Behar (1993, 301) has written of precisely the dilemma faced in feminist ethnographies. Talking of her own work, she has said:

> This feminist ethnography is located on the border between the opposite tendencies to see women as not at all different from one another or as all too different, for to go too far in either direction is to end up *indifferent* to the lives of other women.

The religious movement that I have studied appeared in 1972–1973 to be a male-dominated arena. This was an illusion. Perhaps I might have realized this on my own. As a woman, I was more approachable, and the real forces of the movement—the women—talked to me and let me see them as I suspect they see themselves—as warriors, with battles always raging on several fronts. Gender ideology, which in some distillations favors men, was upheld verbally but very deliberately denied in action. In the place of platitudes, women told me stories of heroic women ancestors. More important, they called upon me to witness their own acts of heroism. They made it impossible for me not to see how hard they must work and how onerous it is for them to write themselves into the national narrative. Perhaps it is my complicity in this effort that has spurred their cooperation. They have certainly witnessed my weaknesses. But that has not been all bad, for without an assessment of my frailties they would not have shown me their strengths.

Acknowledgments

My fieldwork has been supported by the Fulbright Foundation, National Science Foundation, a Brown University Fellowship, the National Endowment for the Humanities in the form of a Travel to Collections Grant in 1987 and a Fellowship for College Teachers in 1990, two sabbatical leaves from Eastern Michigan University, three faculty research fellowships, the World College at Eastern Michigan University, and the Josephine Nevins Keal Awards. I express my gratitude to all of these funding agencies.

Notes

1. This title comes from Anthony Powell's *A dance to the music of time* (1955), a series of twelve novels.

9 Border-crossing in Tonga
Marriage in the Field

TAMAR GORDON

In October 1982 I arrived in western Polynesia in the Kingdom of Tonga as a single, white American graduate student bent on gathering material for a doctoral dissertation on religious and social change. I left in August 1984, a married woman with a Tongan husband, real (not fictive) Tongan relatives, and an additional social identity that changed many Tongans' perceptions of my personhood and my work. My decision to carry on a courtship and marry while doing fieldwork also presented serious challenges to another tradition: my role as researcher and my very classical graduate education. Nothing I ever learned at the University of California, Berkeley, had prepared me for it.

My thoroughly modernist training had taught me that "in the field" I would enter into the interpersonal world of my "informants" in order to gain a functioning cultural empathy. This would allow me to achieve "rapport" while temporarily suspending the certainties of my own world view. I might have friends and contacts among the people I had come to study, but deliberate attempts at blurring or merging researcher self with informant other were taboo.

Different kinds of rapprochements (like the mutual act of falling in love, for example) expose and defy the historical imperative to maintain the outside self/inside other relationship. When revealed in professional writing, these other relationships have the potential to disrupt the authority of anthropological discourse itself. Reports of the messy open-endedness of the ethnographer's subjective experience—the mistakes, betrayals, failed friendships, courtships, animosities, and embarrassments—have traditionally been marginalized in the form of anecdotes that legitimate the fieldwork rite of passage. Such subjective narratives do not fall within the proper boundaries of objective, reconstructed knowledge, but rather are safely excluded from ethnographic writing with its textual closure and indexing of professional expertise. (See Clifford 1988; Clifford and Marcus 1986 for the original critiques of ethnographic writing.) By remaining in this discursive terrain, the anthropologist additionally ensures that breaches in professional ethics will never make themselves known in the public sphere of the academy. Most of us will rest easy that local knowledge of our activities will remain local. Like most of the contributors to this volume, I myself have taken few risks in this regard until this writing.

This chapter describes some of my experiences in Tonga. They compare in some respects with those of Sinclair (chapter 8), another white American woman who married a local person soon after arriving in New Zealand for her first fieldwork among the Maori. Our discussions explore some similar questions. My experiences diverge, however, in at least two important respects. First, they span a single period of two years in the field, in contrast to Sinclair's multiple visits across a twenty-year period. Second, my Tongan experience involved me in an interracial (white American/Polynesian Tongan) as well as cross-national marriage. Sinclair's marriage was an intraracial (white American/white New Zealander) one and thus did not present her with the issue of having married into the family of the people with whom she was working, as mine did. McGrath (chapter 4) and Young Leslie (chapter 3) also report on doing fieldwork in Tonga in the late 1980s as married women, but both were married to North American compatriots, and their husbands accompanied them to Tonga as part of a family fieldwork visit.

Beginnings

Prior to going to Tonga in October 1982, I spent two months in Lā'ie, Hawai'i, in intensive Tongan language learning, and six months in the San Francisco Bay Area getting to know members of the Tongan community in northern California. For the first four months in Tonga, I lived in the home of the Tavake family, who were relatives of my Tongan teacher in Hawai'i. The family comprised Hina, her husband, Mahanga, Hina's father, their teenage daughter, and their seven-year-old son. (All names used in this chapter are pseudonyms.) They lived in a village that had become something of a bedroom community to nearby Nuku'alofa, Tonga's capital town.

I was initially disappointed to realize that the Tavake family did not fit into my prefigured image of traditional Tonga. They were modern, suburban-dwelling, landless, middle-class Tongan commoners: a small, nuclear family whose comfortable, wooden home contained many of the amenities I had been prepared to forego in the service of "authentic" field experience. In addition, since they had lived in New Zealand for several years, the Tavakes spoke English fairly well and were eager to practice. As long as I stayed with them, I was not going to experience the language immersion I needed.

I had come to Tonga to analyze religious politics, particularly the impact of the Mormon church on Tongan national identity. As a way of getting started I spent my first weeks frenetically traveling to different parts of the Nuku'alofa area to interview prominent Mormons. My hard work notwithstanding, I came away with very little. The Tongan Mormon elites had two terrains to protect: their church, which was currently under siege by public opinion, and their Polynesian sense of personal privacy, both of which they preserved by doling out insignificant and incomplete nuggets of information. The proverbial "Friendly Islanders," as the eighteenth-century English explorer Capt. James Cook had dubbed them in response to the pleasant social surfaces he encountered, were not proving to be very friendly by my naive standards. When viewed from my still radically undeveloped sense of Tongan social politics, they were simply not cooperating.

Nearly in tears one evening, I put my woes to Hina while she prepared our dinner on the modern stove top. Her eyes danced with glee as she held up an onion she was peeling. "See this onion? This onion is a Tongan. You peel and peel and you never get to the center." In spite of my discouragement, I laughed delightedly at her ontological metaphor. Feelings of relief flowed. Difference seemed to dissolve in laughter, in mutual appreciation. Hina seemed relieved as well. She had succeeded in lightening the surface of my emotional discomfort with a very Polynesian strategy for coping with anger and depression that I was to experience many times—and eventually offer myself—in the course of my stay.

During those few months there were times when it required an act of will for me to get out of bed and face another day of fieldwork, another day of struggling with the unknowns, especially the extravagantly hidden meanings of conversation and the Byzantine politics of everyday life, another day of denying my personhood and submitting myself to the agenda of others. I was in deep culture shock. Furthermore, my Tongan "family" did not provide me with a respite from what I had come to view as the marketplace of culture "out there" in public. For example, all of my carefully packed nylon slips, soap, plastic shavers, and even dental floss gradually, comically disappeared. My own family was stealing from me! I was not comforted when a trusted Tongan friend responded to my complaints with the local proverb, "You only steal from those you love."

Because of the Tavakes' seeming modernity, the contradictions posed by their attitudes and expectations caught me by surprise. I had to contend with Mahanga's injunctions that I was not to walk anywhere by myself (while their seven-year-old son was sent off alone to the movies) and his orders to speak only English with their daughter so that she might improve her chances with a certain son of a chief who was courting her (while I despaired of ever becoming fluent in Tongan).

I militantly repressed my reactions and my needs because I was deeply committed to maintaining "professional" and therefore "ethical" relationships with my Tongan family and friends. Ethics, to me, meant conforming with the liberal tenets of the anthropological concept of cultural relativism. (See Young Leslie, chapter 3, for an in-depth discussion with reference to fieldwork in Tonga.) This meant eschewing value judgments, avoiding conflict, assimilating as best I could, and being as reciprocal as possible in social exchanges. In the meantime, I was very homesick, seething at times with unexpressed anger at the perceived slights of my hosts and pining for "real" love and missing my "real" family. Looking back on my twenty-seven-year-old self, I can see that I was emotionally unprepared for the participant-observer role that had been thrust upon me by the academy, a role that would result in objective ethnographic description. I wanted and needed to be more of the participant and insider than the properly balanced management of the role allowed.

Courtship

The extradomestic relationships in the life of the Tavake family proved to be my doorway into a more gratifying world. They were bound through friendship, neighborhood, and kinship ties to a tiny private college run by a charismatic Tongan intellectual, an internationally recognized authority on Tongan culture. Mahanga shared with him and his students a weekly kava club—a male social circle that centers around drinking the strained liquid of the kava plant. Thanks to the Tavakes' stewardship, I was able to gain the support of the school's director and consult with him on a regular basis. When I needed more language study, help came in the form of a tutor, a graduate of the college and teacher whom I paid to work with me several hours a day. He would become my husband.

Sojourners in Tonga soon become aware of Tongans' richly loving natures and romantic preoccupations. These qualities are matched, however, by a cultural prescription for rigorous suppression of public intimacy, and this is enforced by means of ridicule and even punishment. The only legitimate forms of courtship in modern Tonga are a visit by a young man to a young woman's house or the opportunity to sit next to her in a kava circle if she is the server. Both are conducted under the watchful eyes of family and friends. Early in my stay, I witnessed a variety of reactions to secret dating—directed at the girl—ranging from laughter and teasing to physical violence. My graduate studies had taught me something of the culture of social hierarchy and control, particularly in relation to women, and finding it firmly in place in Tonga itself had quickly dispelled any lingering illusions I might have entertained about fieldwork in a Polynesian paradise. I was compellingly drawn into an elaborate, hidden discourse of desire. Veiled references to sex and romantic liaisons were everywhere. Love songs composed by Queen Salote, Tonga's late, beloved sovereign-poet could be heard on any night of the week, sung in beautiful harmonies by groups of men as they drank kava. In the course of my stay in Tonga, I served as a go-between for several young couples. When I was invited to be *touʻa,* the unmarried woman who serves the kava, young men always seemed to find seats next to me. I was teased about my availability, and people waited eagerly for me to make slips of the tongue that would signal, in Freudian fashion, my unsatisfied desires. My loud request for a *kila* ('head of a penis') of tuna at the fishmarket instead of a kilo was a source of uproarious merriment for those who heard it and mortifying embarrassment for me. And despite my unmarried status, I was secretly approached by married and unmarried women seeking advice about how to procure birth control devices. True, I was conducting some ancillary research into family planning practices for the United Nations, but as an American, I was dangerously close to the image of the "loose *palangi* (white/European) woman" for whom female Peace Corps volunteers and Hollywood movie stars were the prototype. The fact that I fell simultaneously into the two local social categories—*talavou* 'unmarried youth' and *muli* 'foreigner'—intensified my ambiguity and uncontrollability; I was never viewed primarily as a researcher.

I remained "good" by Tongan and prevailing anthropological standards until, after a month of language lessons, my tutor, Sione, and I fell in love. Gentle and shy by nature, exemplifying the Tongan commoner value of humility, Sione was extremely sensitive to the gossip that soon penetrated the protective cover of our student-teacher relationship. His impulse was to protect us, and his strategy was to limit our contacts together. Safety and secrecy were synonymous for him. I had the opposite need, which was natural enough for a young, single American adult, to display our connection openly. I was learning firsthand, and with considerable hardship, the nature of relationships in Tonga: the secrecy surrounding courtship and stoicism at missed opportunities to be together. I heard for the first time the melancholy fatalism surrounding love so elegantly expressed in the queen's love songs.

Sione was definitely dutiful. He would break appointments with me in order to obey the demands of his powerful paternal aunt with whom he lived. He also spent a great deal of time serving the school and its director, who governed with chiefly authority over his dominion. His friends also took precedence on occasion, lest he endure their ridicule. Again, when looking back over this period, I can only hope that few people saw through my veneer of graciousness. I do know that Sione took the rap both at home and at work for some of my demands on his attention and that he never told me some of the most disturbing gossip about us. Paradoxically, despite my increasing fluency with Tongan culture, my need to experience this relationship as "real" caused me to effect an ignorance of the consequences of my actions on our position within our immediate community.

Sione's parents and siblings lived in Vava'u, the northernmost island group. They all knew about me from the "coconut wireless"—the knowledge flows passed through networks of family and friends—the prime source being Sione's aunt with whom he lived in Nuku'alofa. One of Sione's many ways of protecting me was to exempt me from obligation and, therefore, from servitude to his higher-ranking relatives. He offered me the alternatives of pleasing oneself and expressing freedom of action, both of which are available in the Tongan ideology of social relationships and which I could exploit by asserting my *muli* status. I was, however, eager for his relatives to like me and so I attempted to turn these options into a pleasingly sincere attempt at signifying real respect. I put my competence in the Tongan language to work and spoke with Sione's aunt in a combination of respect-avoidance and joking-warmth styles of interaction. After several months, we had a humorous exchange; she asserted mock authority over me by "ordering" me to get her some tea. I obliged, while addressing her in the high respectful form of Tongan reserved for social superiors. She seemed to enjoy the novelty of a Tongan-speaking American girl with some kind of investment in her goodwill, even though she knew full well that I would never subordinate myself to her interests the way a prospective Tongan wife would. Sione told me that she believed he would repay her sometime in the future for supporting him while he attended school, regardless of the well-known resistance of American spouses to give money to their Tongan in-laws. And since she financed a feast for our modest wedding a year later, the call for our reciprocal *'ofa* 'love' expressed through material contribution would be doubly justified.

My First Visit to Sione's Family

Two months after Sione and I became a couple, I accompanied a friend, the daughter of a chief, on a trip to Vava'u. I wanted to explore the possibilities of relocating my research to a Mormon-dominated village there. I took the bold step of traveling to Sione's home village to visit his family, even though the role of "girlfriend" I was acting out had little meaning or legitimacy in Tonga. Sione had generously written to his family, asking them to welcome me as his friend and student. When I arrived, his mother gently and graciously set about trying to make me fit in, taking me on a walk through the village, telling me about the family and how their house was built. His beloved older sister (who had helped raise Sione more in the manner of a mother than a sister) served a lunch to his father and me while we sat cross-legged on a clean, fragrant mat in the front room. He spoke no English. We talked about things of the world: his sojourn in Fiji as a soldier during World

War II, my travels to Europe, my Jewish background, his love of education, and his admiration for the director of Sione's school. Even though I was dying to tell him how happy their son had made me, the topic of my relationship with Sione was studiously avoided.

As we spoke politely and sparingly of other things over lunch, I was acutely aware of the fact that Sione's older sister was serving us. It went against what I knew of the formal structures of Tongan kinship. As I was to learn in my fieldwork and through my continued contact with Sione's family, status and rank are flexible and contextually redefined as needed. In this case, I was being honored as a visitor (of ambiguous role) to their family, a role that carries temporarily high status. Sione's sister exercised her prerogative to subordinate herself to my needs. It prefigured a fuller welcome of me as a daughter-in-law a year later. When my friend, the chief's daughter, returned with her entourage to take me back to her village, Sione's mother performed a ritual act: she threw a tapa cloth down in front of us.

Riding back to the other village in the truck, I felt elated that I had overcome my fears at meeting Sione's family, but also rather empty. My future mother-in-law's gesture at the end struck me as impersonal, somehow negating my relationship to them. This was because I knew that her presentation of the tapa had little to do with me personally; it was an obligatory act honoring my associate and patron, the chief of the neighboring village. Sione would later express annoyance that his mother had been forced to relinquish a portion of their *koloa* 'ceremonial wealth' on account of my visit. Of course I felt guilty about this but pleased that I had seemingly made a good impression on my future in-laws.

I had wanted to feel close to these people, especially to the sister whom I knew Sione loved and admired so much, and the fact that she alone spoke some English presented additional possibilities for closeness. But the general atmosphere of *ma* 'shy restraint' and the absence of *maheni* 'warm familiarity' left me feeling lonely. I had wanted to make myself "real" to them, but the taboo on discussing with them my personal relationship with Sione ensured an absence of agreement on categories—on who we were to each other. Sione's family, dignified even in their confusion, laid down a grid of Tongan protocol that downplayed the emotions and questions underlying the visit. I will never know how they "really" felt about me on that occasion.

Marriage and Homecoming

Sione and I continued to maintain our relationship during the eight subsequent months I spent in Vava'u—ironically in closer proximity to his family than he was. I visited his family again and sometimes ran into his sister, who taught in the Wesleyan high school in the port town of Neiafu. Sione and I were married in May 1984, three months before we would return together to California. The civil and religious ceremonies—extremely simple and brief affairs—took place in Nuku'alofa. Although his parents could not travel to be there, Sione assured me that they were very happy about the marriage, especially since they both wanted him to obtain his bachelor's degree overseas. Representing the family were his aunt and some cousins of his mother who presented us with wedding *koloa*. These consisted of several large pieces of tapa cloth and some fine woven mats. We made our obligatory appearance in his aunt's church on Sunday, dressed in our wedding mats. Afterward she made a feast for us to which were invited friends and relatives residing in the Nuku'alofa area.

Sione and I returned to Vava'u two weeks later to be received for the first time by his parents as a married couple. We were legitimate at last—no more wagging tongues or missed opportunities. We could live openly together and receive the approving smiles of the people. Knowing my yearning for American-style family bonding, Sione laid down some discursive rules for the first time. He solemnly asked me not to "shame" him by not breaching the all-important respect-avoidance relationship with his sister. I was not to discuss our relationship with her or with anyone else. His family indeed was prepared to love me, but I must not create an embarrassing situation for all of us by blurting out my feelings or by asking his sister personal questions about him. Unbeknownst to Sione, on a previous occasion in Vava'u I had pushed this envelope, so to speak, with his sister. I had haltingly tried to tell her how much I missed him. It was as though I had said nothing at all. When she spoke, it was about something completely unconnected to my statement.

So I resolved to try to "know" them and have them "know" me in conventional Tongan fashion: by building *maheni* slowly on a solid foundation of daily, good-natured interaction and sharing of work. My dream of Tongan familial intimacy would never be realized, however. I would not settle in the village of my husband and perhaps never even see his family again. Sione's father died on the day of our departure for California, and Sione and I divorced four years later.

When we arrived in the village following the wedding in Nuku'alofa, there was a round of feasting, churchgoing, visiting relatives, and conversing about their various households. During our week-long stay, I accompanied Sione to the bush as he tended the family yam gardens, and I helped his two sisters care for their nieces and nephews. His father pointed out the size of their pig herd, the planned improvements on their little house, and the borders of their land with its ancient place names, much of which would someday be Sione's to inherit. He also took me to the village cemetery where members of their *ha'a* 'lineage' were buried. After Sione and I returned to California and I reviewed my memories of this visit, I realized what his father was doing. He was alerting me to the enduring touchstones of their identity, their ties to the land, the family, and the nation. I came to read it as a comment that I must not come between Sione and his profound responsibilities to his family. It was only much later that Sione revealed to me how much his mother had cried when she realized that we would be leaving, perhaps permanently, albeit for greater opportunity. Sione's older brother had already abdicated his right to the family patrimony by becoming a citizen of Australia. She was afraid, rightly so, that Sione would never return to take his place in the family and the village.

Sione's mother revealed none of her concerns to me. She treated me according to the fiction that I was a new bride who had left her dear parents to reside with a strange family. I had observed in other Tongan families that during this sensitive period of time, the new daughter-in-law may develop a joking relationship with her husband's mother to ease the transition. The whole family helps by treating the new bride with deference as if to a high-ranking person, especially when she becomes pregnant. To mitigate what she constructed as my homesickness, Sione's mother quietly organized the two of us into a routine of nightly walks to church choir practice or to relatives' homes. On the fifth night, we had a stereotypic exchange that marked the shift into joking and into *maheni*. When we first arrived, eager to display my talent at gossiping, I had regaled her with stories of Tiamone, an infamous, miserly man in my village study site, who had cheated his neighbors of a share in the revenues for the monthly tourist beach feasts they collectively organized. Now she fished it out as the basis for a mock insult.

> "You are a Tiamone," she said suddenly.
> "You *really* want to be a Tiamone," I rejoined.
> "You're a Tiamone *and* a Sela [Tiamone's wife]." She was poker-faced.
> "You want to be Tiamone while I want to be a member of the *ha'a* Fonua lineage." Now I was really cooking.

My new mother-in-law rewarded my efforts with a reluctant smile of amazement and repeated our exchange to the family over a midnight snack of cocoa and flour dumplings.

My Reception in My Host Village

While Sione remained with his family, I returned for a last, brief stint of fieldwork in the village in which I had established myself over the past year. Returning to this village as a married woman was instructive, albeit disquieting.

Now a seasoned veteran of Tonga, I was able to anticipate and manage veiled expressions of jealousy on the part of my host family, who supposed that I had transferred all my loyalties and resources to my husband's family. However, a part of me still needed to feel that I was an independent agent and that my change in marital status had not affected the access I had worked so hard to achieve. Therefore, when I was no longer invited to serve kava as the "unmarried maiden" or sought out by the young, unmarried women whose company I enjoyed so much, I was hurt. The village Mormons, my primary informants and friends, regarded me strangely when I attended church, as I always had, alone with my host family. People asked me where my husband was and expressed pity for me that he "wouldn't come to church." People were now clearly confused by my presence in the village—far more than when I first arrived—and their moral rancor grew. As I conducted my last household survey, several of the married women pointedly asked me what I was doing in the village. Why was I not with my husband's family, helping them out? By what logic had I returned to their village and not to my husband's? I had no response to offer. It was a rare moment of speechlessness for me. It was of no consequence to my hosts that I still had work to do as a researcher/anthropologist. I had acquired a new insider role, married woman, and was being told that I should behave accordingly. But I was about to leave Tonga, and there would be no chance for the intimacy with other married women in which to learn what being one really entailed and how best to manage the role. Unlike Sinclair (chapter 8), who married during her first fieldwork among the New Zealand Maori, I would not have the opportunity to develop confidences and understandings with other married women across time and life stages. Unlike McGrath (chapter 4), who took her American husband and children with her for fieldwork in Tonga, I could not experience an intimacy derived from discovery of shared knowledge and emotions. Instead, my incorporation into Tongan society as a married woman would remain incomplete and, for the remainder of my time in the field, problematic for my hosts as well as myself. Paradoxically, I had the distinct feeling that I was back to square one as an ignorant neophyte in need of protection and instruction.

Reflections

This is my narrative. What I have chosen to include constructs a reality that would be very different had Sione's voice, or the voices of his family, been included.

The currently popular metaphor of border-crossing perhaps best expresses the naive encounters between myself and my Tongan in-laws, entailing a movement back and forth between two vastly different "countries" of subjectivity. Stripped of the cover of the anthropologist role, I was merely a "quasi-subject." My interpretation of my Tongan experiences is predicated on a "relational form of understanding" (Rosaldo 1989, 206–207) with others that is dramatically without end, without closure. As an anthropological fieldworker in Tonga who married into a local family, I was a quasi-subject in a borderland, actively engaging in the interpretation of cultural behavior along with informant-subjects. Making this explicit not only throws into question the comfortable analytical categories anthropologists construct to systematize other societies and also the means by which this process is mystified and claimed as an exclusive and all-seeing practice. In point of fact, everyone is linked through the global flows of our time. Like "us," natives border-cross all the time, in all their encounters with the nonlocal elements of their world. I have had to come to terms with the political dimension of my relationship with Sione and his family. The conventional professional relationship an anthropologist forms with informants, with its careful reciprocities and sheltering distances, is ultimately weighted in favor of the researcher, for it would take a lifetime to repay the hospitality and cultural knowledge that the anthropologist parlays into a profession. The fact that Sione and I are divorced has ruled out the payback. It has also stifled informants' voices, leaving only mine to sort through this narrative.

When I first embarked on my relationship with Sione, the thought of "going native" was very exciting; it would invite fuller comprehension of another culture while providing me with the love and security I needed to get through the experience of fieldwork and beyond. Of course, marriage to a Tongan *was* in a sense a privileged door into Tongan life. The intimate collaboration between us carried over into my work. I acquired a degree of linguistic fluency that enabled me to communicate and to navigate the complex ground rules for conversation, joking, and the expression of anger. I worked hard to achieve a semblance of cultural assimilation necessary to bridge two different models of intimacy and family relations; indeed, I naively thought Sione's family would love me for my prodigious powers to assimilate. But what was I assimilating *to*? Where would it lead me? What analytical and emotional closure would the process afford me? Instead, the experience proved to be tremendously destabilizing as the ground shifted under me. I lacked the awareness, in Rosaldo's words, to "cope by developing a toleration for contradictions, a tolerance for ambiguity" (1989, 210–211). Instead, I derived satisfaction and comfort through the made-to-fit, fictive commonalities we mutually constructed to deal with each other.

Faced with these experiences, my own borders hardened, and my identities as an anthropologist, as a woman, and as an adult intensified in contexts in which difference and power strongly violated my own values and thwarted my desires; there was little tolerance for "relativity" (a deceptively neutral term for difference that fits the historical aims of anthropology) in these instances.

JanMohamed (1992, 137) is less sanguine than Rosaldo about the possibilities for achieving "authentic" knowledge and insiderhood, writing:

> In theory and effectively in practice, borders are neither inside nor outside the territory they define but simply designate the difference between the two. The border only functions as a mirror, as a site for defining the identity of the group that has constructed it.

To borrow Hina's metaphor, we are all onions, peeling and peeling each other.

Acknowledgments

I thank all people whose pseudonyms appear on these pages—especially "Sione," who chose to make his own journey with me. This period of fieldwork was supported by a University of California Regents Traveling Fellowship and Lowie Scholarships from the Department of Anthropology, University of California at Berkeley. I also wish to thank the expert editors—Juliana Flinn, Leslie Marshall, and Jocelyn Armstrong—who labored to make this a much better chapter.

10 Fictive Families in the Field

DAVID R. COUNTS AND DOROTHY AYERS COUNTS

In an essay on "Language, Anthropology and Cognitive Science," first presented in the prestigious Frazer Lecture series at the London School of Economics, Bloch (1991) says that we anthropologists learn much of what we know about the cultures of the people we study at a visceral, nonlinguistic level achieved by experience. He argues that much of our "cultural knowledge" is a consequence of *doing* things rather than of talking about them. This is the strength and the true heritage of the method of participant observation, especially when it involves long-term research.

In this chapter we build on Bloch's insight. Learning by doing includes learning by making mistakes. When we try to manipulate the cultural system of the people we study, the lessons we learn may reveal the depth of our misunderstanding of them. We may also learn uncomfortable truths about our own ethnocentrism. In our case, we reached enlightenment about the meaning of kinship and family, for the people we were studying and for us, when we tried to construct a fictive family in the field.

The Setting

We have been conducting field research in the Pacific for thirty years, beginning in 1966. All of our work has been in Papua New Guinea, and almost all of it has been done in the village of Kandoka, in the Kaliai area of West New Britain Province. We did our first research in 1966–1967 as graduate students gathering data for our doctoral dissertations. At the time we had been married ten years and had two children: Rebecca, who had her eighth birthday in Kandoka, and Bruce, who was four. We returned to Kandoka four more times, always with children who ranged in age from two to sixteen years, and sometimes with our own graduate students in tow.

It never occurred to us to leave our children behind if they wanted to go. When he was thirteen, our oldest son did choose to remain in North America (with long-suffering grandparents) to avoid losing a year of school. In some ways, we suppose, children are a liability in the field. They get sick, they insist on eating regularly, and—being children—they consume parental time and energy. The demand for endless games of Monopoly, Crazy-Eights, and Fish was continuous. We dedicated a block of time (almost) every evening to bedtime stories, when we really needed to type up our notes. On the other hand, as many others in this volume have noted, the children's contribution to our emotional well-being and to our rapport with the people of the village was beyond calculation. The presence of our children made us vulnerable, nonthreatening, and human. From the first we shared with the villagers the experiences of parenting, and these shared experiences provided rich topics of discussion. Our children made friends in the village, and their friendships eased our integration into the community. And most important—at least from the perspective of this chapter—the villagers interacted with our children on their own terms; they did their best to turn our children into Kandokans and to incorporate them, and us, into their social system.

Family and Kinship in Kaliai

In Kaliai, as in many other societies where anthropologists do research, kin and marriage relationships provide everyone's primary orientation. Persons not connected by blood or marriage are anomalous (Geertz 1973, 364–367). During the colonial period, Germans and other white outsiders who had lived in the Kaliai area were associated with institutions having external links. The Roman Catholic priests and nuns at the nearby mission at Taveliai formed their own enclave as an arm of the church. The mission property was bounded, the structures on it were radically different from village houses, and the father and sisters had little or no informal contact with local people.

The owners/managers who lived at the Iboki plantation, the only freehold plantation in the area, were even more isolated from the local population. In the early 1900s, when the plantation was established, the German owners employed local people. By the time we began our fieldwork, most of that was over. Most Iboki laborers in the 1950s and 1960s were contracted from the New Guinea Highlands. Neither they nor the *Masta* and *Missis* participated much in local life. Kaliai might see the manager tending his trade store, or (less frequently) they might offer to sell him locally produced copra. Otherwise, except for a few specialized and prestigious jobs (tractor driver, foreman, carpenter) Iboki was in, but not of, Kaliai.

In 1966 Kaliai was isolated, and most villagers had limited opportunity to observe whites such as ourselves—especially white children—in their everyday lives. There were (and still are) no roads linking Kaliai with any town or marketing center. Transportation into the area was by irregular tramp copra freighter, government workboat, or mission ship. A few villagers worked in Lae on the north coast of New Guinea or Rabaul at the eastern end of New Britain, and a few students attended high school at Vunapope outside Rabaul. Cash was scarce. The average yearly income from copra sales was twenty U.S. dollars in 1966–1967. Consequently, few villagers owned many manufactured items. There was no working radio or operating trade store in Kandoka when we arrived in 1966 and, therefore, only limited knowledge of or contact with the outside world. For the most part, people depended on their gardens, fishing, and hunting for food, while ceremonial exchanges were the focus of social life.

When we arrived in the village, unannounced, with two small children, intending to live there and wanting to talk to people (endlessly), their problem was what to do with us. The government officials who had approved our research plan had not informed the Kandokans we were coming. We did have external institutional links to our university, but these were invisible and incomprehensible to the people. Their solution to the problem presented by our presence was one that hosts often apply to anthropologists doing exotic field research in kin-focused societies. It is unacceptable to be without kin in a society where relatives define social identity. Therefore, the hosts give relatives to such persons. We were no exception. Furthermore, since members of the same kin group cannot normally marry one another, Dorothy was associated with one group and David with another. Later, following local custom, our children would join David's kin group, Gavu Sae.

Our incorporation into Kandokan kin networks took place slowly and informally. The Kandokans did not give us village names, nor have we ever been ceremonially adopted or affiliated. They did, however, do those things for two of our children. Our daughter, as firstborn child, was the first who could be ritually recognized and ceremonially incorporated into the village. Her completion of the ritual legitimized our younger children as members of the kin group to which David was assigned and made them eligible for ceremonial recognition, incorporation, and naming. Rebecca was not given a local name because a naming ritual was not part of the ceremony given for her. However, when he learned of her birth, David's elder brother Jakob Mua gave Rebecca's firstborn daughter the name Dauan, after his paternal grandmother. Mua's bestowal of this name recognizes Rebecca's daughter and any other of her subsequent children as members of his kin group. After Rebecca's incorporation our other children (all sons) could also be affiliated, but only one— our middle son David Riley—was. Only Riley was both circumcised and present in Kandoka at a time when a ritual to introduce children into the men's house was being held. He was named Sakaili, one of the names customarily given to boys for whom the ritual is done. Should Riley return to northwest New Britain as an adult and identify himself as being named Sakaili, a knowledgeable local person would recognize him as someone who has been formally affiliated into Kaliai society and would know which ritual had been done for him. The Kandokans also invited our youngest son to join his brother in the ritual, but his participation would have required his penis to be supra-incised by the senior men during the ceremony. He vigorously declined.

While our affiliation was informal, it was not arbitrary. Kaliai do not recognize coincidence. They seek explanations to eliminate wherever possible the accidental and arbitrary from their lives. Therefore, it was necessary for the villagers to give us Kandokan relatives. From the early days of our first fieldwork the Kandokans debated how best to bring us into their kinship network. Their debates were not about whether we were kin to some of them. Their problem was to determine who our relatives were. Some of them were (and still are) convinced we were parents or grandparents returned from the dead. They were frustrated that we had forgotten (or would not tell them) our true identities, but our ignorance was not an insurmountable obstacle. There were clues to our identity. To our hosts, our decision to live in Kandoka was not arbitrary; our choice of particular persons as friends was not whimsical; our perceived generosity with our goods—particularly food—was no accident. Finally, our decision to bring our children to live with the people of Kandoka was not coincidental. Our behavior was evidence that we were, in fact, deceased ancestors who had returned to live with our kin. Thus they observed us closely, analyzing our behavior to find similarities with deceased family members, and they watched to see who we chose as friends and informants.

We know that the villagers were discussing our possible identities within six months of our arrival in 1966. Several of them later told us about the initial puzzlement over what we really wanted and who we really were. Also, within six months they had begun to discuss with us the belief—sometimes attributed to "others"—that we were returned ancestors.

By our second trip in 1971, as new faculty members at Canadian universities, the Kandokans had agreed on our identities. While we were generally known outside the village as *Kandoka ele pura* (Kandoka's white/spirit people), within the village we had siblings, nieces, and nephews. Dorothy even had a mother. Our kin relationships in the village did not involve just the two of us, but extended to all our relatives counted by our own calculation. For example, the first time we returned to the village after the death of Dorothy's father in 1978, our friends mourned his passing with her as if he had been their relative, too.

The Kaliai define kinship by shared substance, and they express kin relationships by sharing and exchange. Whereas blood is the metaphor for kinship in Euro-American society, the people of Kaliai consider kinship to be forged through sharing blood, semen, mother's milk, and food (see Counts and Counts 1983; Schneider 1984; Flinn, chapter 7). A fetus is built by its parents who contribute blood and semen to it, and a mother's tie to her child is reinforced when she gives it her milk. Prospective adoptive parents create and legitimize their kinship to their child by bringing food to the birth mother while she is pregnant and lactating, and by providing green coconuts for the child to drink when he or she is old enough.

From our first days in Kandoka, people brought us gifts of food "for the children." In exchange we gave tobacco, rice, tinned fish, and meat. At first we mistakenly thought the villagers were trading with us (see Counts 1990). We also assumed they created a fiction of kinship with us because it was easier for them to deal with us and to establish reciprocal exchange ties with us if we were incorporated into their social system, including their system of kin relations.

We appreciated their incorporating us into their society. Because of the fiction of our kinship, we could share food and resources with members of our Kandokan families and engage in reciprocal exchange with the others. We contributed cash or shell money to the ceremonies sponsored by our village relatives and received wealth items from other groups, just as our kin did. While the entire community was responsible for assuring that we and our children always had a supply of fresh fruits and vegetables, and while everyone answered our questions and suffered our presence with good humor, some were more responsible for us than others. These people, our closest fictive kin, unfailingly provided us with green coconuts, bananas, sugarcane, pineapples, papaya, fish, fresh pork, and vegetables—usually given to us "for the children."

Establishing Our Own Fictive Family

In 1975, on our third research trip to Kaliai, another Canadian, William R. (Bil) Thurston, then our graduate research assistant, accompanied us. It was on this trip that we decided to emulate our Kaliai relatives and create our own fictive family.

By 1975 our place in Kandoka was firmly established. Our periodic return was expected and predictable. In the nine years since our first appearance in Kandoka, we had obtained university appointments and had returned for a short visit in 1971. We had maintained a limited but regular correspondence with some villagers, and they knew we were coming in July to stay for most of another year. We told them that we were bringing three of our four children, the youngest of whom they had never seen, and a graduate student from McMaster University who wanted to study the language of a neighboring group, the Anêm.

The Lusi-speaking Kaliai have long-established links of trade and intermarriage with the Anêm. In 1966 we had found one of the coastal Anêm villages to be especially pleasant, so we wrote our Kandokan friends that Bil Thurston should go to that village for his research. We also asked them to arrange for him to live there.

When we arrived, we found that the Kandokans had vetoed our choice of a research site for Bil. They had better links to Karaiai, another Anêm-Kaliai village located a little farther east down the coast, than the one we had chosen. After a few weeks of acclimation in Kandoka with us, Bil—with no little trepidation—loaded his gear onto a canoe, and with David's relatives to smooth the way, set off on his own adventure. We had arranged that he would come periodically to visit us, and we were delighted when we learned we would see him the following month at Papua New Guinea's Independence Day celebrations at the Roman Catholic mission at Taveliai on September 25, 1975. We also wanted to be able to visit Bil at Karaiai. This would not have been a problem had David been the one to do the visiting. It was likely, however, that Dorothy or Rebecca, our sixteen-year-old daughter who was close to Bil, would visit, quite possibly without David. That, given the assumptions of the Lusi-Kaliai and the Anêm about the inevitable behavior of adult men and women alone together, *was* a problem. They would have interpreted a visit paid by either Dorothy or Rebecca to any unrelated male as impropriety.

Our solution was to create a situation in which we could do the visiting our way as we liked. We wanted to visit each other, share sleeping arrangements, and so on, without scandalizing the people in either village. Just as the Kandokans had created kinship ties for us to make life easier for everyone, we decided to create kinship with Bil. So Bil Thurston became Dorothy's distant relative. We were vague about the exact connection, but this worried no one. After all, they were also vague about the precise ties linking them to distant relatives in other communities, although they were certain of the relationships and depended on them when trading or visiting in distant villages or those in non-Lusi speaking areas—such as in Anêm-land. The arrangement permitted Dorothy and Bil to treat each other as siblings (Dorothy and Bil became *ol sista* in Tok Pisin, the creole spoken as a second language by almost all Kaliai). This made Bil and Rebecca mother's brother/sister's daughter, a close and supportive relationship among both the Lusi and the Anêm. It also accounted for David's providing Bil with a small boat and outboard engine. This was perfectly reasonable since David had received his wife from Bil's family, and the obligations of a man to his wife's kinsfolk never end. Our primary objective was to place Bil in a context that people could recognize and accept, and to simplify our visiting him. Establishing fictive kinship with Bil was a perfect solution. Bil Thurston has written another chapter for this collection, because the Anêm-Kaliai regarded us as *his* family as surely as the Lusi-Kaliai considered him to be ours.

As Independence Day approached, the level of excitement in Kaliai was palpable. There were incipient cargo beliefs rumbling just below the surface, especially among interior groups. Rumors that the mountains would open and give forth all sorts of good things left believers in nervous anticipation. They also gave nonbelievers a lot of comic material to parody for entertainment. Others viewed independence with a mixture of fear and apprehension. Would the departure of the Australians, who had administered the country since the end of World War I, leave them bereft? Would they be required, as members of a modern and independent state, to forgo their systems of reciprocal exchange and follow the "rule of money" on which the cash economy was based? Would they be forced to buy everything, even from their relatives? Despite these contradictory concerns, everyone expected to spend three days celebrating at the mission grounds.

The high point of the event was to be the ceremonial flag raising on the morning of Independence Day. Flag raising was preceded by a pageant by the mission school children illustrating the momentous changes taking place that day. Following the flag raising would be a dance competition entered by every conceivable constituent group in the Kaliai area. Everyone had a role. The Catholic priest, who was a German national, agreed to be master of ceremonies. The Australian Blake family, who owned the Iboki plantation, was to attend, and their son Charles agreed to act as judge of the dance competition. Also offered the chance to serve as judges, we pleaded bias and instead agreed to film the event. Bil and Rebecca had more central roles. Bil, by then established in Karaiai, joined the other unmarried young males as a dancer in the Karaiai's presentation of *boilo,* a dance performed with spears and shields. The young people's club of Kandoka invited Rebecca to join their dance troupe for the competition. Our age-mates privately assured us that, although the young women would be wearing traditional costume and dancing with bare breasts, Rebecca's attire would not offend white standards of modesty. Given the use of shrubbery in traditional dance costume, they would ensure that Rebecca more nearly resembled a bush than a bare-breasted young woman.

August and September are the season of the *Rai* in northwest New Britain, a time of sunny skies and gentle southeasterly breezes from the mountains. September 1975 was a classic month of *Rai* weather, and Rebecca joined the other young people of Kandoka in nightly rehearsals for their performance. Nearly everyone in Kaliai moved to the area near the mission and the village of Taveliai for the three-day party. We, some of our friends from Kandoka, and Bil Thurston were given a house in a satellite village a short walk from Taveliai. Most people camped out, but we enjoyed relative luxury.

Independence Day dawned bright and sunny. The ceremonies, starting about nine o'clock in the morning, went with few hitches, despite some comic moments. The dance competition, following the flag raising at noon, seemed endless, with group after group performing. Bil Thurston, attired as a bush in his own right, stamped his way through *boilo* with his fellow Karaiai, and then joined us in the photographic work.

The Kandoka young people's club entered the field about midafternoon. As they reached the center, arms linked, a moving garden of crotons, bark cloth wraps, and the provocative swaying of woven fringes that characterize the women's dance costume, six older women rushed onto the field from different directions carrying large rolled bundles of pandanus sleeping mats. They threw these on the ground at Rebecca's feet and then ran off. There were a few moments of pandemonium as men, women, and children converged on the field laughing, shouting, and grabbing up the mats to carry them away. We were astonished. We had no idea what was happening. Nor did we have any idea where it would lead.

It is normal for anthropologists in the field to misunderstand what is happening around them. However, figuring out what was going on here took on an added urgency because it was happening to *us*. Our local friends had long since despaired of our being able to remember anything unless we wrote it down. They expected us to be confused because our experience with firstborn celebrations had been limited. As they patiently explained, we had just witnessed the first formal recognition by the villagers of Rebecca's status as firstborn. Among many people of the northwest New Britain coast, virtually everything a firstborn child does for the first time warrants recognition, and these ceremonies reflect strongly on the status of the parents (Scaletta 1985). This was Rebecca's first time dancing publicly as a villager. She was our firstborn; therefore, it was appropriate to recognize her performance. This "first" was honored by the women who made gifts of pandanus mats. While pandanus mats have mundane uses—people sleep on them and use them for protection from the rain—they are most important as women's wealth. They are a local specialty, which, with shell currency, underpins intercoastal trade.

So, all was well. The competition proceeded, and the grand finale saw all of the competing groups on the field together. Dinner for the honored guests at the mission followed the finale, while the exhausted crowds returned to their villages to resume daily life. No mountains had opened and no Draconian laws about the use of money had been proclaimed. Some people were disappointed, while others' fears were relieved.

A few days later, David's elder brother, Jakob Mua, realizing the depths of our ignorance of appropriate behavior, advised us of our debt to the women who had honored Rebecca. One implication of their act was that they had claimed kin rights over Rebecca. They had, in effect, become her mothers. The women were elders from the group to which Dorothy had been assigned and were celebrating the first public dance performance of their child. David, as the father and a member of the group claiming Rebecca as its own, should reciprocate by returning the gifts from Dorothy's group in proper style. This could not be done simply or privately. The honor had been bestowed publicly, so its recognition should be done the same way. Therefore, Mua suggested, this was also a suitable occasion for the ceremony that would formally affiliate Rebecca with Gavu Sae, his and David's men's-house group. He suggested that we hold a *vaulo*.

Among the Lusi-Kaliai kinship is bilateral, but for the most part, descent is patrilineal. When a child reaches the right age (usually seven or eight years), the parents should sponsor a *vaulo* or some other ceremony to incorporate him or her publicly into father's kin group and men's house. The focus of this ceremony is the presentation of gifts from the father's kin group to the mother's. These gifts assert the right of the father's group to claim the child as their own. The ceremony does not end the child's links to its mother's group, whose members retain an active interest in the child throughout its life. It is most significant when the parents are politically ambitious and hold the ceremony for their firstborn child. In that situation, enormous quantities of wealth—shell money, pigs, pandanus mats, carved wooden bowls from the master carvers of the Siasi Islands, clay pots from the renowned potters of Sio on Papua New Guinea's north coast, the same kinds of things used to validate a marriage—are distributed to the mother's family. The focal person in the sponsoring (or *claiming*) group is the child's father. It is his prestige that is on the line. The focal person in the receiving group—the one who is given the most lavish gifts—is the oldest of the mother's brothers. It is particularly important that he receive shell money and a pig.

This is the way that events unfolded. When we set up our fictive kinship with Bil, we did not know that Independence Day was coming. When we learned about the Independence Day celebrations, we did not know that Rebecca would be invited to dance at them. When we and Rebecca agreed that she would dance, we had no idea that it would be a "first" occasion. When Rebecca's mothers honored her, holding a ceremony to reciprocate seemed a simple and appropriate thing to do. When the ceremony became a *vaulo,* events that we set into motion came to unexpected fruition. Rebecca had a mother's brother down the coast in Karaiai. Bil Thurston was about to get a pig.

The *vaulo* was a success. Lusi-Kaliai like parties, and the one sponsored by the local *pura* 'spirits or white people' was to be quite an occasion. Visitors came from all the Lusi-speaking villages in Kaliai, and Bil arrived surrounded by his Anêm supporters. We compensated the women who had claimed Rebecca. Then, surrounded by our Gavu Sae relatives, we spent the night receiving gifts of shell currency and cash from supporters and assessing the situation to see how much and what was needed for presentation to whom.

Two days later, Bil Thurston left in a small boat. He was accompanied by Rebecca, his sister's daughter; a well-trussed and annoyed female pig who complained loudly all the way to Karaiai; ten fathoms of shell money; and fifteen Papua New Guinea kina, then worth about fifteen U.S. dollars. He had a bemused look on his face.

What We Know Now (That We Didn't Know Then)

Taking our children to the field was never part of a research design or strategy for us. We simply never considered any alternative to their accompanying us, especially when they were young. Having children in Kaliai was far easier on us emotionally than leaving them behind would have been. The year our thirteen-year-old son remained in the United States with his "real" grandparents was, by all reports, a good one for both him and them, but we missed him. When we thought about being a family in the field, or when we weighed its advantages and disadvantages, we did so instrumentally. Primarily, we thought our children's presence in the village made it easier to establish rapport with the Kaliai because, as other contributors to this volume have also noted, the common experience of raising children created a link of humanity between us.

Our decision to establish fictive kin links between Bil Thurston and us was instrumental also, but it had ramifications we never foresaw. Until we set in motion the events that culminated in Rebecca's *vaulo,* we thought we understood Kaliai kinship. The consequences of those events surprised us because we assumed our inclusion in the kinship system of the Kaliai was a fiction for them as well as for us. They had, we thought, made us members of their families for the same reason we had made Bil a member of our Canadian family in the field: doing so provided us all with mutually understood guidelines for behavior and made life a bit easier for everyone. Although it was a convenient fiction, in our minds we were no more their *real* kinsfolk than Bil was ours. We were playacting, and we thought they were as well. Our children were our only *real* "family in the field," or so we thought.

At this point our story becomes a cautionary tale. The message is that we must take seriously what people tell us, especially when they are telling us about ourselves. In Orson Scott Card's novel *Speaker for the Dead,* the main character, Ender, tries to warn the resident anthropologists that they are ethnocentric "cultural supremacists to the core." He reproaches them: "You're so busy *pretending* to believe them [the *other,* as it is fashionable to call them], there isn't a chance in the world you could learn anything from them." When an anthropologist protests, "We've devoted our lives to learning about them!" Ender retorts, "Not *from* them" (Card 1986, 248).

So, what did our experience enable us to learn from the people of Kandoka? First, we had not understood the behavioral and emotional content of our kinship ties in Kandoka; we never *believed* in their reality. We knew that kinship and family ties are culturally constructed. *We* would never be so ethnocentric as to need Schneider's warning not to be seduced by the North American assumption that kinship is rooted in biogenetic fact (Schneider 1984). We knew better, at least on the level of what Bloch calls "the dangerous intermediary of language" (1991, 183). We had lectured on it often enough in our introductory anthropology classes. We received our comeuppance.

Second, we learned that when members of our Kandokan family brought us bananas, pineapples, and watermelons, and we gave them rice, fresh bread, and tinned beef, we were not just exchanging groceries. We and they were becoming family. Rebecca's village mothers were the same women who had brought food "for the children." When they fed us and our children and received food from us in return, we were exchanging the stuff of which substance is made: we were *becoming* Kaliai. Rebecca's mothers were not just *calling* us by kin terms. They were creating kinship with us and our children. They were, in fact, becoming Rebecca's mothers. Later, when Mua named Rebecca's daughter—the firstborn of our firstborn—he was giving her the name of his grandmother, and David's grandmother as well. We had a right to use the name, and Mua had the right to bestow it. We are one family.

Third, when we claimed Bil as a family member, our relationship to him was no more fictitious than our relationship with our Kandokan kin. Bil had lived with us and shared meals with us in Canada and in Kandoka. We had shared the substance of which kinship is made; therefore, in Kaliai terms we were family.

Fourth, a consequence of Rebecca's incorporation into her fathers' kin group was that our status as Kandokans was formalized and we became *real* persons. This was brought home to Dorothy six years later when David Riley was introduced into the men's house of one of his grandfathers and given his new name. Women are not permitted to be present when spirits are in the village. Always before, when the women withdrew, Dorothy was permitted to stay in the village. This time, however, one of Rebecca's mothers took Dorothy's arm. "Come on," she urged. "The spirits are coming. We must go." So Dorothy, as a real human woman vulnerable to dangerous spirit power, ran with the others to a sanctuary where they feasted, clowned, and mocked the serious rituals of the men (see Counts and Counts 1992).

Fifth, our experience resulted in an irrevocable shift in the continuum of participant observation. We could no longer be primarily observers; we were participants who had *real* families in the field, with all the entitlements and obligations that entails.

Finally, we learned as participants the stress and sheer terror of trying to meet ceremonial obligations. There is no substitute for bearing full responsibility for the success or failure of a major ceremony. It does wonders to focus the mind. Our academic knowledge of the significance and manner of shell currency exchanges was insignificant in comparison to the experience of trying to determine if we had enough pigs and shell money to avoid losing status. Discovering that he was five fathoms short at five-thirty in the morning and that he must float a loan from a relative or be shamed is an experience David is not likely to forget. Jakob Mua's comment, while made about ceremonial obligations, is also true for our understanding of what it means to have and be family in Kaliai: "Before you just knew about this intellectually," he said. "Now you *feel* it!"

Acknowledgments

The research on which this essay is based was supported in 1966–1967 by predoctoral research grants from the U.S. National Science Foundation and by Southern Illinois University. Research support was provided in 1971 by the University of Waterloo, McMaster University, the Canada Council, and the Wenner-Gren Foundation. In 1981 research was supported by the University of Waterloo, McMaster University, and the Social Sciences and Humanities Research Council of Canada. In 1995–1996 research was supported by the Canada Council, McMaster University, and the University of Waterloo.

11 The Inadvertent Acquisition of Kinship during Ethnographic Fieldwork

WILLIAM R. THURSTON

Cautiously, I descended the unstable ladder with a large bowl of food for Sally, a responsibility thrust upon me unexpectedly by the intercultural translation of a small white lie originally told with good intentions. Lacking any preparation whatsoever for this situation, I was nervously concerned to do the right thing, ashamed for my small part in the naive deception of my new friends, and terrified by the duties I was expected to perform.

Descending a little farther, we locked eyes for the first time. Sally had strikingly beautiful brown eyes and the longest eyelashes I have ever seen. Securely tied to a sturdy post under the house, she was both hungry and helpless. I was worried that the ropes were cutting into her legs as she struggled. I knew no way to communicate my reassurances, to say, "Relax. This is not my fault. I won't hurt you." My mind raced, searching for a way out of this ugly situation, but, short of time travel, I could imagine no escape.

Determined, at the very least, to get some food into her, I stepped slowly toward her, holding the bowl of sweet potatoes and coconut cream well ahead of me tilted toward her so she might understand that I meant her no harm, but her terrified eyes remained fixed on mine, not on the offering. The only sound to penetrate my consciousness was the gritty crunch of sand under my bare feet. Suddenly, still out of range, she let out a bloodcurdling shriek that caused me involuntarily to toss the bowl into the air, dumping its contents over her head as I fled back up the stairs, aware only of the need to escape and to breathe.

As Sally scrambled for the sweet potatoes, now covered with sand, laughter from several quarters informed me that my first bungling ministrations to her had been observed. It would not be long before everyone knew that the newest anthropologist in the area had been intimidated by a pig.

People Are Inalienable

Although it is considered presumptuous in some circles to speak in such terms, most anthropologists return from fieldwork, especially their first fieldwork, speaking about the people they have studied within a framework of kinship. This follows from the principle that, in small communities organized around kinship, outsiders must be incorporated, and it is only within the framework of the prevailing kinship system that outsiders can be assigned a workable identity within community life. Without changing the social structure of the host community by instituting new identities, only those identities provided by the kinship system are available for the incoming anthropologist(s). In turn, as noted by Carucci (chapter 12), the identity assigned determines which facets of the host community are likely to be exposed for anthropological investigation. If anthropologists working in such communities cannot provide explanations for their place in the general scheme of things to the satisfaction of their hosts, people of the host community are likely to take clues from the behavior of the anthropologists to deduce what kinship connections must be in operation. Consequently, in a society where kinship is a prime organizational principle, no anthropologist can evade the acquisition of kinship in the field. Moreover, whereas anthropologists (like myself) raised within a Western context tend to treat such acquired families as instances of fictive kinship, this trivializes the seriousness of the relationships created reciprocally with the people we study and, at the same time, highlights the Eurocentric bias in the dominant model of kinship where real kin are connected by either birth or marriage.

Between 1975 and 1988, I conducted five periods of ethnographic field research in the Kaliai and Bariai Census Divisions of West New Britain Province, Papua New Guinea. In the course of these trips, my hosts have incorporated me and my traveling companions according to various principles of social organization into an extensive, crabgrass-like social network. In 1975, David Counts (one of my professors at McMaster University in Canada) and Dorothy Counts (University of Waterloo) invited me to join them on their third period of field research in West New Britain. While they resumed research in the Lusi-speaking village of Kandoka, my task was to initiate the study of Anêm, a non-Austronesian language spoken about twenty-five kilometers down the coast to the west in the village of Karaiai. In 1978, I invited my partner, Rick Goulden, to return with me. After settling in, Rick (a graduate in linguistics from the University of Toronto) took over the collection and analysis of data in Lusi, while I concentrated on Anêm. This worked so well that we returned together in 1981 as a subunit of a larger project that included David and Dorothy Counts and Naomi McPherson (formerly Scaletta, then a doctoral student in anthropology at McMaster University). On this trip, Rick and I conducted an extensive grammatical, lexical, and ethnographic survey of all the known languages in the Kaliai and Bariai Census Divisions of West New Britain, while the Counts resumed work in Kandoka, and Naomi initiated fieldwork among speakers of Kabana in Kokopo, Bariai. The following year, Naomi, Rick, and I returned so that Rick and I could continue the survey while Naomi spent a full year of ethnographic research in Kokopo. Finally, in 1988, Rick and I returned to concentrate on a few pressing questions that had arisen from our survey.

In the course of these field trips, our hosts constructed kinship relationships for us by concatenating information provided directly by us, clues from our personal characteristics, and events of recent and legendary history. Without a place in their social world, we would be disconnected fragments, and we would not have been able to live in their communities asking the sorts of questions that anthropologists ask. For New Britainers, both grammatically and intellectually, people are like body parts. Like a disconnected human hand that might wash up on some beach (grim metaphor intended), people without a social network are disquieting, perhaps not even really human. Whereas Westerners are prepared to accept strangers into their homes on the basis of rather superficial statements of occupation, New Britainers follow the Pacific pattern (see, e.g., Howard 1990) and appear to require integration into a kinship system specifically. No anthropologist can work in this area for more than a month or so without acquiring some sort of family.

Sally

In 1975, David and Dorothy Counts already had plans to travel to West New Britain with their sixteen-year-old daughter, Rebecca, and their two youngest sons. Since Rebecca and I were both students, however, we were eligible to take advantage of cheap student fares and so traveled separately from her parents to Port Moresby, capital of Papua New Guinea. During the week of endless shopping for research supplies in Lae (a major town on the north coast of New Guinea and a departure point for West New Britain), Rebecca announced that she was afraid she would become bored if she were stuck in Kandoka for the entire eight months and that she expected to visit me in my Anêm village. David and Dorothy, worrying how a visit between two young people of different sexes would be viewed in our host communities, devised a plan to make appearances locally respectable.

We conspired on a small fabrication, the white lie mentioned earlier, namely that my father and Dorothy's father were trading partners related by some presumed but unknown kinship tie. By extension, I became Dorothy's sibling, David's brother-in-law, and their children's mother's brother. This would also explain why they brought me along in the first place. It seemed like a trivial white lie, one that would make everyone feel more comfortable. We failed, however, to follow its logic through to the same socioeconomic conclusions that our Lusi and Anêm friends would. Informally, David had already been incorporated into a kin group, and, as his firstborn, Rebecca's ritual processing was already long overdue. The sudden appearance of her mother's brother, a key figure in the ritual, provided an opportunity that David's Lusi relatives could not resist. The Counts' perspective on these events is presented in detail in chapter 10.

Under the supervision of David and Dorothy, I spent my first month of field research in Kandoka learning Tok Pisin (the lingua franca of most of Papua New Guinea) and gently getting used to life in a small West New Britain village. I also managed to start collecting linguistic data in Anêm by working with speakers in neighboring villages. During these day trips, I was often greeted by older men who had mistaken me for David, but my traveling companions would clarify who I was by introducing me as David's brother-in-law. The fiction seemed to be very useful, and, at the end of the month in Kandoka, I departed for Karaiai with an important element of kinship identity in hand.

A couple of months later, I received a note from Dorothy informing me that I was expected in Kandoka in a few days to attend a ritual for Rebecca and that I should bring a couple of sticks of tobacco. My Anêm friends tried to explain what I was in for, but I was still far too dense to understand all their concerns about firstborns, in-laws, and pigs, because at that time I still labeled myself a linguist, not an anthropologist. The Anêm did manage to get through a warning, however, that the ritual to be performed was very serious, and they helped me roll several pounds of tobacco for the occasion. On the way there, they also trolled for fish, saying that I should not arrive without meat.

At dusk, groups of dancers arrived from neighboring villages, and the ritual began in earnest. Although I have never performed as an actor, I could not shake the image that this was opening night of an elaborate stage production. In my mind, the producers had cast me to play a major role but had neglected to give me a copy of the script. At intervals throughout the night they handed me the appropriate props, fed me lines in Lusi to memorize, and pushed me on stage. Finally, after a night without sleep, a complete stranger grabbed my hand and dragged me at a running clip around the village until we came to an abrupt halt in front of an enormous pig, Sally, tied under someone's house. He then presented her to me formally. I have no memory of how and when I also received strands of shell money—I was too worried about what to do with the pig.

After a few hours of unrestful sleep in the tropical daytime, I awoke to firm instructions about Sally. She was given to me as a special kind of gift that incurs no debt, but she had to be killed and distributed among my kin in Karaiai, and anyone who ate part of her would have to compensate me. Until then, she was my responsibility. Being a city boy, my mind raced to comprehend the content of these duties. Without a garden, where would I get food for her? What are the four major food groups for a pig? Did I have to take her for walks? Did I have to touch her? She was huge, and I was afraid of being bitten. How was I going to get such a bulky animal twenty-five kilometers down the coast to Karaiai, where surely someone would help me cope?

We decided that Rebecca would return to Karaiai with me for a week, so David and I traded boats because his was larger and would accommodate the extra person and a pig. The morning we left, Sally was unceremoniously strapped onto a pole and tied upside down across the gunwales. When we finally arrived in Karaiai, two women, by then identified as my mothers, took on responsibility for Sally's feeding and general care, while my fathers and I decided that she would be on the menu at my going away party.

Sally highlighted the network of kinship into which we had been incorporated. Since David had acquired shell money and pigs from his kin group, his relationship with them was confirmed, and they became my in-laws. On every subsequent field trip, the exchange of information, goods, and services with my Lusi in-laws has continued. Meanwhile, I had my own Anêm network, and by virtue of their relationship to me, Dorothy and Rebecca were Anêm. The incorporation through kinship symbolized by Sally, however, was only a fragment of a much larger picture.

A Pilgrimage to the Sleeping Place of Titikolo

During my first month in Kandoka, people were already talking to me about a legendary hero, Titikolo. According to the legend (Thurston 1994), a long time ago, no one worked, became sick, or died. When people aged, they just shed their skin like snakes and rejuvenated their bodies. At that time, Titikolo lived among the Anêm ancestors, and by virtue of his knowledge the Anêm lived well. Then, a series of calamities resulted in the Anêm ancestors' trying to kill Titikolo. In disgust, he departed but left the Anêm cursed with sickness, sorcery, warfare, death, the pain of childbirth, and hard labor simply to get food. The legend is central to the Anêm understanding of their relative poverty in comparison with any Westerner. Many Anêm view Western wealth and power as an indication that, when Titikolo left West New Britain, he must have landed among Westerners, and although Titikolo did not promise to return, many Anêm are primed to view any Westerner as a possible emissary from Titikolo sent to check whether the Anêm deserve to be reintegrated into a life of bounty and comfort.

In the mountains behind the strip of coast the Anêm now occupy is the site where Titikolo once lived. To appreciate what it means to be Anêm, I had to visit this site. In 1975, while I was a mere linguist, however, West New Britain mythology was David and Dorothy's territory, so from my perspective it was equally important that they also visit the site. While making plans with Boswell, one of my Anêm fathers and leader of the expedition, I worried that he would resist having outsiders, especially Lusi, participate in the adventure, but his only concern was that Dorothy and Rebecca might not be sturdy enough to make the climb. In retrospect, it makes perfect sense that I should bring along my kin—if I had acquired an Anêm identity, then so had they.

The entire expedition was exhausting and dangerous. For four days Dorothy, Rebecca, Maxwell (one of my Lusi in-laws), Lydia (Maxwell's wife), Boswell, and assorted Anêm from Karaiai and Pudêlîng (a large Anêm village east of Karaiai) trekked up and down slippery mountain slopes. All of us ended up slashed and bruised, and a week later both Dorothy and I were taking antibiotics. Nevertheless, events both during the trip and in the aftermath have led to a better understanding of our host communities.

For instance, during the trip, Victor (one of my Anêm friends) became somewhat of a nuisance with angry outbursts that made no sense to me at the time. In retrospect, however, I realize that the tension devolved from a conflict between his extension of the kinship system on one hand and my effort to streamline the expedition on the other. Since the two of us shared a father, Victor was one of my brothers. It had not occurred to me to take this into consideration when packing for the hike. To reduce our share of the cargo to a bare minimum, Dorothy, Rebecca, and I had arranged to share a large blanket, a sleeping mat, plates, soap, and other things. From Victor's perspective, I was sleeping with my sister (in the vicinity of Dorothy), eating in full view of my brother-in-law (Maxwell), and sharing sleeping space with a married couple (Maxwell and Lydia)—all strictly taboo. Following the formality of fraternal protocol, it fell to Victor to shame me into behaving properly, but all I saw at the time was Victor having erratic emotional outbursts.

Similarly, on the final leg of the return journey Victor and I argued about the path. Victor insisted that we retrace our path over the mountain ridges, but by this time Maxwell had pointed out that we could save hours of mountain climbing by following the ridge we were on straight down to the coast into the Lusi village of Atiatu, whence we could take a canoe. From the perspective of our Anêm guides, all of us except Maxwell and Lydia were Anêm, and it was unthinkable that we should cross into Lusi land and then put ourselves into the demeaning position of having to request transportation from the Lusi. At the fork in the road, not understanding one another, we separated into two groups with palpable tension. My Anêm friends were annoyed with me, and I with them. Had it occurred to me to think in terms of kinship, much of this tension might have been avoided.

The Young Men on My Porch

My personal diary from this first period in the field is full of what I now recognize as classic culture shock. I felt that I was being treated badly in my host community. I felt that, had I been part of a family unit, I would have been given the respect I thought I deserved and that I perceived the Counts family was enjoying in Kandoka. David and Dorothy and their children had a house to themselves, with dinner times and control over their own menu. At bedtime, all guests left. Several other contributors to this volume, who went as family units, describe similar situations.

In contrast, although I had my own house, it was constantly littered with young men engaged in raucous behavior or just lounging around. Whenever I started to cook anything, it became a communal operation, and plates of extraneous food would suddenly appear from elsewhere, as though I was not being allowed to eat my own food. People came to my house in a constant stream to demand rice, kerosene, and tobacco. When I went to bed, the party on my porch usually continued, and in the morning either I had to tiptoe around bodies while making coffee or the party was already in progress again. Except in my outhouse, I was literally never alone for more than five consecutive minutes. While I had the advantage of a constant supply of informants, and while we did have fun, and while I did become very fond of those young men, it also meant that any serious analysis of my data was conducted under the sheets with a flashlight in the dead of night on those rare occasions when the young men on my porch were all asleep. In my diary, written in stolen moments and full of unfinished paragraphs, I constantly bemoan the lack of privacy and the lack of control over my diet. I dreamed about fresh raw vegetables that would crunch between my teeth.

At first, I mistakenly interpreted this as an ethnic difference between the Anêm and the Lusi. Whereas the Lusi were reserved and respectful, I had observed, the Anêm were much more informal—to the point of being pushy. Toward the end of the research period, however, it became clear that, among other things, it was my marital status that was at issue. As a single, twenty-five-year-old male clearly past the age of initiation, my status was very low. When the bachelors were sent out to cut floorboards in the forest, I was sent, too, the only major difference being that, since it had been decided I was not to be trusted with sharp objects, I was usually allocated to a corner out of harm's way with a small child appointed to keep me out of trouble. Since men do not cook except under especially stressful conditions, my attempts to cook were interpreted as a public comment on my neglectful Anêm mothers who let me go hungry all the time. When I gave away the surplus food that my mothers had sent to make amends, the young men on my porch got into trouble, because they were eating all of my food and letting me go hungry. If word got out to people in neighboring villages that I was not being looked after properly, it would bring shame on the entire village.

Aside from the issue of the missing wife and children, my Anêm hosts also believed that I should never be left alone, because people are vulnerable to an assortment of spirits when they are alone. The young men on my porch constituted a twenty-four-hour security system that I was not allowed to do without. If anything happened to me, the village would be held responsible. With this news, I vowed to myself never to return without someone from my own culture for company. The vow is similar to that made by Petersen (chapter 6) after his first fieldwork as a single male, although our reasons for making it differ somewhat.

Not Quite a Wife, But He'll Do

Despite the litany of problems during my first fieldwork, within a year of returning to Canada I entered a doctoral program in anthropology so I could plan to go back to West New Britain. In a course in historical linguistics, I met Rick, then an undergraduate student of linguistics. Aside from my professors, he was the first person I had ever met who admitted to a genuine interest in the structure of language per se. During that year, our friendship and mutual trust grew to the point where I felt both confident about inviting him for eight months of near-claustrophobia in Karaiai and reluctant to leave him behind. As part of a preliminary screening process, David, Dorothy, and I tested him by showing him grisly slides out of context and telling him the most disgusting stories, but we could not discourage him. Not only did he agree to the adventure, but he enrolled in anthropology courses for additional preparation.

Aside from his good company, I reasoned that Rick would be important in the field for several reasons: without the need to baby-sit me around the clock, the Anêm would be relieved of an unfair burden while I conducted research. Without the young men on the porch, I would gain time to conduct my analysis more efficiently. Finally, I would be able to take advantage of Rick's training in linguistics.

The experiment worked. No sooner had we arrived than the village elders announced that, since I already knew my way around, Rick would be entrusted into my care. In the intervening three years, most of the young men on the porch from the previous trip had acquired wives, and no replacements for them ever materialized. Whenever people went to work in the gardens or in the forest, Rick and I would be left with much of the day to ourselves to work unimpeded. After a month or so in the field, Rick gained competence in Tok Pisin and took over most of the research on the Lusi language, freeing me to concentrate on Anêm.

This second trip was very different. Rick and I could gather our laundry and dirty dishes and walk, unaccompanied, into the forest to the river. While I washed laundry and the fish in the river did the dishes, Rick read novel after novel aloud to me. Although plates of sweet potato and coconut cream still poured in during the early evening, no one seemed to take it personally when we cooked meals for ourselves, and when we went to bed at night, we generally had the house to ourselves.

For a while, to relieve what we saw as the burden on women collecting water for us, we took to carrying buckets to the spring ourselves, but this was stopped when I became terribly sick and divination revealed that my soul had been snared by a lonely spirit that inhabits the area near the spring. Otherwise, the two of us set up house, looked after ourselves to a high degree, and worked almost constantly. We collected most of our new data by interview in the evening and performed analysis and cataloging during the day when most people were busy elsewhere. Before long, people started to make comments to the effect that we behaved like a married couple.

Determined not to repeat the mistake of kinship fabrication, we tried to explain our relationship in terms of being originally from the same school, but the official interpretation, we later learned, was again constructed in terms of kinship. Since my social position had previously been established, it was Rick who needed to be incorporated. One day, on the way to the daily bath in the river, we were accompanied by Victor and a young Kove man visiting from the nearby village. Victor was explaining to him that Rick was a cousin on my mother's side. To clarify the matter, I broke in explaining that we were not relatives, that we had just met in school, and that we were just friends. Almost simultaneously, Victor and the Kove man repeated to one another "cousin," with a knowing look that indicated they knew better. Rick and I were just too friendly with one another. We joked a lot, made fun of one another in front of other people, and played tricks on one another using anyone who happened to be near as an accomplice. Taking clues from our behavior, our West New Britain friends looked beyond our claims of "fact" and interpreted our relationship as that typical of cousins. We did not fit the more formal relationship found among brothers, the only other available slot in the kinship system for two males close in age.

At the same time, cousins are also potential marital partners, and our domestic behavior also fit into this mold. Throughout the area, Rick and I acquired names in the local languages that mean, simply, 'the two of them.' In terms of our divergent research interests, I remained associated with the Anêm, while Rick became nominally Lusi. Meanwhile, still other threads of connection were being woven for us.

A Ghost in the Family

In 1975, only a few months before news of my first impending visit reached the Anêm, Maud, a woman with two teenage sons, Tony and Perry, was tending to her husband on his deathbed. His last words to her were, "Watch for a man who will come soon." Then I arrived. I was not aware of this until several field trips later, and then, piece by piece, the following sad picture emerged.

The timing of my arrival, several personal quirks, and a mole on my chin convinced Maud (and several others) that I was her dead husband come back to check on her. During the 1975 and 1978 field trips, Maud frequently left her home in Pudêlîng to spend as much time as possible in Karaiai where I was living. On each trip, she made a point of smoking reef fish to bring as a special treat just for me. Even the usual mundane sweet potato and coconut cream she garnished for me with pumpkin greens and other treats. Whenever I visited Pudêlîng, she was right there with a fresh sleeping mat and a package of special foods, making sure that I received the very best accommodation.

My relationship with Maud lacked much of the formality and awkwardness that characterized my relationships with most women in West New Britain. Also, more than anyone else, Maud was determined that I should speak Anêm. Although she would resort to Tok Pisin when I was too confused, she pressed me on all occasions to speak and to behave Anêm. The only time she expressed even mild annoyance with me was when I was trying to show off my new knowledge of Mouk, a language spoken in the interior and known to many Anêm. She said, "To hell with Lusi; to hell with Mouk; just speak Anêm." To my sadness, I learned from others that she believed I was her dead husband always playing cruel tricks on her by pretending not to understand Anêm.

Except for Maud's son Tony, the Anêm almost never touched me on those first field trips. Some kept their distance because that is the way they have learned to behave with whites. Others, believing that I was a spirit (alias animated corpse), found the notion of touching me creepy. In my 1975 diary, having noted with admiration that West New Britain men are so openly and so unselfconsciously affectionate with their friends, I complain about sensory deprivation, because almost no one would touch me or allow me to touch them—except Tony. Even though I was unaware of it, Tony believed I was his father and behaved accordingly. Several times while in Karaiai I would step down out of my bed and be surprised to find him sleeping on the floor. One night in Pudêlîng, while I slept on the floor in the men's lodge, he curled up in the small of my back. When Rick and I returned in 1988, Maud had died. Even though Tony no longer believed I was his father, he was restless and irritable until we had an opportunity to hug and cry together in grief.

In some eyes, my status as a ghost made quite rational sense. I had come back from the dead to spy on the Anêm to see whether they were worthy of a return to the kind of life they had enjoyed during the time of Titikolo. If I were not Anêm, why would I come all that way? Prolonged exposure to me in the flesh, however, has since convinced most people that I am, after all, just human.

From Ghosts and Cousins to Wantoks

When I returned for my third visit in 1981, six years of independence had seen a remarkable amount of social and cultural change in West New Britain. In much greater numbers, people from northwestern New Britain traveled and worked for cash. Towns were transformed from colonial outposts into Papua New Guinean cities. More young people went to high school. An elected representative to the National House of Assembly from Bariai spent two weeks in Vancouver attending an international conference. People who found work in towns also found that they had to contend with a constant stream of long-term guests from their original community. They found themselves responsible not only for visiting kinsfolk, but, by extension, anyone who spoke the same language—people known in Tok Pisin as wantok.

In 1981, we returned to West New Britain en masse. David, Dorothy, their two youngest sons, Naomi, Rick, and I all landed on Kandoka together, and from there eventually dispersed to our field sites. Although inquiries were made about Naomi's husband and son to establish what category of woman she was, no one seemed driven to connect her with the rest of us through the traditional kinship system.

Naomi moved into a corrugated iron structure in the Bariai village of Kokopo. As part of our language survey, Rick and I spent weeks at a time sharing the same building with her. No one seemed to balk at the notion; no one even suggested that Rick and I should sleep in a men's lodge while visiting Naomi's village.

Without the intellectual isolation imposed by colonialism, the personal experiences of many New Britainers made it more and more difficult to support the old cosmology in which it was rational to believe that we were spirits. Although there were always holdouts in every community in which we worked (right up until 1988), our relationships seemed more and more to be construed within the wantok system, rather than within traditional kinship, and people stopped referring to us according to kinship terminology. Almost with a tone of bemused apology, friends in West New Britain admitted to me that, although they once thought of me as the spirit of a particular man, they no longer believed it. The wantok system made a more convenient scheme for integrating us, alleviating the intellectual necessity of attributing us to traditional kinship categories. At the same time, each of us achieved a sort of dual citizenship within the wantok system. While we are wantok among ourselves, I still retained the status of Anêm; Rick, Lusi; and Naomi, Kabana.

Among our Lusi friends, as the idiom of family shifted to an idiom of wantoks, Rick and I came under increasing pressure to create a biologically based kinship network; they wanted the ultimate of souvenirs—babies. Offering a case of beer as a bribe, one friend tried to get us to spend a night on a small island with a couple of young women who, he assured us, would be more than happy to get involved, but Rick and I could not get beyond the basic ethical tangle to give any serious thought to the proposal, and our friends were disappointed.

The Nature of Families and the Other Lie

In order to be truly human, one must be integrated into a social system, and the basic principle of social organization in northwestern New Britain remains kinship, but what counts as "real" kinship for Euro-Westerners and anthropologists is clearly not the same as what counts in West New Britain. Euro-Westerners hang "real" kinship on the act of heterosexual procreation—"real" families consist of a genitor, a genetrix, and the offspring of their mating (Schneider 1980). Other "real" kin are calculated by extrapolating this prototype across generations. In Euro-Western societies, the logic of this procreative bias provokes crass paternity suits to define legally who is obliged to support a baby financially; it drives adopted children to search for their "real" parents; it provides parents with the self-righteousness needed to disown their gay children and to deny kinship with the families created by their gay children; and it leads most anthropologists to construct a list of possible kinship relationships, some of which are construed as "real," while others are demoted to the category of "fictive."

In contrast with the Euro-Western model, kinship ties in northwestern New Britain can be created according to several mechanisms over the course of a person's lifetime. Primary, of course, as the basic building block of social organization in all primate groups is the actual tie of shared blood between a mother and her child, but kinship in northwestern New Britain is also built on processes other than sex and on substances other than blood and semen. For example, women who provide food build motherhood by physically contributing to the composition of one's body, and, by extension, their husbands simultaneously build fatherhood through their expenditure of sweat and labor in horticulture or hunting. Each plate of sweet potatoes we ate in West New Britain built kinship with our hosts (see Counts and Counts 1983 and chapter 10 for more detail). During the early periods of research there, our hosts urgently needed guidelines for how to behave toward us, and it took little to start the process of building kinship. The 1975 fib simply provided a convenient framework for our friends with which to work. The last words of a dying man and the cosmological framework embodied in the legend of Titikolo provided the starting point for others to believe that I was the spirit of a dead husband, an Anêm myself, come back to check up on them. With independence, the wantok system that had operated on plantations for over a century provided an additional category within the kinship system of the village. The crucial point we failed to appreciate is that the relationships built by these processes are real kinship relationships in our host communities, not fictive—that is, the prime factors involved in identifying a kinship relationship in northwestern New Britain are social, not biological.

Essentially the same issue has already been presaged in the literature. For example, Feinberg (1981; 1990) cites data from Melanesia, Micronesia, and Polynesia in support of his argument that kinship throughout the Pacific area involves both genealogy and a code for conduct. On one hand, if the love and cooperation expected of kin are not forthcoming, the kinship relationship is nullified, while on the other hand, genealogically unrelated people can acquire a particular kin status by taking on the behavior expected of people related through that particular role. Similarly, in her treatise on lesbian and gay kinship in the United States, Weston observes that cultural anthropologists "have tended to overlook certain bonds regarded as kin by the 'natives' themselves" (1991, 2) and that "discourse on gay families critiques many of the procreative assumptions that inform hegemonic notions of kinship in the United States" (1991, 17). She argues further that relationships of blood or marriage in the United States can be and are nullified by acts of disowning and divorce, and that gay people build families using the idioms of choice and love. That is, even in a Euro-Western society where kinship is treated as biology at the level of ideology and law, real kinship at the level that governs actual behavior is very much conditional upon social conduct. Almost all of the contributors to this volume converge, from different perspectives, on the same realization that is surprising only because our Euro-Western culture predisposes us to filter nonblood kinship out of our perceptions, and because the intellectual tools normally at the disposal of anthropologists need reworking to highlight this bias in kinship theory. Before I wrote this, I thought that kinship was a fairly straightforward domain, that I understood it, but my confidence in this has been shaken, at both professional and personal levels.

My work involves me in being a real person interacting with other real people living in another society according to the rules of another culture that I am supposed to figure out. The missing unanalyzed covert assumption that I took with me into the field, however, was that, because I am gay, I was not quite a real person—not in my own society, and certainly not in this other society. Until Herdt (1981a), the subject of homosexual behavior, not to mention gay identity, was virtually taboo as a topic for anthropologists. In my undergraduate lectures, I can recall only a single reference to homosexuality, and that only to disqualify gay couples a place on kinship charts. According to my own education, homosexual behavior did not occur in non–Euro-Western societies; gay identity was a cultural peculiarity (or disease) of Euro-Western societies; and, in traditional, coherent, nondysfunctional real societies, real families were built around heterosexuality and procreation. Even to mention differences in sexual behavior among other peoples could be construed as pejorative. In order to come to an understanding of the real families I would encounter in West New Britain, I would have to continue to play the role I was used to playing in my home society, and herein lies the other lie.

Several years ago, I astonished one of my Canadian students by turning up at one of the local gay dances. She confided in me that although she was really interested in anthropology, she had considered the discipline closed to her professionally, because gay people could not possibly do fieldwork in other societies. In part, she is correct. Colleagues have warned me not even to think about conducting fieldwork in certain places, because the people are so homophobic that they would arrange for me to have "an unfortunate accident." This has been reinforced by meeting lesbians and gay men from other countries who claim that in their birthplaces gay people must leave home, stay in the closet, or commit suicide. At the same time, I know there are other lesbian and gay anthropologists out there doing ethnography. Yet, unless the study population consists of gay men or lesbians (e.g., Miller 1993 or Weston 1991), the gay identity of an ethnographer remains unacknowledged, and consequently gay and lesbian anthropologists continue to be invisible.

From the point of view of personal safety or of difficulty in establishing rapport, I see gay identity as equivalent to other considerations about the identity of the ethnographer as they relate to the proposed research—women wishing to study male initiation rights or African Americans contemplating fieldwork among white supremacist groups, for example. I found it difficult to imagine my West New Britain friends being anything but welcoming, but just in case, even before I mentioned to Rick that I wanted him to go to Papua New Guinea with me, I asked David Counts to comment on the proposal as my mentor. His comfortingly nonplussed response went something like, "I see no problem with taking Rick. It is not as though you two are going to have sex in public." This leads to another question, one I have been asked frequently.

Rick and I did not have sex in the field, because there was no Euro-Western–style privacy. Even though we often had our own house, the walls were so permeable to sight and sound and the houses so close together that, for all practical purposes, we had our own screened-in area, but no real space apart. The fact that we slept together (literally) was certainly known, but men in West New Britain often sleep together, sharing space and body warmth against the cold at night if necessary. I do not really know whether they were aware of the sexuality involved in my relationship with Rick, but if they were, they seemed to disregard it, looking instead to the social nature of our relationship, labeling it according to their nearest prototype, and behaving with us accordingly. If they passed judgment on us, no one ever exposed us to any unpleasantness about it. The only real concern seemed to be with our lack of offspring, and, as mentioned above, they were even prepared to help remedy that.

What about my ethical responsibility as an anthropologist to be entirely open and honest with my West New Britain hosts? I have no answer to this, but people in West New Britain were also extremely private about personal matters. Almost all discussion about sex, and there was a lot, was conducted at an entirely abstract level without personal references. I believe our friends in West New Britain would have found it grotesque had we announced our sexuality simply to be honest. I just let them assume whatever they assumed about me personally, a pattern I have had training in for as long as I can remember, and it seemed to be all right.

Finally, as Berreman (1962) suggests and as Linnekin explains in chapter 5, much of this story is really about impression management and failed impression management in the field. In 1975, the Counts family and I created fictive kinship to avoid the impression of being morally loose, and our hosts astonished us by acting as though the kin labels were real, not simply convenient. Subsequently, Rick and I denied any formal kinship relationship in an effort to be honest and were assigned a kinship relationship anyway. Throughout our fieldwork together, we lived the lie of omission by not explicitly divulging the sexual component of our relationship and were treated like a married couple anyway. Despite our role-playing, our West New Britain friends interpreted the substance of our relationships, using our formal descriptions only as a guide. That is, they reacted according to the social and behavioral substance of the relationships, rather than to genealogy in a strictly biological sense.

Acknowledgments

I am grateful to the Social Sciences and Humanities Research Council of Canada for funding much of the research on which this chapter is based. I would also like to thank David and Dorothy Counts, Naomi McPherson, and Rick Goulden for sharing their lives with me and for allowing me to write about the experience. I would also like to thank the people of northwestern New Britain for putting up with such a weird foreigner so graciously and for teaching me so much with such kindness.

12 Shifting Stances, Differing Glances

Reflections on Anthropological Practice in the Marshall Islands

LAURENCE MARSHALL CARUCCI

As anthropologists bring the authority of the texts they produce into question, the shifting interpersonal complexities of each researcher's field situation provide us with important ways to contextualize the wide array of texts that are produced in the process of doing ethnography. Personal accounts of field situations, even in their general outline, can help destroy the myths of objectivity and synchrony that typify many accounts. Such accounts encourage readers to consider the conditions under which the negotiated outcomes of day-to-day practices in any community are generalized. They also bring to the level of consciousness something of the manner in which an outsider, the ethnographer, is fashioned into an object of meaning and value in a local system of social and cultural production.

Each ethnographer undoubtedly approaches this topic with a certain amount of trepidation. The self-doubts are well founded since in the process of questioning the supposed objective conditions of our own cultural production we must expose the discontinuous segments of interpersonal activity that we have woven into logically consistent accounts projecting continuity and wholeness (Clifford 1988, 92–113). Even though the outcomes of this soul-searching will be incomplete, the resultant accounts are bound to increase our understanding of both the research process and of the ethnographers involved.

My purpose here is to outline the shifting conditions under which I have conducted research in the Republic of the Marshall Islands over the past twenty years. I hope to show how different pragmatic conditions have provided a variety of structuring influences on my research that are directly related to the types of information I was able to record. In many instances these research conditions were beyond my control, and in all cases they were far from what I might have predicted in advance. Not only was the "lens" I used to create images of this community constantly being readjusted through phases of my incorporation into a local family, but at most I controlled the shutter. Aperture, focal length, film advance, and reloading were set by local people. Each incremental shift in the process of making me a member of a certain family within the Ujelang community was part of an ongoing negotiation. My perspective, as outlined here, overvalues my position in the process since it is the primary way for me to present a viable and cohesive, if contingent, identity.

From my personal journal it is clear that these negotiated positions occurred not only on the sweeping level already discussed, but at the level of momentary occurrences. By doubly transforming the occurrences into events (giving them conscious form and then writing them down) I overvalued certain images and interpretations, lending them viability and power (Bourdieu 1991, 223). The systematic arrangement of these fragments of practical encounters then allowed me to fashion an empowered image of myself in this community, an image connected to others' views of me, but in no sense the same as those views (Goffman 1971).

Destination Ujelang: From First Contacts to Incorporation

I began my fieldwork as a graduate student from the University of Chicago in 1976 with a short stay on Majuro, the administrative center of the Marshall Islands in the central western Pacific. I hoped to work on issues of culture change with Ujelang people, displaced from their home, Enewetak Atoll, by nuclear testing and other military uses since 1947. A few days after arrival, I met with the Enewetak/Ujelang senator and was taken to a family dwelling in "Ujelang Town" on a crowded section of Majuro. I sat, shared food, offered prolific thank yous in return (one of the few Marshallese words I had learned), and pieced together fragments of a story about how I would marry into the Ujelang community. Without rejecting the possibility, I feebly suggested that my primary interest was in learning the language and lifestyle, and that I had a strong and long-term relationship with a female student at the university in America. With seeming disregard for my "unmarried but unavailable" explanations, those seated within the house immediately reiterated that I would, indeed, marry into the Ujelang community.[1]

Within two weeks I was on Enewetak Atoll to ask the chiefs and council members if I could accompany them to Ujelang to conduct my research. The first evening, the senator introduced me to the Enewetak (Jitoken) chief, his brother's father by adoption. I had hoped he would give his blessing to my research. Instead—as if research permission were not an issue—he immediately *told me* I would take an Ujelang wife. This would be a good thing. Using hand gestures, he noted the sexually satisfying nature of this arrangement. Through an inexperienced translator, he also noted that he expected me to marry a favorite offspring of his who would link me directly to the chiefly line. The tenor of his initial proposal had been lighthearted, but as he publicly reannounced the conditions of the posited union several times in coming days, I worried that the very approval of my research project might depend upon my marrying the favored granddaughter of the chief. My apprehensions were allayed when the chiefs and council approved my research plan without objection. Although I reiterated the stories about my University of Chicago companion, the old chief never wavered in his plan to link me to the Enewetak/Ujelang community through his own line up until the time of his death a few years later.

After years of experience living with members of the Enewetak and Ujelang community, their initial attempts to use marriage strategies to bridge the chasm between *ruwamwaijet* 'foreigner or stranger' and *di anin* 'person of this atoll' seem routine. Enewetak people have employed the strategy from the early colonial period until the present. Indeed, it is simultaneously the most controllable and empowering strategy to normalize the contradictions between long-term community residence and the status of "foreigner." While the in-marrying person never fully becomes a local (see Carucci 1987), she or he has a defined status and a concomitant code for conduct that provide preauthorized symbolic templates and resources on which the newcomer and community members can depend as the foreigner becomes enmeshed in the local community. The successful manipulation of the "discourses of love" (see Sahlins 1985; Gordon, chapter 9) that bring marriage to an Ujelang person into being serves as proof of the irresistibility of the local lover and demonstrates the desirability of Ujelang spouses and of the community as a whole. In this society with matriclans where women "domesticate" young men by bringing them within a family unit that requires the young man's daily labors as a provider, marriages are often described as "battles" that young women "win" (Carucci 1993).

While my rank among Enewetak/Ujelang residents is perhaps uniquely marked by their interpretations of my educational status, it also rests on my status as a white American. All unions between Enewetak/Ujelang women and white persons *(diPalle)* or Japanese *(diNippon)* are described as desirable marriages to a "high" person. The values of such unions are multiple. First, in each circumstance the marriage provides a direct pathway to the group of foreign ruling chiefs who controlled the Marshall Islands during a particular colonial era. More important, however, in accord with their ideology in which one's core identity is acquired from and vested in one's matriclan, control of the United States by Ujelang people could result from such a union. In the words of one close friend, "If you and Lijanin were to have a baby, and that child became president, then a bit of power or ability [*maron*] over every location in the United States would be in the hands of Ujelang people." Ujelang people had no doubts about the power of the United States. They had personally experienced this foreign controlled force in three particularly memorable events: when Christian missionaries first brought the word of God, when Americans took the atoll from the Japanese during World War II, and when islets on Enewetak were "evaporated" during the nuclear testing era.

My outside "marriage commitment" prevented the local incorporation schemata from being operationalized. Nevertheless, Ujelang people watched me closely, secure in their knowledge that lack of sexual fulfillment would eventually cause me to take an Ujelang wife. The only options were death or lunacy, the certain fates of men who become overly "full" of sperm. Several respected elders worried about my health. They continued to suggest that I marry a local woman throughout my initial twenty-five-month residence and even during my second twelve-month stay in 1982–1983.

My failure to *koba* 'combine or marry' caused local people to come up with alternate strategies to eliminate the ambiguities presented by my single, foreign status. The second, less desirable, incorporation strategy, although still with significant potentials for empowerment of local people, was adoption. Many Pacific researchers in the region have noted the high rates, desirability, and value of adoption (Carroll 1970). Adoption expands and solidifies ties of interpersonal relationship. The *social practice* of "residence with" and "providing for" a certain group demonstrates an adoptee's primary family affiliation. Some Ujelang adoptees in the 1970s chose to reside with their relatives by birth, others moved back and forth between their natal and adopted families, and some resided solely with their adopted kin. With only two instances of Ujelang divorce in the remembered past, in 1976 marriage was, incontestably, a more effective way to incorporate others, control them, and gain access to their potentials for power.

My adoption into a local family formally came about seven weeks after reaching Ujelang. Nonetheless, it was presaged by representations that are themselves features of family identity—shared land, labor, food, a common cookhouse, shared time, and evidences of "caring for." Other core representations of identity that could be bestowed only by family were also involved: a sleeping house, a sleeping mat, and a pillow. The process began my first day on Ujelang when I took up residence in Lobet, a land parcel near the middle of town. Having ousted a local family from their dwelling, my sense of imposition was allayed slightly when I discovered that the family had a larger house where they normally lived.

With ideas of self-sufficiency and the avoidance of burden set in my mind, I initially cooked for myself, scrubbed my few dishes, and did my own laundry. However, the husband of the woman who headed my urban land parcel assisted me on trips to their bushlands to collect coconut spathes for my cookfire every day. In addition to assisting with kindling, the land parcel overseer brought me a sleeping mat made by his wife's daughter, claiming it was "no good" to recline on the sleeping platform wrapped solely in a sheet.

After a few weeks I began to lose weight from a bout with intestinal parasites, and Ujelang residents, who use corpulence as a representation of healthfulness, began to comment on the unhealthy state of my increasingly slim form. For them, my parasite-host condition was moving too quickly from 'illness' (a loose translation of *nañenmij*) to 'near death' (the literal translation of *nañenmij*). Therefore, the old woman sent her husband to insist that I eat with them. Initially, I stuck by my plan to cook for myself so as not to impose, but each subsequent day the old woman sent her daughter (adopted granddaughter) and her husband to repeat the offer.

My self-sufficiency stance must have seemed ludicrous to Ujelang people. Local single males wander from cookhouse to cookhouse among their relatives, accepting invitations to eat or simply helping themselves. They know how to cook basic meals but do so only occasionally. They lack the sophisticated culinary skills of their female age-mates, who transform foods from raw to cooked for most of the community every day. While my own cooking experience was extensive, I also knew that to refuse local food was to refuse local sociality. Therefore, I finally accepted the invitation of the woman's husband, making it clear that if I became an imposition, I would return to the separate cooking arrangement. The compromise allowed me to ease my own guilt in sacrificing my initial vow of self-reliance and yet honor their desire to normalize my actions in their community.

My move into the cookhouse was critical because, as Mason (1954, 180) notes, a "household" is defined primarily by shared cooking arrangements (even though the members may have separate sleeping houses), and the "cooking group" is the primary unit that governs a family's daily activity during most of the year.[2] All members eat together, and all except the very old and very young contribute to gathering, fishing, or cooking. Initially, my skills as a fisherman and coconut thrower were undeveloped, so my primary contribution to meals came from sharing my supplies of canned meat and assisting with firewood collection. As imports became sparse, I supplemented the supplies provided to my cooking group with small shares of imported staples like rice and flour. The matriarch's adopted daughter, who did the cooking, insisted I keep the foods in *my* house to prevent depredation by relatives. She shared the cooked food in whatever way she deemed appropriate and did not have to hide uncooked family food from her relatives. Instead, she could say of me, truthfully, that I still had a small amount of food that I shared with the family. Later, as my obligations to others in the community began to increase, I would honor requests for uncooked food from them as well.[3]

The cookhouse provided a new mode of understanding the local community. People not only ate there, they just sat, gossiped *(kamao)*, observed, and commented on the movements of other community members. I soon learned that I could access a wide array of relatives as well as the entire cookhouse group by extending the time of breakfasts and suppers. By now the extended family knew that I had an interest in interpersonal relationships, so as soon as a guest departed, someone would comment on the guest's demeanor and fit him or her into the matriarch's kin network for me.

One day, weeks after I had begun to eat at the cookhouse, the aged household matriarch invited me to come and speak with her. After discussing other things, she then expressed her wish to adopt me. I was thrilled, yet overwhelmed. She kept saying she would call me *nejo* 'offspring' and I was to call her *jino* 'mother.' She then noted the terms to use when I spoke to others in my new family. Later that evening, the daughter and her husband clarified some of what had been said, and the next day my mother's husband repeated many of the details. I now had a real place in the community. It was a most memorable and joyous day, although, in hindsight, it became clear that many of the constituting elements of the relationship had already come into being over the past weeks.

My adoption normalized a set of already existing behaviors at the same time that it gave these relationships a specific form, and I could then refer to her as "Mama Biola." As the head of the extended family, only she could authorize and give substance to the construction of these classificatory forms (Bourdieu 1991, 107–126). While fortuitous in some ways, the shape she gave them brought into effect a certain order with counterbalancing negative effects. Formerly a person of unclear status, I was now positioned within her family and, therefore, within the entire community. My position in the community could be metaphorically manipulated with a wide array of "kinship games" (see Carucci 1989), but without additional ritual transformations, it could not be changed. At the time, one positive attribute of the adoption for me was that it positioned me in the community as a member of an important family, but not a *chiefly* one. My prefield training had emphasized the importance of these associations to the type of information I would get. It would be difficult to obtain the commoner's knowledge of the society that I desired if I were too closely associated with the chiefs or resident missionaries.

Within a month, the outlines of the extended family of which I was now a part became apparent. It was, indeed, *extended,* including all but two Ujelang people. At its most extended level, it was the most powerful family on the atoll precisely because it was the most inclusive. But even my segment of this family (the descendants of one of seven original founding sisters) was overrepresented in the ranks of the community's central political actors. This seemed less fortuitous, since I had hoped to find a middle ground from which to come to understand the perimeters. Nonetheless, within the huge family, Biola was descended from a younger sibling of the seven, which helped compensate for the community's high valuation of several of its living members. Moreover, Biola was the youngest of four siblings in her immediate family, and I was nearly the youngest of her offspring. All of this juniority counterbalanced the superordinate weight given to the island-encompassing extended family.

During the first years of my research, I also felt it was fortuitous that my generation level was high. Reckoning through my mother's mother, I was the next-to-the-youngest member of the generation who controlled the daily operation of atoll affairs in the 1970s. The negative side of my generational position has become apparent more recently as my chronological age-mates have moved into positions of power within the community. Classed as sons, daughters of my clan, or nieces and nephews, some of them are reticent to tell me stories in precisely the way they might share them with other members of their own generation. These taboos can be overcome, in many cases, if I can find another pathway, through one of the other eleven large extended families, to establish a different generational connection to a consultant. But, particularly among the young, there is a disproportionate reliance on the most inclusive *bwij* 'extended family' to trace relationships to others.

The manner in which I was integrated into the Ujelang community had a direct effect on the constructions of it that I was able to produce. Not only was more time spent with members of my family and closely related families, but the relatively central cookhouse location gave me a particular view of village affairs. Furthermore, an entire set of preexisting permissive categories and taboos were brought to bear on me in certain ways as a result of my interpersonal categorization within the community. Communal marginality, a position that itself stood in opposition to community cohesion, was necessarily replaced by *an internal* stance, and the entire shape of my first written constructs of "Ujelang culture" are contextually grounded by the interpersonal and community circumstance created for me by community members.

Elaboration of Interpersonal Pathways

By the next summer the nature of my project was relatively transparent to Biola. With increased language skills, perhaps the equivalent of a six-year-old, I was largely independent of the group of mediators who had introduced me to Ujelang. One day, following an argument I had had with her current husband, my mother informed me that I need not "really" consider him my father. As she reminded me, I was "her offspring, her adoptee." "Go out from *Lokijbad* [the land parcel she shared with Onil, her current husband]," she said, and "eat from" the lands of the children of her first marriage. She knew her instructions would allow time for the dispute between Onil and me to die down, but equally, I believe, she had figured out that my interest in the community required extended access to interpersonal connections. By clearing new paths of relationship for me through her first husband, George, she doubled my kin connectedness, since Onil was an outsider (although recognized as "part of the Ujelang people"). When I subsequently asked "mama," as I came to call her, about certain potential consultants, her insistence on using the new kin linkages she had established for me reinforced my opinion that she could see the value to me of having a broad array of closely linked relatives.

After a few days, the argument with Onil passed, and while we continued to have our disagreements, I knew he would be offended if I did not treat him as a father. In any case, George's other offspring also called him "father" in spite of their own ambivalent relationships with him. Moreover, Onil and Biola's eldest son, Tebi, then still alive, might have viewed his mother's strategy as an attempt on my part to usurp his older sibling position. Therefore, I continued to treat Tebi as older sibling until his death in 1990. My decision to maintain my younger sibling identity ultimately proved beneficial since, in the autumn of 1977, after I had been in the field just over one year, Onil began to stress how closely related I was to a family in the other half of the village with whom I had become closely acquainted. He indicated that the wife in the family was his adopted daughter, and that therefore I was her younger sibling. Thus the dual ties of adoption through Onil (ties not established through Biola) legitimized my increasing presence in the other half of the village; that half—the Jitoen half—had been underrepresented during my first year of research in favor of the Jitoken half.[4]

My mother died in the autumn of 1977. I have explained the circumstances surrounding her death elsewhere (Carucci 1992). Perhaps confirming the efficacy of all rituals of death, the event drew me closer to the remaining members of my Ujelang family even though, in some categorical sense, it was only through her that I had any real claims of family identity. Existentially and pragmatically, other claims now existed—claims vested in spending time with, in laboring with, and in sharing with the family—and it is these claims that, through the years, have maintained my position in *this* extended family. These alternate codings of oneness were particularly stressed by all family members in the months after my mother's death.[5]

Marriage Revisited

Adoption into an Ujelang family did not circumvent attempts to get me to marry into the community. It simply provided a new structure in terms of which a marriage would need to be negotiated. While the old chief continued in his attempt to pair me with his granddaughter, his wife began to joke with him that I was actually *her* cousin. This was, in fact, the case if one adopted the standard pathways that linked our great-grandmothers. By referring to me as her "marriage-class item," the chieftainess could construct a relationship between us in which joking was expected. In much the same way that the kin path to my mother's second husband's adopted daughter gave me substantial freedom to explore the Jitoen half of the community, the joking relationship with the Jitoken chief's wife gave me reason to visit their household. The chief's daughter, a jokester in her own right, was aware of the chief's designs for his granddaughter, and she frequently referred to me as her "offspring" and invited me to their home to "clean the path" that would link me to her family.

During my second research year (1977–1978), I actively participated in most community affairs, including the major project, building a new church. I was committed to the community and willing to consider an Ujelang spouse. After nearly three years of separation, my Chicago partner and I were drifting apart. Nevertheless, I remained ambivalent about marriage into the Ujelang community due to my own idealistic beliefs about equal partnerships. The educational status of the pool of unmarried Ujelang women was of greatest concern. The most highly educated Ujelang women had only high school degrees obtained in Majuro, the government center.

Nevertheless, my personal journal entries began to reflect my belief that my refusal to marry locally served as a self-fulfilling story that distanced me from Ujelang people. Local people definitely viewed my claims about my graduate school relationship as a form of rejection since several times each week I rejected local attempts to care for what they considered my increasingly degenerate health due to lack of sexual release. Some simply said, "Perhaps you thought that Ujelang women were no good." No one spoke in white/nonwhite terms, yet I feared they might also see my refusals as essentially racist. Both of these interpretations disturbed me since they were the antithesis of the affection I had come to feel for the community and its members.[6]

During the church construction period, the women of Jitoken or Jitoen labored each day on noontime meal preparation while the men worked on the church. Most foods were made communally, but they were delivered to each carpenter and brick mason by individual women in a manner that posited great public joking relationships, really pseudomarriages. These public displays involved the necessary exchange of male and female labor, and were compared to the joking relationships of Christmas when men and women playfully captured ritual marriage mates in the games of *karate* and *kamolu* (see Carucci 1980 and forthcoming). For the first weeks, a variety of women delivered my meals, but then a young woman from Jitoen routinely brought my meals for each alternate noon food fest. As I feebly attempted to mimic others' successful antics of humorous acceptance, the community clapped and wildly voiced their approval. Quickly, they detected that I found the young woman attractive. Within three days several men and women stopped by my house to say something about Jenet. Some noted that she was in precisely the same kin category as the chief's favored granddaughter—a permissible marriage partner. Others, who had heard my idealistic discussions about egalitarian marriage relationships and equal education, noted that she was the most promising graduate of the local school and would go to high school the next year, and then "I" could take her to a U.S. college. Meant to be consoling, such talk was very frightening since, at that time, Jenet was a teenager and just over half my age. "This is meaningless! This separation of years makes no difference. She is 'old' [mature]. The good thing is she is 'the perfect size' [fit] for you!" Such talk was typical of the local rationalizations.

Within a week, a sizable segment of the community had, in their persuasive joking way, reordered the set of kin terms they used for me in a manner that took my marriage to Jenet for granted. Shocked by the transition, I began to reiterate to my closest relatives that I was really "one with" them, and the new talk was all in jest. In an equally real sense, however, the other talk brought a new identity into being that contested the old one and required me to consider what the new positioning meant *for me*. Even my closest relatives supported the matchmaking, noting that I would continue to remember and provide for them and simultaneously watch over Jenet and bring her family goods. Two of my consultants, knowledgeable genealogists, found alternate paths to use to transform my granddaughter into a marriageable cousin. In spite of my verbal protests, they knew they had sparked my interest.

The community led me to spend far more time in Jenet's half of the village, with invitations to eat with some relative or another who lived in Jitoen. These were not overt matchmakings but provided the context in which any local boy would have to pass by his lover's house after the invitation and would make contact with his paramour, signaling to her as she relaxed after dinner to meet him on the ocean side. The sight of the resident anthropologist creeping up to the open window of a (very) young woman to propose such a tête-à-tête did not strike me as viable, and it never happened. Nonetheless, my research came to include residents of the downwind "towns" of Ujelang village far more than it would have otherwise because the community refocused my schedule and reformulated my entire persona. Close relatives of Jenet's who lived in other parts of the village also began to invite me to their houses, thus providing new and different interactions on which to ground my research.

The church project continued until the chiefs, elders, council members, and I traveled to Enewetak Atoll to recreate the land parcel boundaries in the summer of 1978. The group also returned with supplies needed to finish the church roof. Jenet departed for Majuro to begin high school while the council was on Enewetak, and after the return to Ujelang, my remaining time was spent in a settled manner with my adopted family. Only occasionally was Jenet mentioned. Our relationship continued to be taken for granted, however. As my departure neared, I gave a final atoll-wide party to thank the community for their hospitality; my closest relatives who were distributing food ceremonially delivered a plate to Jenet's family in a manner that signified the link between her family and mine. When I shrugged my shoulders in recognition, the gesture drew far more laughter than the most humorous parts of my thank-you speech.

In a setting where departures were not easily handled, the days prior to my leaving were filled with a plethora of disjointed and ambivalent messages. I had become close to the community, yet many of them were certain they would never see me again. My pleas to the contrary had been heard too many times before from Peace Corps volunteers and other well-intentioned Americans to be believable. Someone in my family asked if I were leaving my twenty remaining pigs for Jenet. Again, the degree to which local people had realigned me with Jenet amazed me. Looking back, however, I believe such statements reflect the greater trust Ujelang people place in marital "cement" as compared to the bonding capabilities of adoption. After some discussion, we agreed that one pig would go to my father, one to a man who had recently performed some Marshallese medicine for me, and nine each to others in my family and to Jenet.

When I reached Majuro, my symbolic marriage to Jenet seemed to be fully orchestrated in advance. After two days' residence in Ujelang Town, my sister's husband, a close relative of Jenet, invited me for a picnic in a land district where Jenet's father held land. The entire event, sparsely attended, had obviously been planned for Jenet and me. At day's end my sister and her husband indicated I should remain with Jenet's family for two days. At bedtime, Jenet's mother insisted that we all sleep inside in case of rain (unlikely in August). I was placed on the low-ranked lagoon side with Jenet's father in the most distant ocean side position. Next to Jenet's mother was her older brother, then her youngest brother, her sister, and Jenet, next to me. The representations were all in line. My naive thought was that if I simply shivered in my sheet and kept to myself, it would send some signals about my remaining ambivalence vis-à-vis Jenet. Undoubtedly, however, my inappropriate actions simply fit into a collection of already existing stories about the sexual inadequacies and inabilities of white foreigners. The next day I made it clear to Jenet's mother that Jenet would have to complete high school and college if at some point in the future we were to marry. Rather than being upset, she agreed fully[7] and suggested that I go to America and find a university for Jenet. After my next trip, both of us would travel to America. As a professor, I would then "watch over" and "care for" her daughter while she went to college.

Altered Relationships

I departed for Hawai'i in September 1978 and did not return to the Marshalls until May 1982, when I traveled to Enewetak Atoll to spend another year with the now repatriated Enewetak/Ujelang people. In the interim, however, I mailed letters and gifts to my closest relatives. Jenet had been designated as my most faithful correspondent. While in my mind my return to the community was certain, the history of return visitors to Ujelang led them to a different view. After a couple of years, their replies to my letters became increasingly spotty, signifying, I believe, that Ujelang people had given up hope of my return. Given the time orientations of Ujelang and Enewetak people, my *planned* return four or five years in advance must have seemed infinite.

While government supply ships frequented Ujelang every two to four months in the late 1970s, by 1982 Enewetak was served by twice-a-month Airline of the Marshall Islands flights. After a brief stay at my adopted sister's house in Ujelang Town (Majuro), I was on Enewetak, living with my younger sibling at our house in Lobet. After a few days, I went to visit Jenet's mother and grandparents. As with many Enewetak people, they voiced surprise at my return, but they were also overtly overjoyed. They indicated that Jenet would soon arrive on Enewetak, "when she returned from school," and her mother suggested, almost jokingly, however, that I would then come and live with them. Yet I had heard from others that Jenet was now married to a young man from Majuro, had dropped out of school, and was going to have a child. When Jenet did return in June, talk about our relationship was again resurrected, but members of my adopted family began seriously to counsel me to pay no attention. They contended with increased certainty that she was pregnant and things "would never be any good," even though her parents and grandparents wanted me to marry her.

These new strategies of empowerment differed from the days surrounding my departure in 1978. My own Enewetak/Ujelang family had obviously discovered that the adoptive "cement" had been adequate to keep me in contact with them and cause me to return. While Jenet's family had to rely on what they saw as an agreed-upon union to gain access to a substantial share of the goods or opportunities I might bring into the community, my own family's share of the symbolic capital would be diminished by the union. Many Ujelang people, particularly members of my extended family, had placed Jenet in the "sacred maiden" position, a suitable mate who would secure the long-term loyalties of the foreign professor/"chief." Indeed, the Enewetak chief had first conjured up this scenario for me vis-à-vis his granddaughter. But, as Mead points out for Samoa (1973, 51 et seq., 275), the expectations and restrictions for the sacred maiden are far more strict than those that apply to young commoner women. If Jenet were pregnant, she could no longer fill this role.

To clarify the gossip, I asked Jenet's mother about Jenet's marriage. She, too, had heard that her daughter was pregnant but denied she was married. Furthermore, she said: "It means nothing. It is *my* child. . . . You will still take Jenet to be solely yours." The adoption of her daughter's unborn child was the ordinary strategy used to free young women of children born in early experimental marriages. It was her way of telling me that marriage to her daughter was still viable. Such strategies do not work for sacred maidens, however, and it was on this basis that other community members argued that Jenet had irreconcilably damaged our "marriage."

In some sense I was relieved because, like Jenet, I had found another friend. While my new relationship was at the time far from marriage, we had become very close friends. In August, Mary joined me in the field as a research assistant. Her training as a nutritionist fit in with my research: one major dimension of social change on Enewetak was from shifts in food acquisition and consumption brought about by stripping the residence islets of all vegetation during the cleanup of radioactive wastes. The Marshall Islands interested Mary, and she agreed to assist with work on family food histories as part of my proposed research. She was well aware of my adopted family in the Marshalls and of the ambiguities in my relationship with Jenet.

Construction of a Marriage

I arranged to meet Mary in Majuro, where we resided for two weeks with my younger sibling, waiting for a boat to take us back to Enewetak. The days spent in Laura on the leeward end of Majuro provided the first context in which Enewetak people would begin to impute a "married" status to the two of us. In spite of our assertions to the contrary, the fact that we shared a single sleeping room on Majuro was interpreted to mean exactly the same thing as my sharing a sleeping mat with Jenet four years earlier. Naively, I had hoped to make American categories understandable to Marshallese: male and female, anthropological and nutrition researchers, close friends, coresident but *not* married. For Marshallese, however, coresident men and women, unless constrained by taboo, *were* intimate. The strict Marshallese interpersonal avoidances between opposite-sex siblings themselves represent a way to address the idea that unconstrained postpubescent men and women will find each other sexually irresistible.

The boat to Enewetak provided an ideal context to introduce Mary to island life. As I had done many times, we stayed on deck with Enewetak people, sleeping on adjacent mats and sharing food cooked over a common kerosene stove. This setting only reinforced Enewetak people's interpretation of us as "married." Ironically, Jenet's mother slept next to us during the trip, watching over Mary as she faced the trials of life on the field trip ship. Later she would say she did not believe, as did others, that Mary and I were "together" because, even though my mat was spread out next to Mary's, I did not "grab her." Ultimately, Jenet's mother and Mary became lasting friends.

On Enewetak, Mary and I shared the single available room in my family's Lobet house. While other household members knew we were not married, the shared private space again caused the community as a whole to believe we were married. We finally played along with the common interpretation since our constant denials left others unsettled and in disbelief. The community devised several ways to bring our relationship within normal categories. Mary was asked to join Radikdoon, the women's church group reserved for church *members*—celibate single communicants or married women. By February, Mary was also asked to become someone's adoptee. As in my case, an older community member of opposite gender asked to adopt her, but instead of adopting along a standard lineal path, Mary was adopted as the man's younger sibling. The man and I were related as cousins in a way that made Mary and me, in our locally fashioned married state, "proper" marriage partners. Once again my relationship to other community members was restructured. I encouraged Mary to support her brother by providing goods and foods, and by spending time with him. "Cleaning (or weeding) the path" in this way strengthened the relationship, and soon I was spending more time asking her brother and his close relatives questions about matters of land, community relationship, and recent changes in custom and demeanor. These discussions with "in-laws" vastly altered my view of the Enewetak community.

The conjugal family that had been created out of the ambiguous relationship between Mary and me contained its own ambivalences. It served to distance me to a degree from the community since, in comparison to the proposed "marriage" with Jenet, my "marriage" to Mary was only marginally under community control. Clan identity is only tenuously transmitted by adoption, and any subsequent offspring of our marriage would not be intimately linked by clan to Enewetak. Thus local people could not, with assurance, gain dominion over the United States through an offspring born to Mary and me. If Jenet were the mother, the implications of power would follow. On the other hand, a certain sense of settlement and maturity is bestowed upon married Marshallese, and even in this union of their own making, Mary and I jointly benefited from being classed more fully as "true adults." Concomitantly, questions about my sexuality and, therefore, my health, were no longer of concern to the community. In some sense, marauding young males are a threat to community solidarity. As a way to deal with its collective fear, the community brings some control to bear on the lack of constraint manifest among young males by engaging them in marriages. While my own demeanor in the Marshalls had been oriented to contradict local theories of the nature of male sexuality, it could not come close to changing the stereotypes.

The constructed marriage thus changed the fundamental character of research for both Mary and me, shifting the grounds for its conduct toward the community of settled couples. While on Ujelang, people who entered my door included an overrepresentation of young men and women, and while my research necessarily led me to learn a good deal about smoking, coconut toddy production, and alcohol consumption, a much more staid crowd of married church members now stopped by to talk. I had to seek out the young drinkers, and they began to question my motives in being around them.

The 1982–1983 research also tested the developing friendship between Mary and me for two major reasons: (1) the contradictions that emerged as a result of differences between our role as "friends" and the unequal relationship we occupied as "research assistant" and "project director"; and (2) our substantially different knowledge levels of Marshall Islands culture and language. As friends, Mary and I had worked to establish a very equal division of labor, yet as project director I had to make decisions about the design and implementation of the nutritional component of the research that threatened this equality. We were both trapped between feelings of uneasiness and inadequacy in the formal and informal parts of our now multifaceted relationship. The disconcerting sense that equality had been replaced with hierarchy was also influenced by our differential knowledge of Marshallese language and culture. I was fluent in Marshallese, and Mary was just beginning. To gain fluency, she had to speak the language constantly. Yet the more I spoke with Mary in Marshallese, the more my established linguistic knowledge made her feel subordinate. To communicate as equals we had to communicate in a language in which we shared similar levels of competence. Yet speaking to each other in English only perpetuated the underlying cause of inequality. Ultimately I relented, and the contradiction remains even today. Overall, while the "family" relationship Mary and I shared in 1982–1983 placed the Enewetak community at ease, the alignment of all of the categories of empowerment and their placement in my hands made that same relationship internally difficult for both Mary and me.

Weaving Additional Family Ties

I did not return to Enewetak until 1989, two years after Mary and I were married in the United States. Our wedding had surprised no one on the atoll since, for them, it was simply a church-sanctioned confirmation of the *koba* 'common-law marriage' that had long existed. My single presence on the atoll in 1989 was more worrisome, and many people attributed my slenderness to illness rooted in sadness. Others thought I was lying about being married since, in their eyes, I had not aged. A married person could not look the same as in 1982–1983 since the marriage would cause the person to look aged. These experiences confirmed for me the universal applicability of local ideas about human development.

Along with the earlier trips, a series of annual research visits between 1989 and 1993, and more extended research trips in 1990–1991 and 1996, have done much to ensure that I am "a piece of the Enewetak/Ujelang people." My membership in an Ujelang family is the most common idiom used to express the general statement about shared family/community identity. My residence on Enewetak is so established in Lobet that, without asking, whoever transports me from the airport automatically stops their truck in front of the Lobet house. Nonetheless, my position in the community has continued to change. The year 1990 marked my fourth "Christmas" celebration on Ujelang or Enewetak. While I had always been a member of Yeolab, the "middle" competitive songfest group, population increases required the addition of new groups. With my younger brother and me both absent from Enewetak, Biola's adopted daughter, Yula, and her family had become long-standing residents of the Lobet dwelling. Residence at Lobet with Yula and her family has given me the ability in some contexts to "move down" to the generation of Yula's family. In 1990, this meant shifting alliances to Kane Ekaal, a new local songfest group supported by Yula's family, while most of my older-generation cohorts remained with Yeolab. The multilayered components of Enewetak family identity allow for these negotiated possibilities, not only on my part but for all local people. In this view, family is not solely a unit in which one claims membership, but is a multifaceted participatory resource to be used in the construction of personal identity. It provides potential pathways of common clan identity through females, of common "blood" through males, and of additional shared features that are just as personally embodied: adoption, shared food, and shared space, including residence.

During the research period I spent on Majuro in 1990 and 1991, I resided with my sister's son and his family in Ujelang Town, an extremely crowded urban settlement. He held a good job with the credit union and supported his own household and many other relatives. The shift to an extended period of urban research refashioned my position in the community and exposed me to the innovative representations that embodied challenges to the urban Ujelang family's existence. While someone was always "at home," food and other movable objects were locked, as was the core family's room, enshrining the sacred air conditioner, television, and stereo, and separating the room's residents from all others. I was welcomed into the household but paid seventy-five dollars per week to compensate for food and inconvenience. These mediated symbols of sharing were never comfortable, either for me or for my sister's son. The cash payment seemed like rent, yet it was detached from the task of provisioning, as had been the case on Ujelang. The money moved in a contorted way from older to younger to allow my sister's son to retain his position as family head. Moreover, in my research I was working with senior men and women from all over the Marshall Islands. In one way this brought into question my standing as solely an Enewetak/Ujelang person, only "their" professor/anthropologist, but at the same time it increased my rank for some members of the community who saw me as becoming *bunbun* 'famous.' Not only did my position on Enewetak and in Majuro shift, but the ambivalences of life in Ujelang Town came to represent for me the surreal shapes of a Marshallese family confronted with the challenges of an urban existence in the 1990s.

In 1991 Mary, our daughter, Iliana, and I returned to Enewetak. For the first time, Mary and I were true adults who, in local terms, had altered our generational status by reproductively replacing ourselves with a subsequent generation. All questions about the legitimacy of our marriage ended with the birth of an offspring, although, in fine Enewetak fashion, some people contended that our daughter looked like Jenet—an indication that she was the "dream genetrix" who had been in my mind during the time the fetus was being formed. This claim on Iliana's identity was not simply a statement about my own past. It constructed a local history for my daughter, placing her within the relationship in which claims of power had been negotiated since my first day on the atoll. It condensed the community's past plans for me, drew them into the present day, and projected them as future hopes onto the scripted outlines of my daughter's life. When we returned in 1992, Iliana had begun to speak, and some of her clearest words were Marshallese, uttered in an acceptable Ujelang dialect. Enewetak people were overjoyed. For some, her utterances proved that Jenet was her hidden genetrix, thus reinforcing their claims of common clan identity with her. For others, Iliana's words were taken as more straightforward evidence that someday she, too, would be a "true Enewetak person."

Similar to our experiences with Iliana, when we returned to the atoll with our young son as well as our daughter in 1993, local people drew on unfulfilled desires as a source of promise for Enewetak people in the future. We had given our son both Marshallese and Enewetak names, Akeo Lekkeya, and their iteration became a kind of mesmerizing chant for children and adults alike. During our first visit, my sister said she wanted to adopt Iliana and raise her as a "real Enewetak child." I declined but indicated that, if we had more than two children, she could ask for the third. With Akeo, she again reiterated her wish to adopt him. I reminded her that the third would be hers. This time, however, the old Enewetak chief's oldest granddaughter told my sister that I had given Akeo to her. While this was not true, her adoption of my son would have fulfilled the old chief's dream of paths to America through his great-grandchildren. Both women would use the adoption in a very typical way, to strengthen bonds between already existing kin, but in this case power would also be gained over the United States through a direct family tie. At the same time, our refusal to give our children freely to these women re-represents the unequal nature of the colonial encounter. No matter how much we desire our children to grow up with multicultural exposure and understanding, ultimately we failed to give "our" children to them in the same way that Enewetak volunteer to allow us to adopt their children for perceived educational gain. In this contest over the educational construction of categories (Bourdieu 1991, 48 et seq.), the structures of domination that produced the research situation as a possibility are reiterated in comfortable talk about third children we do not intend to have. (See Young Leslie, chapter 3, for another fieldworker's rather different experience and management of a host community's interest in adopting and raising her young child.)

While the recent research trips have reinforced for Enewetak people our enduring commitment to the community, they have also served to point out the real distance that separates my family and me from them. The Enewetak view of solidarity is ultimately measured by "time spent with." Visits of limited duration therefore set us apart as outsiders to a much greater degree than my one- and two-year research periods of the 1970s and 1980s.

Not surprisingly, the focus of Mary's projects in the Marshalls on issues of nutritional change has altered the direction of my research, and the presence of our children in the field has equally had an effect on the amount of time I spend on topics related to children. While childbirth, child rearing, and children were always of concern, the presence of my own children shifted my experiential world and facilitated work on child-related topics. Concomitantly, the rapid shifts in and out of the field, often during the summer, have brought out the contrasts between American and Marshallese child socialization models. Whereas American children are enculturated into a culture of childhood and adolescence, a world of play defined largely in opposition to adult demeanor, Marshall Islanders orient their child rearing primarily toward the attainment of adulthood.

The internal dynamics of the family situation for Mary and me are now more settled than in the past. My knowledge of Enewetak has continued to increase at a more rapid rate than Mary's due to more frequent interactions, but on our trips in 1991, 1992, 1993, and 1996, Mary has been the director of a nutrition education program for Enewetak people, providing a balance of power that was not present in the early 1980s. My position has been to serve as translator, assist with her program design, and perform a variety of odd tasks for the community and their legal representative. Furthermore, it is the Enewetak people, represented by their council, who are our employers. They pay Mary for her consulting services, and ultimately they select the voices they would like to have address them on issues of nutrition. Each of these families, just like each of the families of which I have been a part over the last twenty years, is part of an ongoing negotiation among several parties to construct empowered senses of self in relationships with others and to lend to those selves a voice that deserves to be heard in an ever-changing world.

From the beginning, my research experiences have been deeply affected by altered political agendas and renegotiations in the balance of power between Euro-American and Pacific peoples. My initial proposal to conduct research in the eastern Solomon Islands had to be altered when I could not obtain a research permit during the era of Solomon Islands independence. In 1976, when I began research in the Marshall Islands, I hoped to discover a set of symbolic fields that were simply "out there" to be analyzed with the ostensibly altruistic aim of promoting cross-cultural understanding. Yet from the moment I arrived in the Marshall Islands, my research experiences were far more complex than I had imagined. As part of this complexity, Enewetak and Ujelang people shaped me into a person of symbolic and pragmatic benefit to themselves. Often they did so through the use of a variety of tropes and metaphors that centered on the family. Indeed, the way in which our lives have been interwoven is very complex, leaving little room for the maintenance of guises of distant objectivity. Yet if an accounting of these ongoing negotiations of persons and identities increases the complexity of doing anthropological research, or of doing it well, an exploration of the multilayered symbolic constructions allows for vastly enriched ethnography. These are emergent and discontinuous processes that involve intricate human relationships. By exploring the familial and interpersonal dimensions of these relationships, the analysis of supposedly distant others is brought close to home, clarified, and made far more human.

Acknowledgments

Research for this chapter was funded by grants from the National Science Foundation (1976–1978) and the National Endowment for the Humanities (1982–1983 and 1990–1991), by the Enewetak/Ujelang local government council, and by Montana State University. While the work could not have been conducted without their support, all interpretations are my own and should not be taken to represent the views of these agencies.

Notes

1. During the period of my initial research with the Enewetak/Ujelang community, most of the community lived on Ujelang Atoll, with the exception of the small expatriate community on Majuro. Originally relocated to

allow the United States to conduct nuclear tests on Enewetak Atoll, some residents were allowed to return to Enewetak under a temporary settlement program in 1977, and Ujelang residents as a whole returned to Enewetak in 1980. I shall use primary residence as a referent of identity, as is local practice, even though residence shifts during the periods of time I have lived with the community during the last eighteen years.

2. From late September through January, the community is rearranged into *jepta* for the celebration of *Kurijmoj* 'Christmas,' which alters food collection and preparation in systematic ways (Carucci 1980; 1992; forthcoming).

3. There is a larger sense in which I was indebted to the entire community for allowing me to conduct research on Ujelang, but they did not see the situation in this way. Instead, I became the responsibility of the family who was sponsoring me. Such sponsorship had certain costs and brought certain benefits. This pattern was very unlike the other local pattern for dealing with foreigners, which had been based on the visiting chief model, then extended to pastors and to former anthropologists. Using the later schema, the community fed and maintained foreigners as extended and privileged guests, and each "town" provided meals for a set period of time in rotation. From the beginning, I worked to avoid the "honored guest" designation. Therefore, the household sponsorship pattern was applied. It had been modified for use during the Peace Corps era, and, while several community members knew I was not a Peace Corps volunteer, I fit local stereotypes about Peace Corps all too well: young, often single, often male, lacking any locally meaningful occupation. It is not surprising that for the first few months many who did not know me well continued to ask if I was not a new Peace Corps volunteer.

4. It is clear that I was manipulating ties of relationship for my own benefit throughout my research. While this is true, I believe it is doubly justifiable. First, Ujelang people themselves adopt this strategy, although for somewhat different ends. Second, it is the negotiated exchange of symbolic capital, from goods and services to honorific forms of address and "thank yous," that lends an extant form to the community. My manipulations could only take place as part of an ongoing exchange to which I contributed labor and goods that were deemed valuable at the time by those who welcomed me into their homes and families.

5. My attempt to make readers aware of the relevance of these negotiationally situated selves to the research process also makes it appear as though I always judged my interactions with local people based on what sort of effect they might have on field research. Certainly this was not true. In becoming part of this community, my relationships were as emotionally charged and personally involving as any I have been a part of in the United States. I took few myths about the objectivity of the research process to the field with me. Indeed, as an overt strategy to separate myself from former Marshall Islands

researchers, I conducted no formal interviews, hired no interpreters, and never requested a consultant to come to my house for an interview. Virtually all of my research was designed to capture interaction in the contexts of its own generation.

6. While some readers may see my decisions about marriage as evidence of an exclusively male sexual license, I believe this to be an overly simplistic, Eurocentric reading of the situation. Indeed, young Marshallese males and females are equally active (and apparently equally successful) in pursuing amorous encounters. Moreover, I was hardly acting as a typical young American male out to "get laid." In a manner reminiscent of how Turner (1987) describes the way her Polish ethnic identity influenced choices she made in the field, and the way Flinn (chapter 7) describes class differences as influencing the different ways she and her husband interacted in the field, my own ethnic, class, and religious identity had definite effects on my action. Far from overly sexualized, my own demeanor was governed by extreme restraint, a strategy I had adopted as an adolescent to prove that theories of inherent ethnicity, particularly talk about Latin "hot-bloodedness," did not apply to me. This had been a critical part of my own adolescent self-presentation inasmuch as I grew up in a white middle-class setting in Colorado, as an all-too-conservative Protestant, with no connection to an Italian community and tangential ties to my father's partly Italian family. My mother's family, with its British, German, and French ancestry and claims of all-American status, formed the context for my bland midwestern-grounded socialization and middle-class aspirations. While college and graduate school provided the context for me to negate some of my parents' Protestant prudery and engage in critiques of class-constrained action, my own investment in the work ethic and in the demonstrated denial of Latin ethnic stereotypes through overcompensation, particularly the avoidance of the sexual component of cross-gender interactions, have continued to the current day.

7. I had used the word *pelele* 'to marry' to talk about what might happen in the future. But representationally, *pelele* did not separate those who were *koba* 'combined, common-law married' from those who had *komari* 'wed, taken marriage vows in the church.' When Jenet's parents allowed me to "sleep with" their daughter, the conditions required for *koba* in local terms were fulfilled. Some young *koba* couples simply set up a household together without the permission of both parents. Long-term coresidence allowed these marriages to become recognized over time. In spite of my protestations—we were not truly married, but perhaps some time in the future, or, I needed to obtain my birth parents' permission before I could marry (*koba*)—people simply said that Jenet and I were "combined." The boundaries around marriage are so fluid in practice that the precision I wanted to demand from the representations simply made no difference in local people's classifications.

Reflections on Families and Fieldwork

ANNE MARIE TIETJEN

As I read the chapters in this volume, I felt a personal resonance for the fascinating stories they contain. I found myself recalling my own experiences as an American child in an unfamiliar culture, an unaccompanied fieldworker, a fieldworker accompanied by a spouse, a spouse of a fieldworker in the field, a fieldworker's spouse left at home, and a mother introducing her child to an unfamiliar culture. As a child I lived in Europe for three years and in Okinawa for two. My first fieldwork experience was in England as an undergraduate student, and I later conducted doctoral dissertation research in Sweden. In 1981 my anthropologist husband, John Barker, and I arrived in the village of Uiaku, in Papua New Guinea, and began our individual but inseparable research projects there. John returned to Uiaku alone for three months in 1986 while I stayed behind in the United States. We now have a seven-year-old son who has not been to Uiaku yet, but he has spent two weeks in Sweden and two months getting to know an elder from Uiaku who lived in our home recently while working on a project with John.

Although fieldwork is often the purview of the anthropologist, I am trained as a psychologist. I began as a developmental psychologist, studying with Urie Bronfenbrenner the cultural and ecological contexts of human development. Since 1989 I have been in private practice as a clinical psychologist, and I am frequently aware of bringing some of the knowledge I gained working in other cultures to my work with troubled adults and children. The ways in which people make meaning of their experiences is what I endeavor to understand, both in fieldwork and in psychotherapy.

The chapters in this volume are all authored by North American anthropologists but represent diverse generations, genders, developmental stages, and degrees of formal involvement in fieldwork. A common thread among them, however, is that all are about the tensions produced by trying to combine fieldwork and family and about the ways in which the two influence one another. Some writers have emphasized the effects of fieldwork on family members, while others have focused more on the effects of family on their fieldwork. And, although not all of the authors have made it explicit, the chapters are also about the personal and professional growth and development of the writers as they have grappled with the often conflicting demands of what are probably the two most important aspects of their lives.

Influences of Fieldwork on Family

Each of the authors who took family members to the field believed that in doing so they would be providing their children with invaluable experiences that would enable them to understand important things about the world. A fieldwork experience characteristically offers exposure to different cultural values and ways of understanding the world and its events, economic comparisons between the first and third worlds, exposure to languages other than English, and so on. It was with the best intentions and highest hopes that families described in these chapters undertook going to the field. Many parents also had concerns about the possible negative effects of the fieldwork experience on their families. Health and safety issues and the possibility of falling behind in schoolwork seemed to head the list of anticipated risks. Precautions were taken to minimize these risks by carefully choosing the field site and the length and timing of the stay, and by bringing along medical supplies and school materials.

On balance, it seems, what can be said after the fact is that most parents who took children to the field felt their children gained something, although it was sometimes hard for both parents and children to put into words just what they had gained or what the long-term implications would be. Most writers seemed to feel the experience brought their families closer together (Flinn, Goodenough, McGrath, Petersen and Garcia). Several writers reported that there were some unanticipated benefits from the experience, such as opportunities to interact with people of different ages and to meet and learn from such diverse adults as mapmakers, botanists, and storytellers (Goodenough). There were painful experiences, as well, however, such as leaving family members behind (Goodenough), dealing with a child who had unpleasant experiences in the field (Gilmore), and removing a child from a secure and valued host culture (Young Leslie).

Some of the factors that seem to have influenced fieldworkers' and children's feelings about the experience include the ages of the children, the length of the stay in the field, the presence or absence of a second parent, the role of the second parent, and, of course, characteristics of the field site and host culture. It is difficult to make generalizations about the effects of these factors. This is in part because the factors interact with one another and in part because of the relatively small number of children involved. Some tentative generalizations, however, can be made. The presence of a nonfieldworking parent was usually an advantage (Flinn, Goodenough, McGrath, Petersen and Garcia), although not a necessity (Flinn, Linnekin, Sinclair). Many children did well with fieldwork stays of many months' duration, whereas at least one was eager to return home after a few weeks (Gilmore).

The experiences of families with children at various developmental stages can be seen as reflecting developmental differences in children as well as in their parents and host cultures. Kegan's (1982) view of human development as a dialectic process involving the achievement of a succession of balances between inclusion and individuation, or integration and differentiation, is useful here. In this view, individuals develop by proceeding along a helix that alternately emphasizes integration and differentiation at different stages.

Kegan describes infancy as a period of inclusion, where the self is just beginning to be differentiated from others. Infants are adaptable and malleable. In the field, infants and toddlers are building up their first notions about how the world works rather than comparing cultures. They have not yet established expectations and habits based on the ways of their birth culture that contrast with their field experiences. Additionally, they learn from their own senses and actions and direct experiences to a greater extent than do older children, who become increasingly influenced by the use of language and representative thought (Piaget and Inhelder 1969; Vygotsky 1978). (Counts and Counts make the point in their chapter that some of the most important knowledge gained by anthropologists conducting fieldwork is obtained through direct involvement and experience, as children tend to learn things, rather than through talking.)

Young Leslie describes her infant daughter's experiences in the field as becoming a member of the host culture. The child's early difficulties in Tonga most likely occurred because she was old enough to have begun developing some expectations of the world during her first eighteen months of life in North America. In this respect her experience contrasts with that of children taken to the field at ages less than twelve months, who seem to have eased naturally into the local culture (see Turner 1987 for a Pacific example). In a relatively short period of time, however, Young Leslie's daughter became so attuned to and comfortable with the ways of her host culture that her mother found herself with unexpected internal conflicts concerning her values and assumptions about such basic things as motherhood and cultural relativism, and with feelings of estrangement and discontinuity between herself and her daughter. Young Leslie's expectations of her child's behavior, based largely on North American norms, were challenged as she watched her daughter learn the local language and customs in ways she herself sometimes envied.

Although the experiences Young Leslie describes are very similar to those of Turner (1987), who took her nine-month-old daughter to Fiji, others in this volume (Counts and Counts, Flinn) describe a very different kind of experience with their young children in the field. Counts and Counts emphasize that their children's presence in the field "created a link of humanity" for them with the Kaliai. Flinn was keenly aware of the benefits to her nineteen-month-old son of living in a culture where he would receive lots of attention from adults and other children and experience a degree of freedom unusual for North American children his age. She assumed that his experiences in Pollap would contribute to his sensitivity and adaptability, values she was eager for him to develop. She reports experiencing none of the estrangement and discontinuity mentioned by Young Leslie or Turner (1987). By way of explaining this contrast she cites her own very positive experience in another culture as a child, which gave rise to positive expectations about her son's experience, as well as her Pollapese hosts' accepting attitudes, and, perhaps, the supportive role of her accompanying husband. Clearly the age of the child interacts with characteristics of the parents and the host culture. The internal conflicts described by Young Leslie and Turner (1987) could also occur at home, where other socializing agents such as grandparents, teachers, and baby-sitters can be perceived as instilling values that conflict with those of the parents.

A concept from cross-cultural developmental psychology that may help to illuminate the experience of parents and children in the field is Super and Harkness' (1986, 1994) notion of the "developmental niche." The three components of the developmental niche are (1) the physical and social settings of everyday life, which include the company a child keeps as well as the physical characteristics of the places in which children are found; (2) customs of childcare, including ways of handling everyday situations; and (3) the psychology of the caregivers, or the cultural ways of thinking and feeling of those caring for children. According to Super and Harkness (1994, 98), "Parents' cultural belief systems and related emotions underlie the customs of child rearing and validate the organization of physical and social settings of life for children." One way of viewing the difficulties experienced by Young Leslie is in terms of a mismatch or discontinuity between the psychology of the parents as caregivers and the settings and customs to which their children were being exposed.

New parents are also in an important developmental phase. Learning the role of parent while also learning the role of fieldworker, as well as learning a new culture, is almost certain to produce some degree of role conflict and feelings of frustration. Studies of the experiences of new parents in the United States have emphasized the importance of social support in the transition to parenthood (e.g., Crockenberg 1981). Although most of the parents contributing to this volume were receiving social support in many forms from their

Pacific hosts, it was sometimes support for values and preferences quite different from their own.

Early work on infants' emotional attachments (e.g., Bowlby 1969) emphasized the importance of the mother as the primary caregiver and presented infants as capable of forming only one primary emotional attachment. In contrast, recent research has suggested that infants may have the capacity to achieve a sense of connectedness to several people at an early age. Tronick, Morelli, and Ivey (1992) found that Efe infants in Zaire spend about half of their time in social contact with individuals who are not their mothers and that Efe three-year-olds spend 70 percent of their time in such company. Tronick and his colleagues suggest that patterns of caring for children develop out of the social and physical ecology of a culture and, in turn, may be associated with particular developmental experiences and ways of conceptualizing self and others.

The community-based child rearing described by Tronick et al. is not unlike that which occurs in many Pacific cultures and perhaps fits the experiences of the young children described in this volume. Cared for by local adults as well as by their North American parents, they very likely became attached to their local caregivers and learned much from them. How or whether these experiences affected their sense of self and community in lasting ways would be interesting to know.

None of the contributors to this volume who took older children to the field reported experiencing a sense of estrangement and discontinuity from their children. North American children of school age arriving in Pacific cultures for the first time with their parents have already firmly established primary relationships with their parents, expectations of the world based on experience with Western cultural and behavioral patterns, and a sense of their own identity that is less malleable and less focused on inclusion and integration with others than that of infants. Flinn commented on the importance of privacy to her eight-year-old son. McGrath's children, at ages three, six, and nine, apparently were able to make friends with local children but did not become Tongan. Nonetheless, McGrath offers cogent examples of children's ways of being in their experiences rather than having them, or feeling their experiences rather than analyzing them, as adults tend to do.

Both Emily Sinclair and Rebecca Counts—the only adolescents discussed in this volume—had gone to their parents' field sites since early childhood. Given the geographic moves Emily Sinclair had experienced within the United States, returning to New Zealand with her mother to live again with the Maori was experienced as a homecoming. Nonetheless, Emily's experiences during her stay with the Maori as an adolescent reflect her developmental status and suggest why taking an adolescent to do fieldwork for the first time is perhaps not often undertaken.

Writers in this volume describe the experience of fieldwork as being at times stressful and lonely, and as requiring that the fieldworker and companions give up or suspend portions of identity temporarily for the enterprise to succeed. For North American adolescents, finding one's identity among peers and increasing one's independence from parents are considered to be among the important developmental tasks. The fieldwork experience may provide too few opportunities for appropriate individuation from parents and perhaps too many opportunities for feeling separate from peers unless being part of the host culture has been an aspect of the adolescent's identity since childhood, as it had for both Rebecca Counts and Emily Sinclair. The personal identities of these two young women appear to have been greatly enhanced, rather than threatened, by fieldwork. Here, too, the child's age interacts with parental and cultural factors.

Influences of Family on Fieldwork

Turning to a consideration of the effects of family members on fieldwork, it seems clear that many of these effects were not anticipated or planned. As Flinn points out in the introduction, there is very little to be read ahead of time about family and fieldwork.

The most obvious and concrete way in which families affect fieldwork is that they make demands on fieldworkers' time and energy. Unaccompanied fieldworkers have more freedom to make decisions about their work without having to take into account the effects on their family members. It is worth noting, however, that none of the writers here reported that the presence of family members prevented them from doing work they would otherwise have done, or prolonged the fieldwork unreasonably. Perhaps that is due to selection factors in the sample, or perhaps it is due to the nature of fieldwork. Fieldwork is a fluid process in which the fieldworker expects and deals with the unexpected constantly. The needs and demands of family members, in most cases, are dealt with as the need arises, along with "other uncontrollables," as Linnekin calls them.

Dealing with the needs and demands of family members, however, is often of necessity done in full view of one's hosts and informants, and this factor has its own effects on the fieldwork. As Linnekin points out, it poses problems for managing the impression one wants to present and maintain. Emotionally charged interactions with one's children can expose aspects of oneself and one's views of the host culture in ways that make it more difficult to maintain the "polite fictions" that are traditionally seen to make fieldwork go smoothly. McGrath points out, however, that just such a situation provided a breakthrough for her in her relationship with an important informant, which resulted in richer and more realistic information than she might otherwise have obtained. Several writers mentioned that having children in the field increased the empathy between themselves and their hosts. David and Dorothy Counts assert that the shared experience of parenting provided rich topics for discussion with hosts. What the hosts learn about the fieldworker appears to have an effect on what the fieldworker will learn about the hosts. Several of the chapters also make it clear that the age of one's children also influences the nature of what the fieldworker will learn about the host culture.

Chapters by Thurston, Carucci, Counts and Counts, and others indicate that whether a fieldworker arrives in the field with or without family members, he or she is likely to be provided with family by the host culture. This may be more important to the hosts if one arrives alone, since unconnected individuals are anomalous in the Pacific cultures under report. In any case, adoption by the hosts provides rich opportunities for learning about social categories and their meanings, as Carucci, Counts and Counts, and Thurston have shown. Dealing with family in the field, whether biological or acquired, provides knowledge that is felt, as well as known.

Several writers have commented on the importance of acknowledging the effects of having family members in the field on the way fieldwork is defined and carried out, suggesting that traditional, ideal fieldwork is impossible when family members are present, and that notions of fieldwork should be revised to account for the realities of families' presence in the field. Any further comments on how this should be done I will leave to anthropologists.

Influences of Family in the Field on the Fieldworker

According to the traditional model, fieldwork is a "transforming experience" for the lone fieldworker because he or she becomes immersed in the host culture and comes to know human experience in profoundly new and different ways. Whether one feels, on balance, that bringing family members to the field increases or decreases one's ability to become immersed in the host culture, it is clear from the contributions to this volume that coordinating the demands of family and fieldwork was a transforming experience for many of the writers. Personal growth was as important an outcome of the fieldwork experience as professional growth for several writers.

At the same time, insofar as it involves a loss or suspension of aspects of one's identity, living in an unfamiliar culture heightens one's awareness of oneself. Removed from our own cultural backdrop, we stand out in higher relief against the new surroundings. Several writers in this volume experienced greater awareness of their own needs and values. Flinn observed an increased awareness of her need to express herself and to be appreciated and understood by others when she was alone in the field after having first experienced fieldwork accompanied by her husband and son. Gordon and Linnekin both mused about the need to feel in control of something while doing fieldwork, because one's sense of control is so diminished. Glenn Petersen and Victoria Garcia eloquently describe a sense of lost identity in the field. Glenn describes the experience of the lone fieldworker as feeling "without guideposts," while Victoria writes, "I had to learn everything again, without the indulgence provided to infants."

Away from our familiar surroundings and routines, where we and those around us know the rules, we are more likely to consider why we think, feel, and act as we do, and perhaps to take more individual responsibility for our values and choices than we might have to at home. Surrounded by people whose values differ from ours, we become increasingly aware of just what our values are. Gordon found her identity intensified in the face of strong differences in values. Others became aware of inconsistencies in their value systems, often prompted by their children's reactions, and found themselves reexamining their assumptions and "comfortable fictions" (Sinclair). Perhaps this is especially true for people who are actively engaged in trying to pass on their values to their children. For several writers, value conflicts with members of the host culture or their own families led to reexamination of their experiences in their families of origin (Flinn, Garcia, Goodenough) and, in turn, of their own identities. Identity issues may be most salient for those taking very young children to the field because they are building new identities as parents at the same time they are building new identities as fieldworkers and participants in unfamiliar cultures.

Kegan's (1982) model of human development as a process of negotiating balances between independence and inclusion, or between differentiation and integration, seems to speak to the experiences of many of the authors here. The conflicts described in many of the chapters may be seen as involving these two aspects of human experience. For example, the fieldwork process itself requires the researcher to achieve and maintain a balance between inclusion in the host culture and independence from it. In another sense, the traditional model of fieldwork emphasizes a lone individual in the process of becoming or being an independent professional, while family life demands an orientation toward integration and inclusion with family members. Garcia's balance included introducing aspects of her own culture to Pohnpei friends in the field, and later, back home, introducing forms of community cooperation and childcare learned in the field to her American neighbors.

One of the strengths of these chapters is the personal openness with which the authors have told their stories and reflected on their experiences. They show us with their hearts and minds how finding a balance between fieldwork and family provides rich new dimensions to the development of the family, the fieldwork, and the fieldworker.

Fieldwork Relations and Ethnographic Presence

MICHÈLE D. DOMINY

In examining families in the field—primarily those accompanying us but also those absorbing us when there—these chapters contribute to the analytic power of the autobiography of fieldwork, and they contribute to the ways in which reflexivity can tell us something pragmatically and methodologically about us as anthropologists, but also theoretically about the people with whom we work and the unique and complicated relationships generated by our shared lives.[1] We might call this reflexivity an interfamilial dialogic; Jane Bachnik (1986, 75) defines dialogic as a text that is the

> by-product of relationships established with a series of people who actually do more than inform. Their personal interaction creates a "ground" or a tie, within which cultural knowledge is defined and understood.

By interfamilial dialogic I refer to an even more complex nexus of relationships established within and between field families. Thus the volume invites us to examine how processes of knowledge construction provide ethnographic insights into the behavioral world of relationship and connectivity in affect-laden contexts.

In the opening chapter of *Notes on Love in a Tamil Family*, "What Led Me to Them," Margaret Trawick (1990, 48) traces how she came to see that her key informant's textual interpretations

> were hooked into the everyday affairs of his family—his life in the family gave the ancient poetry the meaning it had for him. . . . I learned that in the everyday life of the members of this household, and especially for Themozhiyar and his sister-in-law who formed its emotional center, the principle of love, *anpu*, was not just a high ideal, it was the way they lived.

The only certainty she discovers is that relationships exist in a permanent negotiated tension that binds one to another within and between families; her family of procreation is no less implicated in these processes. Not only does Trawick find the meaning of sacred texts revealed in the culturally specific patterns of ambiguity in extended family life—primarily in twinning/mirroring, where individuals are linked together through opposition and complementarity in pairs of matched sets—but she paints Tamil Nadu life against the backdrop of her own nuclear family of procreation, one stressed and strained eventually to breaking point amid the structural and emotional constraints and rigors of fieldwork and its aftermath. *Notes* provides a metacommentary on the fragile autonomous constitution of North American nuclear family life, on the conditions of work where the personal and the professional defy separation, and on the hidden logistics of fieldwork when the anthropologist is embedded in multiple families. This work helps us to understand why it "is wrong to decide a priori that a diverse array of social units we call families fulfill the same set of functions or that their primary function is the same" and to resist "the conviction that we can construct a precise reduced definition for what are inherently complex multifunctional institutions imbued with a diverse array of cultural principles and meanings" (Yanagisako 1979, 199).[2]

Relating Autobiography

Judith Okely provides an appropriate theoretical backdrop against which we can read these accounts. She writes, "The autobiography of fieldwork is about lived interactions, participatory experience and embodied knowledge; whose aspects ethnographers have not fully theorised" (1992, 3). Suggesting that this kind of embodied knowledge can "dismantle the positivist machine," she urges us to think of the personal as theoretical, rescuing it from the periphery of scientific and interpretive work and placing it center stage as more than political and subjective. The familial personal is often physically, strategically, and conceptually separated from the ethnographic professional in our fieldwork accounts and analyses, and the contributions in *Fieldwork and Families* face the challenge of bridging these domains and addressing the ways in which ethnographers are multiply positioned subjects within and between both their own Euro-American families and their fieldwork families. Our families from home potentially create a more complex nexus of relationships in the field when we go accompanied, or when they live in our field areas, as did Gordon's and Sinclair's in-laws, sometimes demanding that as we negotiate between identities, some assert themselves more loudly than others and confound our attempts at impression management as we take "performance risks" (Linnekin). Family relationships demand that we separate, recognize, and factor in the interplay of multiple identities as we negotiate our social worlds. Families, both our own and those we join, therefore, mediate knowledge for us much as does the self; furthermore, as Hastrup (1992, 120) argues for the self, they are reinvented in fieldwork.

Many of these chapters bridge the relationship between anthropology and autobiography by linking self-knowledge and social knowledge through the analysis of a nexus of family relationships. Taken together these chapters span a continuum of emphasis from purer narratives of experience conveying the immediacy of fieldwork conditions, to methodologically focused inquiries, to explorations of data, to the analysis of indigenous kinship constructions. For example, Counts and Counts effectively use materials to provide theoretical insight into Kaliai kinship dynamics and cultural practices for marking the status of their daughter, Rebecca, as a firstborn. Their engaging narrative tells us about the behavioral and emotional content of their kinship ties in West New Britain and illustrates what happens when we play our informants' cultures out by trying to be players in their social systems, while not quite appreciating its nuanced complexity until we are caught up short. Alma Gottlieb has written about this search for the ethnographer's magic in her Ivory Coast research as the quest for how to "be an embodied Beng—to inhabit a Beng body" (Gottlieb and Graham 1993, 266), or, as Thurston puts it, "what it means to be Anêm." This happens to all of us as we think we approach understanding, only to be knocked back because we do not, and only to gain incremental understanding from our failures rather than from our more systematic attempts to discover the sociocultural system. Thurston analyzes the changes in his own treatment in the field as a socially positioned actor within a kin network to illustrate changing social relations and structural principles for the Kaliai and Anêm people he studied. Here again, readers learn as much or more about them than about Thurston's exploits as he provides insights into changes in the old cosmology in which it was rational to assume the fieldworkers were spirits. In all of these cases, kinship is the organizing principle for the research participants, and the anthropologist has to engage with that in their terms, which enables him to cast the analysis in Kaliai rather than highly personal terms.

Most significantly, the Counts and Counts and Thurston chapters, read together, ask us to think critically about our analytical distinctions between so-called fictive and real kin. And more important, they challenge us not to assume the fictitiousness of our own social location within the fieldwork context. Despite thinking that we are marginal, not quite players, within the kinship system, in fact we are players simply by being there and inserting ourselves in the lives of others who may then try to link the anthropologist into their system of relationships through what Carucci characterizes as "indigenous metaphoric ties." Thurston notes that the modern, more open system "made a more convenient scheme for integrating us, alleviating the intellectual necessity of attributing us to traditional kinship categories" (164). Because we are marginal players does not mean that we are not social actors; perhaps we think we are marginal more than we are. Bachnik's discussion of intersubjectivity in fieldwork can be extended to include families: "the ethnographer [with family] is part of the universe of discourse which the natives construct from their varied relationships (including that with the ethnographer [and family]) and which becomes their social world" (Bachnik 1986, 81). We need to acknowledge not only our, and their, cultural and historical positioning, but also our, and their, parallel and distinctive social, sexual, and affective positioning.

Most of the contributions to this volume document and reveal vulnerabilities, emotions, private writings and experiences, and details of family dynamics and tensions that are privatized within kinship and domestic domains, reflecting a time-honored culturally constituted divide that Hugh-Jones (1987) refers to as that between "familial" and "professional." The cultural specificity of such a division is all the more reason the family is traditionally excluded and all the more reason we should include it. Linking home and the field through the inclusion of family arrangements and practices provides a corrective in demanding that we integrate what has been so carefully differentiated and privatized (see also Tietjen, this volume). McGrath correctly notes in her chapter that the family presence in fieldwork is not new; it has just been hidden so that what is being revealed in volumes such as this one has been there all along but not acknowledged and, more significantly, not theorized. As we write openly about our own varieties of family, about courtships, partnerships and formalized marriage, children, divorce, and custody, we break rules. This volume is an invitation to other fieldworkers to develop a tradition, illustrated powerfully and eloquently in the honesty of Trawick (1992), Gottlieb and Graham (1993), and Behar (1993) about their accompanied fieldwork, to break those rules not just by breaking silence, but through innovative multivocal textual strategies in which different family voices speak to each other explicitly within the text (Petersen, Garcia, and Petersen), or implicitly (Flinn, Goodenough, Sinclair), or even between texts (Counts and Counts, Thurston). Logistically, an explicit collectively authored familial format is difficult, as many contributors found when trying to elicit written contributions from their children:[3] some have only vague memories or prefer not to recall, others do not want anyone to "mess with" their prose, others are protected by parent fieldworkers who do not want to impose the strictures of their own narrative lines on their children. Especially useful can be the juxtaposition of a variety of literary forms such as letters, journals, reminiscences, and fieldnotes (see Sanjek 1990; Cesara 1982; Wolf 1992). Counts and Counts and Thurston talk about an experience in the same region of West New Britain from different perspectives, and that can happen between separately authored chapters or indeed within chapters. What to do with the personal is an ongoing challenge, and most of the chapters in this volume embrace it to some extent by revealing individual backgrounds and personalities (Goodenough; Petersen, Garcia, and Petersen; see also Wylie 1987) as part of an intellectual tradition in North American anthropology that dates back to Margaret Mead, Ruth Benedict, and Edward Sapir.

Gendered Fieldwork and Families

As Diane Bell (1993a, 11) notes in *Gendered Fields: Women, Men and Ethnography*, men's production of a more self-conscious ethnography has dominated disciplinary accounts of reflexivity, and yet the earlier personal accounts often are authored or edited by women. Like Cassell's (1987b) edited volume, *Children in the Field, Fieldwork and Families* presents more female than male contributors, as did the sequence of sessions at the ASAO meetings that produced this volume. Bell draws upon Cesara's (1982) strongly reflexive experimental account to suggest that the gender imbalance in these kinds of autobiographical accounts can be explained by the greater ease (or necessity) with which women integrate the personal, that is, the family, and the professional;[4] in the present Pacific cases it may also be explained by host societies' expectations of women, as they are more tightly yoked physically and conceptually to their accompanying families. A focus on families demands that we address more than the question of why women (or men) may write about the personal in particularly gendered ways, but also how the family as an analytic category and conceptual unit engenders us in ways that shape what and how we can know what we do. Families especially serve as yardsticks for measuring differences and similarities among ethnographers, research participants, and their social units.

The genderedness of many of the experiences recounted in this volume takes different forms: Goodenough and Garcia were accompanying female spouses; Sinclair and Gordon coped with accompanying or indigenous male spouses; Linnekin and Gilmore were fieldworker mothers with accompanying children; and McGrath, Flinn, and Sinclair document being both fieldworking spouses and mothers, while some contributors were members of fieldwork partnerships sometimes with children, sometimes not—Carucci, Counts and Counts, Thurston, Tietjen, Young Leslie, and Petersen and Garcia. Accompanied (heterosexual) fieldwork is highly gendered in ways that cannot be masked and may be more gendered than unaccompanied fieldwork (Carucci and Petersen). For example, Young Leslie notes that we need to think comparatively about the elaboration of women as mothers in other cultural systems by juxtaposing them with our own North American notions of motherhood and by considering the implications such elaboration has for the female ethnographer (see especially discussions by Linnekin and Sinclair). In this way we can more precisely situate ourselves as knowers. This volume reminds us that we must explicitly "recognize gender in order to control for bias" (Okely 1992, 6), but more important, it invites us to manage for bias by thinking about family (or its absence) as an analytic category rather than a conceptual given.

Inflected Kinship: Family as Concept

Some imaginative thinking about the conceptualization of families characterizes these accounts as families both gender us and engender fieldwork.[5] The volume provides the opportunity for rethinking our understandings of family with its procreative bias (Schneider 1980, 1984), especially because we cannot assume our host families to be analogues of our own. It invites us to factor in geographic, socioemotional, and genealogical dimensions of attachment, as Kath Weston (1991, 52) has done in her concept of "families we choose." Marshall (1994) provided the lead in our ASAO symposium with her treatment of family broadly conceived to include adopted birds and other pets as family members, and Flinn reflexively traces and interweaves her notion of family with that of the Pollapese while simultaneously juxtaposing her North American middle-class definitions with those of a spouse with working-class origins; Flinn recognizes gradations within Western notions of family. Thurston, in his discussion of Kaliai interpretations of his relationship with his partner, Rick, helps us to see the more flexible conceptualizations of family that some of our informants engage. Sinclair's simultaneous engagement in a marriage with a Pakeha (white) New Zealander and involvement with the Mareikura family in the Maori community she studied granted her admirable independence from cultural conventions, an independence sustained by her daughter in her own cultivated interstitial categories of cultural identity and of relative. In many of these accounts, use of the terms accompanied and unaccompanied fieldworkers is a useful device to solve the boundedness of the "homogenized" Western notion of "family." And a blurring of the distinction between real families and fictive families is productively explored in contributions by Counts and Counts, Gordon, and Sinclair.

While some of these authors (such as McGrath and Young Leslie) reinforce the disciplinarily established (and sometimes essentialized) distinction of consanguineal and affinal (blood and marriage) kinship from fictive kinship in the Pacific—where studies of adoption and fosterage are well established (see especially Carroll 1970 and Brady 1976)—some provocatively conflate fictive kinship in its traditional sense with fictive kinship in the sense of imagined or constructed kinship in the fieldwork context, especially when no other way exists to imagine how an anthropologist (and accompanying others) might fit in (see especially Carucci, Counts and Counts, and Thurston). Interpretive approaches in anthropology have eliminated the concept of fictive kin as we have realized that "all kinship is in some sense fictional—that is, meaningfully constituted" (Weston 1991, 105), and as we have examined biology "as symbol rather than substance" (Weston 1991, 34; see Schneider 1980, 1984). The authors in this volume invite us to consider the varying ways in which kinship is inflected for the Pacific fieldworker both as a network of relationships that we scrutinize and that is flexible enough to incorporate us in diverse ways. As Gottlieb has discovered in her African Beng work, her challenge as a fieldworker was not a "matter of slotting into the system" but of becoming a player in social relationships that are "continually dismantled and reconstructed" (Gottlieb and Graham 1993, 236).

In the New Zealand high-country farming valley where I have worked since 1986, there was no preestablished kinship framework ("fictive" or otherwise) into which I could fit. As an unaccompanied woman then in her early thirties, I was unrecognizable to many in a way that was most clearly expressed to me early in fieldwork by a five-year-old girl from a neighboring property who came into my hut to find my family. She asked where my husband was, where my children were, and, finding no nuclear family, excitedly rushed out with bemusement to tell her mother that I had none. What were they to do with an unentangled woman who wanted to go places where women usually did not go, such as high-country musters (round ups)? A nongendered cultural category was not a recognized option as it has been for other nonmarried women fieldworkers such as Nancy McDowell and Jane Goodale in Melanesia (Tumulty 1994). A family of procreation, accompanying me or not, would have complicated my fieldwork, perhaps making it impossible to do well. My field families and I have discussed this openly. They are fairly certain people would not have thought well of me if I had had children and left them with a spouse in the United States. They are equally certain that accompanied fieldwork would have forced me into social categories of wife and mother, thereby restricting my ability to move between sex-segregated events. They are aware, however, that being an unaccompanied professional woman also initially made me unapproachable.

I became a situationally defined member of the family but uniquely defined without a particular kinship status or extant nuclear role of parent or child or sibling. This was most clearly marked when I moved physically from my hut to the station homestead, to make room for a nephew hired to do some casual labor during the school holidays; when I politely resisted, they said no, telling me that "it is only fitting that you move into the house." So I did with a flash of that proverbially triumphant being-there moment—"they-have-made-me-kin"; but knowing that, as individually conceptualized rather than culturally recognized kin, I am not kin. I move back into "my" old room on return visits, and I accept the designation of family member as a privilege earned, signifying a singular attachment and belonging to both a nuclear and extended family, and the place and life of which it is a part. The degree to which one is included and excluded, or one is considered intimate or distant, is constantly negotiated in high-country life and expressed especially in ritual moments of celebration and grief, when it serves as a measure of relatedness. Thus social formations are constructed transactionally through the patterned choices of positioned players; the anthropologist's negotiated inclusion and exclusion is experienced individually without the certainty that an ascribed status provides. My degree of nearness and farness feels constantly marked, measured, and displayed. While inclusion ensures "being there" physically, exclusion often ensures "being there" conceptually; my marked otherness in numerous contexts led to people telling me what they claimed not to be able to tell each other—time and again people would say, "Well, we can tell you this because you aren't a New Zealander," or "because you are an outsider," or because, in effect, I am not an interested player in a tight nexus of social relationships. This configuration invites us to ask new questions of the lone ethnographer model: what are the implications of being marked by *not* having "family" in the field or perhaps at home?

For Carucci it meant that his Ujelang hosts used incorporation strategies of marriage and adoption to capture the potency of a foreign line and to shape him "into an object of meaning and value in a local system of social and cultural production" (169). For gay anthropologists under similar circumstances, the risk of losing access by revealing who has been left at home may force the fieldworker to be secretive in ways that might be anathema in one's own cultural context; Weston (1991, 202) notes that while Anglo-European notions of genealogical descent engage in "procreative interpretations of kinship," gay families use selectivity as an organizing principle, where the signs of enduring solidarity include symbolic demonstrations of love, shared history, and material or emotional assistance (Weston 1991, 109). This is linked to the converse case of most of the present contributions—the unaccompanied fieldworker in a context where the biological family is so salient in people's lives that our hosts can imagine no alternative to family.

If our kin statuses and roles are varyingly inflected in the field in highly specific ways, they are no less so when we return to our countries of habitation, where friends and families of orientation are different from, but simultaneously similar to, our field families in terms of their affective significance. The categories are not coterminous, but the affect and power of connection sometimes is of the same order. Many chapters in this volume illustrate the conflation of the anthropologist's field host families and home families, as well as the conflation of the anthropologist's accompanying nuclear family of procreation and the host families (see especially Carucci, Counts and Counts, McGrath, Sinclair, Thurston, Young Leslie).

Familial Bonds and Children

Many of these chapters document the emotional, financial, pragmatic, and ideological factors shaping decisions about whether to take children to the field (see especially Gilmore, Goodenough, Sinclair). What does anthropological fieldwork ask of accompanying families and of those left behind? Cassell (1987a, 258) tells us that we are doubly at risk when our children are in the field. In exposing ourselves, we expose them (both children and spouses), but in exposing them, we also expose ourselves both negatively and positively. Sinclair's field families will never forget when the Maori queen visited their community, and Sinclair's husband, Mike, went sailing, thus revealing her inability to control her spouse. Gilmore's daughter, Elaine, suffered unbearable homesickness, and her mother had to find a way to make her premature and unanticipated departure comprehensible to her Tahitian hosts in their terms of rank and *fiu* (boredom). Goodenough's children benefited and suffered in quite different ways from one another, and her analysis points to the importance of her children's placement in the developmental cycle in terms of their need to accompany or not accompany us. Emily Sinclair's development and sense of self is embedded in her life in the Maori settlement in Ohakune, but now as her opportunities and choices diverge from her Maori age-mates, she will not return until she, too, is a mother like them with her own family of procreation. These accounts document the costs and benefits to our personal lives and to the entangled lives of those we call relatives.

With the eye of an adult anthropologist, Wylie (1987, 115) writes of his experiences in France as a field child and explains the particular challenges to field children: "a child's initial sense of *depaysement* [expatriation] is worse than an adult's, since it is unbuffered by such intellectual constructs as 'another culture' and by such exercises as keeping a journal." As anthropologists, we spend our careers working our ways through an alien culture; this is an emotional and intellectual immersion closed to our children. Wylie calls his article "Daddy's Little Wedges" and, like Young Leslie in this volume, asks how entitled are we to use children for our purposes, to illustrate the tension between the specificity of the ethnographer's task and the family's daily lived experiences—tensions also well documented by Garcia and Goodenough in this volume. Although many of these contributions challenge the value placed on the Malinowskian model of the so-called lone male fieldworker, such a model (regardless of how it is engendered) suggests that our primary identity as fieldworker, as anthropologist, when unaccompanied may shield us from the stresses that confront field families and accompanied fieldworkers; the identity—stripped free from suspended home-based statuses and roles—shields us from confrontation with difference as we allow ourselves through total immersion to accept, and do, and hear anything and everything (see Petersen's and Carucci's accounts of unaccompanied fieldwork). For Young Leslie, Linnekin, and McGrath, their own commitments to cultural relativism were at times jarred precisely because of their urges to protect their young children from being too native (see Turner 1987). Children in the field often "go native" as they are socialized, achieving an ethnographic intimacy with their hosts that parents often cannot match. Trawick (1990), Turner (1987), and Young Leslie write of children becoming the other better and of indigenous offers to adopt their offspring. On the other hand, socialization of older children, such as Emily Sinclair and Oliver Goodenough, creates for some children an analogous experience to that of the parent fieldworker, one that can be mined as a resource for personal and intellectual growth, rendering the child's perspective anthropological in scope and vision. Families can reinforce their own boundaries when abroad, drawing in upon themselves and providing an unthreatening retreat that may constrain adolescent children at the very moment in their development when they need to separate (see Tietjen, this volume).

Expressions of Intimacy

Accompanying families can highlight the ways in which cultural models and expressions of intimacy vary. In exploring expressions of emotion, Linnekin, McGrath, and Gordon give "an at least partially reflexive analysis in which we see the emotional life of the ethnographer and his or her society reflected as an exotic phenomenon in the eyes of the people encountered" (Lutz 1988, 6). Linnekin's "ballistic" and frantic moment when her son fell from the house of her family's high chief into a rubbish dump unveiled her "polite fictions" and embarrassed her through its indirect insults to Samoan sanitary conditions. McGrath's loss of temper at her fractious children enabled her to reveal herself in ways that she thinks led to a deeper relationship with another local mother despite expectations of greater emotional restraint in Tonga. And in a very personal account of her courtship and marriage to a Tongan and her attempts to affiliate with his family, Gordon focuses on tensions between her own need to "blurt out" her feelings and ask personal questions to establish intimacy, and her husband's desire that she honor sister-in-law respect-avoidance and not offend her more restrained Tongan in-laws. Gordon's experience provides a way into the cultural system of familial meaning in Tonga where, as in Micronesian Ifaluk, "emotion is seen as a component of social situations or relationships," not of the individual (Lutz 1988, 41). Indigenous models of emotion, linked and parallel to indigenous models of family, similarly may constrain our behaviors in the field. Families force us to act out our own emotional configurations, revealing us in spite of ourselves and forcing us to be more honest about our other selves.

The "Briggs Theme": We Cannot Become the Other

In what ways does an anthropology of familial autobiography enhance our claims to ethnographic authority, our experience of ethnographic presence? In 1974, as a third-year undergraduate student, I read Jean Briggs' *Never in Anger: Portrait of an Eskimo Family* for a course in culture and personality; it was by far the most engaging ethnography I had read, and it affected me then with the same kind of force that Trawick's *Notes on Love in a Tamil Family* seemed to affect my own undergraduate students in introductory anthropology in 1995. *Never in Anger* is a forerunner to *Fieldwork and Families*. Briggs teaches us about Utku Inuit constructions of emotion through personal experience by narrating her own missteps in directly and forcefully expressing her own desires—her need for solitude, for privacy, for direct expression. She teaches us about Utku Inuit conceptions of the family by showing how her behaviors marked her as a bad daughter who violated kinship norms. We learn much about her family in the field; we learn much about the conditions of fieldwork, about doing anthropology, about what ethnographic authority is. We learn in the end how she could not be Utku Inuit. We feel the disciplinary burden none of us can shed—the impossibility of being an "embodied Beng," the knowledge that "our eyes are not Beng" (Gottlieb and Graham 1993, 196).

The Briggs theme raises an issue central to this volume: "the degree to which the anthropologist's identity and gendered presence is part of the process of collection, documentation, experience and presentation of data during fieldwork" (Tumulty 1994, 7). By extension we can ask: what is the role of the anthropologist's identity as a family member in shaping fieldwork and, by extension, theory? Briggs highlights for us, as do many of the chapters in this volume, the tension that exists between the multiple identities the anthropologist holds in the field—identities that are not only gendered, but are defined further through our relationships with intimates.

The "Performance Risk" Theme

Linnekin, Sinclair, and Young Leslie in particular wonder: do families keep us more honest? Do they unmask us? McGrath notes that children challenge our confident assertions of cultural relativism. Linnekin explores the ways in which close companions complicate "impression management"; children in particular make this kind of control difficult, which may account for why so many of these chapters focus on children, sometimes to the exclusion of spouses and other categories of significant others. Gilmore claims better insights as a "repositioned other with children." The honesty at stake, potentially compromised by sentimental accounts of family relationships, may not so much refer to the revelation of who we are as much as to the honesty of our vision. Sinclair eloquently illustrates the point:

> Emily has unmasked us: she has revealed my inadequacies (at least in Maori terms) with the effect of making me more human.... Emily's cello playing, her failure to stand aloof, her unmitigated enthusiasm ... for the people, for the culture have proved to be revelatory and certainly stand in opposition to what would have been my choice of relative reserve ... I have nowhere to hide. There are no literal or metaphorical walls to conceal my emotions, and Emily's reactions keep me honest. The clarity of her recognition of racism, of class, and of privilege has forced me to understand that these elements are integral parts of my research. (127–128)

Perhaps families keep us not more honest, but honest in different and complementary ways. The unaccompanied fieldworker may not so much be disadvantaged in her solitude (see, for example, stages in the fieldwork of Carucci, Flinn, Linnekin, and Petersen), but instead, stripped of familiar relationships from home, the unaccompanied fieldworker often controls or neutralizes or denies emotions, including those of guilt for and emotional deprivation from leaving partners and children behind, and with only the self at stake can suspend moral judgment, weaving herself interstitially into the cracks of culture. These stripped-downed selves are not fictions; we experience them repeatedly as part of who we are as anthropologists. They can liberate us from our cultural selves, othering us as embodied Utku Inuit, or Beng, or Anêm; they can in fact free us from impression management. Families render us neither more nor less neutral, neither more nor less honest. Rather, they provide the opportunity for degrees of increasing inclusiveness under varying circumstances and conditions. The ways in which families intensify and detract from our ethnographic presence are quite culturally specific.

Anthony Cohen (1992, 226) urges anthropologists to exploit the "intrusive self as an ethnographic resource rather than suffer it as a methodological hindrance." To explore the complexity of self, to explore personhood, he writes, is to acknowledge that of others. This volume's authors similarly urge us to exploit "intrusive" families and entanglements as an ethnographic resource rather than a methodological impediment. To explore families, to explore kinship and household, is to acknowledge the complexities of other familial systems; like Counts and Counts and Thurston, we may be humbled in the face of the complexities of their kinship systems; we may find them not to be, or to be, analogues of our own.

Notes

1. For illustrations of the theoretical force in engaging an autobiography of fieldwork, see especially Okely and Callaway (1992) and Bell, Caplan, and Karim (1993).

2. See also Thorne (1982) and Yanagisako and Collier (1987).

3. For a productive and successful example, see daughter Linda's contribution to Annette Weiner's *Women of Value, Men of Renown* (1976).

4. See, for example, Bowen (1954), Briggs (1970), Butler and Turner (1987b), Cassell (1987b), Golde (1986), Powdermaker (1966), and Whitehead and Conaway (1986).

5. Callaway (1992, 35) asserts that the autobiography of the anthropologist must unfold "in terms of gendered experience," and, by extension, Kulick (1995, 6) and Seizer (1995) add the fieldworker's erotic subjectivity to the autobiographical agenda; these elements are all the more salient when we speak of the autobiography of families.

References

Asad, Talal
    1986   The Concept of Cultural Translation in British Social Anthropology. In *Writing Culture: The Politics and Poetics of Ethnography,* ed. James Clifford and George E. Marcus, 141–164. Berkeley: University of California Press.

Bachnik, Jane
    1986   Native Perspectives of Distance and Anthropological Perspectives on Culture. *Anthropological Quarterly* 59:75–83.

Back, Les
    1993   Gendered Participation: Masculinity and Fieldwork in a South London Adolescent Community. In *Gendered Fields: Women, Men, and Ethnography,* ed. Diane Bell, Pat Caplan, and Wazir Jahan Karim, 215–233. London and New York: Routledge.

Banks, David J.
    1983   From Structure to History in Malaya. In *Fieldwork: The Human Experience,* ed. Robert Lawless, Vinson H. Sutlive, Jr., and Mario D. Zamora, 35–48. New York: Gordon and Breach Science Publishers.

Bartholemew, Robert E.
    1993   Whose Ethics? *Anthropology Newsletter* 34(7):2

Behar, Ruth
    1993   *Translated Woman: Crossing the Border with Esperanza's Story.* Boston: Beacon Press.

Bell, Diane
    1993a   Introduction 1: The Context. In *Gendered Fields: Women, Men, and Ethnography,* ed. Diane Bell, Pat Caplan, and Wazir Jahan Karim, 1–18. London and New York: Routledge.
    1993b   Yes, Virginia, There Is a Feminist Ethnography: Reflections from Three Australian Fields. In *Gendered Fields: Women, Men, and Ethnography,* ed. Diane Bell, Pat Caplan, and Wazir Jahan Karim, 28–43. London and New York: Routledge.

Bell, Diane, Pat Caplan, and Wazir Jahan Karim, eds.
    1993   *Gendered Fields: Women, Men, and Ethnography.* London and New York: Routledge.

Benedict, Ruth
   1934   *Patterns of Culture.* Boston: Houghton Mifflin.
Benhabib, Seyla, and Drucilla Cornell
   1987   Introduction: Beyond the Politics of Gender. In *Feminism as Critique: On the Politics of Gender,* ed. Seyla Benhabib and Drucilla Cornell, 1–15. Minneapolis: University of Minnesota Press.
Bernard, H. Russell
   1994   *Research Methods in Anthropology: Qualitative and Quantitative Approaches.* 2d ed. Thousand Oaks, Calif.: Sage Publications.
Berreman, Gerald D.
   1962   *Behind Many Masks: Ethnography and Impression Management in a Himalayan Village.* Ithaca, NY: Society for Applied Anthropology Monograph No. 4.
Bloch, Maurice
   1991   Language, Anthropology and Cognitive Science. *Man* 26(2):183–198.
Boas, Franz
   1901   The Mind of Primitive Man. *Journal of American Folklore* 14:1–11. Revised 1938. New York: Free Press.
Bourdieu, Pierre
   1991   *Language and Symbolic Power.* Cambridge, Mass.: Harvard University Press.
Bowen, Elenore Smith
   1954   *Return to Laughter.* New York: Harper.
Bowlby, John
   1969   *Attachment and Loss.* Vol. 1. New York: Basic Books.
Brady, Ivan, ed.
   1976   *Transactions in Kinship: Adoption and Fosterage in Oceania.* ASAO Monograph No. 4. Honolulu: University Press of Hawai'i.
Briggs, Jean L.
   1970   *Never in Anger: Portrait of an Eskimo Family.* Cambridge, Mass.: Harvard University Press.
Butler, Barbara, and Diane Michalski Turner
   1987a   Children and Anthropological Research: An Overview. In *Children and Anthropological Research,* ed. Barbara Butler and Diane Michalski Turner, 3–30. New York and London: Plenum Press.
Butler, Barbara, and Diane Michalski Turner, eds.
   1987b   *Children and Anthropological Research.* New York and London: Plenum Press.
Callaway, Helen
   1992   Ethnography and Experience: Gender Implications in Fieldwork and Texts. In *Anthropology and Autobiography,* ed. Judith Okely and Helen Callaway, 29–49. ASA Monographs 29. London and New York: Routledge.

Caplan, Pat
> 1993 Learning Gender: Fieldwork in a Tanzanian Coastal Village, 1965–85. In *Gendered Fields: Women, Men, and Ethnography,* ed. Diane Bell, Pat Caplan, and Wazir Jahan Karim, 168–181. London and New York: Routledge.

Card, Orson Scott
> 1986 *Speaker for the Dead.* New York: Tom Doherty Associates.

Carrier, Achsah
> 1985 Infant Care and Family Relations on Ponam Island, Manus Province, Papua New Guinea. In *Infant Care and Feeding in the South Pacific,* ed. Leslie Marshall, 189–205. New York: Gordon and Breach Science Publishers.

Carroll, Vern, ed.
> 1970 *Adoption in Eastern Oceania.* ASAO Monograph No. 1. Honolulu: University of Hawai'i Press.

Carucci, Laurence M.
> 1980 The Renewal of Life: A Ritual Encounter in the Marshall Islands. Ph.D. dissertation. Department of Anthropology, University of Chicago.
> 1987 "Ruwamwaijet im RiAnin: Outsiders becoming Insiders." Paper delivered at the annual meetings of the ASAO, Monterey, California.
> 1989 "Joking with Gender on Ujelang Atoll." Paper delivered at the annual meetings of the ASAO, San Antonio, Texas.
> 1992 "We Planted Mama on Jeptan: Constructing Continuities and Situating Identities on Enewetak Atoll." *Pacific History: Papers from the 8th Pacific History Association Conference,* ed. Donald H. Rubinstein, 191–199. Mangilao, Guam: University of Guam and the Micronesian Area Research Center.
> 1993 "An Atoll Called Desire: Women, Wars, and the Language of Welcome on Arno Atoll." *Proceedings of the Montana Academy of Sciences* 52: 119–128.
> forthcoming *The First Hour of Tomorrow: Ritual Renewal in an Island World.* DeKalb: Northern Illinois University Press.

Cassell, Joan
> 1987a Conclusion. In *Children in the Field: Anthropological Experiences,* ed. Joan Cassell, 257–270. Philadelphia: Temple University Press.

Cassell, Joan, ed.
> 1987b *Children in the Field: Anthropological Experiences.* Philadelphia: Temple University Press.

Cesara, Manda
> 1982 *Reflections of a Woman Anthropologist: No Hiding Place.* New York: Academic Press.

Cheater, A. P.
   1987   The Anthropologist as Citizen: the Diffracted Self? In *Anthropology at Home,* ed. Anthony Jackson, 64–179. ASA Monographs 25. London: Tavistock.

Clifford, James
   1986   Introduction: Partial Truths. In *Writing Culture: The Poetics and Politics of Ethnography,* ed. James Clifford and George E. Marcus, 1–26. Berkeley: University of California Press.
   1988   *The Predicament of Culture: Twentieth Century Ethnography, Literature and Art.* Cambridge, Mass.: Harvard University Press.

Clifford, James, and George E. Marcus, eds.
   1986   *Writing Culture: The Poetics and Politics of Ethnography.* Berkeley: University of California Press.

Cohen, Anthony
   1992   Self-conscious Anthropology. In *Anthropology and Autobiography,* ed. Judith Okely and Helen Callaway, 221–241. ASA Monographs 29. London and New York: Routledge.

Collier, Jane, Michelle Z. Rosaldo, and Sylvia Yanagisako
   1993   Is There a Family? New Anthropological Views. In *Talking about People: Readings in Contemporary Cultural Anthropology,* ed. William A. Haviland and Robert J. Gordon, 151–158. Mountain View, Calif.: Mayfield Publishing Company.

Comaroff, John, and Jean Comaroff
   1992   *Ethnography and the Historical Imagination.* Boulder, Colo.: Westview Press.

Counts, David R.
   1990   Too Many Bananas, Not Enough Pineapples, and No Watermelon At All: Three Object Lessons in Living with Reciprocity. In *The Humbled Anthropologist: Tales from the Pacific,* ed. Phil DeVita, 18-24. Belmont, Calif.: Wadsworth.

Counts, David R., and Dorothy Ayers Counts
   1992   Exaggeration and Reversal: Clowning among the Lusi-Kaliai. In *Clowning as Critical Practice: Performance Humor in the South Pacific,* ed. William Mitchell, 88–103. ASAO Monograph No. 13. Pittsburgh: University of Pittsburgh Press.

Counts, Dorothy Ayers, and David R. Counts
   1983   Father's Water Equals Mother's Milk: The Conception of Parentage in Kaliai, West New Britain. *Mankind* 14:46–56.

Crandon-Malamud, Libbet
   1991   *From the Fat of Our Souls: Social Change, Political Process, and Medical Pluralism in Bolivia.* Berkeley: University of California Press.

Crews, Frederick C.
    1965   *The Pooh Perplex.* New York: NAL Dutton.

Crockenberg, S.
    1981   Infant Irritability, Mother Responsiveness, and Social Support Influences on the Security of Infant-Mother Attachment. *Child Development* 52:857–865.

Dettwyler, Katherine A.
    1994   *Dancing Skeletons: Life and Death in West Africa.* Prospect Heights, Ill.: Waveland Press.

DeVita, Philip R., ed.
    1990   *The Humbled Anthropologist: Tales from the Pacific.* Belmont, Calif.: Wadsworth Publishing Company.
    1992   *The Naked Anthropologist: Tales from around the World.* Belmont, Calif.: Wadsworth Publishing Company.

Dickinson, George E., and Michael R. Leming
    1990   *Understanding Families: Diversity, Continuity, and Change.* Boston: Allyn and Bacon.

Dumont, Jean-Paul
    1978   *The Headman and I: Ambiguity and Ambivalence in the Fieldworking Experience.* Austin: University of Texas Press.

Edgerton, Robert B.
    1985   *Rules, Exceptions, and Social Order.* Berkeley: University of California Press.

Eshleman, J. Ross
    1991   *The Family: An Introduction.* 6th ed. Boston: Allyn and Bacon.

Evans, Mike
    1996   Gifts and Commodities on a Tongan Atoll: Understanding Intention and Action in a MIRAB Economy. Ph.D. dissertation. McMaster University.

Evans, Mike, and Heather Young Leslie
    1993   Remaking History, Anytime: History and Its Telling in the Kingdom of Tonga. Paper presented at Canadian Anthropology Society/ Société Canadienne d'Anthropologie, North York, Canada, May 1993.

Fabian, Johannes
    1983   *Time and the Other: How Anthropology Makes Its Object.* New York: Columbia University Press.

Feinberg, Richard
    1981   What is Polynesian Kinship All About? *Ethnology* 20(2):115–131.
    1990   New Guinea Models on a Polynesian Outlier? *Ethnology* 29(1): 83–96.

Flores-Meiser, Enya P.
  1983 Field Experience in Three Societies. In *Fieldwork: The Human Experience,* ed. Robert Lawless, Vinson H. Sutlive, Jr., and Mario D. Zamora, 49–61. New York: Gordon and Breach Science Publishers.

Foucault, Michel
  1980 *Power/Knowledge: Selected Interviews and Other Writings 1972–1977,* ed. Colin Gordon. New York: Pantheon Books.

Fowler, Don D., and Donald L. Hardesty, eds.
  1994 *Others Knowing Others: Perspectives on Ethnographic Careers.* Washington, D.C.: Smithsonian Institution Press.

Freeman, Derek
  1983 *Margaret Mead and Samoa: The Making and Unmaking of an Anthropological Myth.* New York: Penguin Books.

Freilich, Morris, ed.
  1970 *Marginal Natives: Anthropologists at Work.* New York: Harper and Row.

Geertz, Clifford
  1973 *The Interpretation of Cultures.* New York: Basic Books.
  1984 From the Native's Point of View: On the Nature of Anthropological Understanding. In *Culture Theory: Essays on Mind, Self, and Emotion,* ed. Richard A. Shweder and Robert A. LeVine, 123–136. Cambridge: Cambridge University Press.

General Anthropology Bulletin Board
  1993–1994
       Postings to ANTHRO-L. <Anthro-L@ubvm.cc.buffalo.edu>

Gerber, Eleanor Ruth
  1985 Rage and Obligation: Samoan Emotion in Conflict. In *Person, Self, and Experience: Exploring Pacific Ethnopsychologies,* ed. Geoffrey M. White and John Kirkpatrick, 121–167. Berkeley: University of California Press.

Gilligan, Carol
  1982 *In a Different Voice: Psychological Theory and Women's Development.* Cambridge, Mass.: Harvard University Press.

Goffman, Erving
  1971 *Relations in Public.* New York: Harper and Row.
  1973 [1959]
       The Presentation of Self in Everyday Life. Woodstock, NY: The Overlook Press.

Golde, Peggy, ed.
  1986 *Women in the Field: Anthropological Experiences.* 2d ed., expanded and updated. Berkeley: University of California Press.

Goodenough, Ruth Gallagher
  1970   Adoption on Romonum, Truk. In *Adoption in Eastern Oceania,* ed. Vern Carroll, 314–340. ASAO Monograph No. 1. Honolulu: University of Hawai'i Press.
Goodenough, Ward H.
  1951   *Property, Kin, and Community on Truk.* Yale University Publications in Anthropology, No. 46. New Haven, Conn.: Yale University Press.
Gordon, Daniel
  1991   Female Circumcision and Genital Operations in Egypt and the Sudan: A Dilemma for Medical Anthropology. *Medical Anthropology Quarterly* 5(1):3–14.
Gordon, Deborah
  1988   Writing Culture, Writing Feminism: The Poetics and Politics of Experimental Ethnography. *Inscriptions* 3(4):7–24.
Gottlieb, Alma
  1995   Beyond the Lonely Anthropologist: Collaboration in Research and Writing. *American Anthropologist* 97(1):21–26.
Gottlieb, Alma, and Philip Graham
  1993   *Parallel Worlds: An Anthropologist and a Writer Encounter Africa.* New York: Crown.
Hammel, E. A.
  1994   Meeting the Minotaur. *Anthropology Newsletter* 35(4):48.
Hammersley, Martyn, and Paul Atkinson
  1983   *Ethnography: Principles in Practice.* London and New York: Tavistock.
Handler, Richard, and Jocelyn Linnekin
  1984   Tradition, Genuine or Spurious. *Journal of American Folklore* 97:273–290.
Harding, Sandra
  1986   *The Science Question in Feminism.* Ithaca, NY: Cornell University Press.
Hastrup, Kirsten
  1992   Writing Ethnography: State of the Art. In *Anthropology and Autobiography,* ed. Judith Okely and Helen Callaway, 116–133. ASA Monographs 29. London and New York: Routledge.
Hatch, Elvin
  1983   *Culture and Morality: The Relativity of Values in Anthropology.* New York: Columbia University Press.
Herdt, Gilbert
  1981a *Guardians of the Flutes: Idioms of Masculinity.* New York: McGraw-Hill.
  1981b *The Sambia: Ritual and Gender in New Guinea.* New York: Holt, Rinehart and Winston.

Herskovits, Melville J.
 1947 *Man and His Works.* New York: Knopf.
 1973 *Cultural Relativism: Perspectives in Cultural Pluralism.* New York: Vintage Books.

Hitchcock, Patricia
 1987 Our Vileri Child. In *Children in the Field: Anthropological Experiences,* ed. Joan Cassell, 173–183. Philadelphia: Temple University Press.

Hooper, Antony
 1970 Adoption in the Society Islands. In *Adoption in Eastern Oceania,* ed. Vern Carroll, 52–70. ASAO Monograph No. 1. Honolulu: University of Hawai'i Press.

Howard, Alan
 1990 Cultural Paradigms, History, and the Search for Identity in Oceania. In *Cultural Identity and Ethnicity in the Pacific,* ed. Jocelyn Linnekin and Lin Poyer, 259–279. Honolulu: University of Hawai'i Press.

Howard, Alan, and John Kirkpatrick
 1989 Social Organization. In *Developments in Polynesian Ethnology,* ed. Alan Howard and Robert Borofsky, 47–94. Honolulu: University of Hawai'i Press.

Hugh-Jones, Christine
 1987 Children in the Amazon. In *Children in the Field: Anthropological Experiences,* ed. Joan Cassell, 27–64. Philadelphia: Temple University Press.

Hughes, Daniel T.
 1983 Contrasting Experiences in Fieldwork. In *Fieldwork: The Human Experience,* ed. Robert Lawless, Vinson H. Sutlive, Jr., and Mario D. Zamora, 81–89. New York: Gordon and Breach Science Publishers.

Hymes, Dell, ed.
 1969 *Reinventing Anthropology.* New York: Random House.

Institut Territorial de la Statistique
 1983 *Tableaux Normalisés du Recensement Général de la Population: Résultats de la Commune de Tahaa: Territoire de la Polynésie Française.* Papeete, Tahiti: Institut Territorial de la Statistique.
 n.d. *Évolution de la Population Légale de la Commune de Polynésie Française de 1971 à 1988.* Papeete, Tahiti: Institut Territorial de la Statistique.

Jackson, Jean E.
 1990 "I Am a Fieldnote": Fieldnotes as a Symbol of Professional Identity. In *Fieldnotes: The Makings of Anthropology,* ed. Roger Sanjek, 3–33. Ithaca, NY: Cornell University Press.

JanMohamed, Abdul R.
 1992 Worldliness-without-World, Homelessness-as-Home: Toward a Definition of the Specular Border Intellectual. In *Edward Said: A Critical*

Reader, ed. Michael Sprinker, 96–120. Cambridge, Mass.: Basil Blackwell Publishers.

Karim, Wazir Jahan
- 1993 With *Moyang Melur* in Carey Island: More Endangered, More Engendered. In *Gendered Fields: Women, Men, and Ethnography,* ed. Diane Bell, Pat Caplan, and Wazir Jahan Karim, 78–92. London and New York: Routledge.

Kavapalu, Helen
- 1993 Dealing with the Dark Side in the Ethnography of Childhood: Child Punishment in Tonga. *Oceania* 63(4):313.

Kegan, Robert
- 1982 *The Evolving Self: Problem and Process in Human Development.* Cambridge, Mass.: Harvard University Press.

Kennedy, Elizabeth Lapovsky
- 1995 In Pursuit of Connection: Reflections on Collaborative Work. *American Anthropologist* 97(1):26–33.

Keyes, Charles F.
- 1983 The Observer Observed: Changing Identities of Ethnographers in a Northeastern Thai Village. In *Fieldwork: The Human Experience,* ed. Robert Lawless, Vinson H. Sutlive, Jr., and Mario D. Zamora, 169–194. New York: Gordon and Breach Science Publishers.

Korn, Fred, and Shulamit R. Decktor Korn
- 1983 Where People Don't Promise. *Ethics* 93:445–450.

Kulick, Don
- 1995 Introduction. The Sexual Life of Anthropologists: Erotic Subjectivity and Ethnographic Work. In *Taboo: Sex, Identity and Erotic Subjectivity in Anthropological Fieldwork,* ed. Don Kulick and Margaret Wilson, 1–28. London: Routledge.

Lawless, Robert, Vinson H. Sutlive, Jr., and Mario D. Zamora, eds.
- 1983 *Fieldwork: The Human Experience.* New York: Gordon and Breach Science Publishers.

Levy, Robert I.
- 1973 *Tahitians: Mind and Experience in the Society Islands.* Chicago: University of Chicago Press.

Lincoln, Y. S., and Guba, E. G.
- 1985 *Naturalistic Inquiry.* Beverly Hills, Calif.: Sage.

Linnekin, Jocelyn
- 1983 Defining Tradition: Variations on the Hawaiian Identity. *American Ethnologist* 10:241–252.
- 1985 *Children of the Land: Exchange and Status in a Hawaiian Community.* New Brunswick, NJ: Rutgers University Press.

Lutz, Catherine A.
    1988   *Unnatural Emotions: Everyday Sentiments on a Micronesian Atoll and Their Challenge to Western Theory.* Chicago: University of Chicago Press.

MacIntyre, Alasdair
    1993   Ethical Dilemmas: Notes from Outside the Field. *Anthropology Newsletter* 34 (7): 5–6.

Macintyre, Martha
    1993   Fictive Kinship or Mistaken Identity? Fieldwork on Tubetube Island, Papua New Guinea. In *Gendered Fields: Women, Men, and Ethnography*, ed. Diane Bell, Pat Caplan, and Wazir Jahan Karim, 44–62. London and New York: Routledge.

MacKinnon, Catharine A.
    1987   *Feminism Unmodified: Discourses on Life and Law.* Cambridge, Mass.: Harvard University Press.

Malinowski, Bronislaw
    1961   *Argonauts of the Western Pacific.* New York: E. P. Dutton. Originally published in 1922.

Marcus, George E., and Michael M. J. Fischer
    1986   *Anthropology as Cultural Critique: An Experimental Moment in the Human Sciences.* Chicago: University of Chicago Press.

Marshall, Leslie
    1994   Feathered Family: Pets and Fieldwork in the Pacific. Paper presented at the 23rd annual meeting of the ASAO, San Diego, California, February 9–13.

Marshall, Mac
    1977   The Nature of Nurture. *American Ethnologist* 4(4):643–662.

Mason, Leonard
    1954   Relocation of the Bikini Marshallese: A Study in Group Migration. Ph.D. dissertation. Department of Anthropology, Yale University.

McGrath, Barbara Burns
    1993   Making Meaning of Illness, Dying and Death in the Kingdom of Tonga. Ph.D. dissertation. University of Washington.

McNeill, William H.
    1963   *The Rise of the West: A History of the Human Community.* Chicago: University of Chicago Press.

Mead, Margaret
    1973   *Coming of Age in Samoa: A Psychological Study of Primitive Youth for Western Civilization.* 6th ed. New York: Morrow Quill. Originally published in 1928.

Miller, Neil
    1993   *Out in the World: Gay and Lesbian Life from Buenos Aires to Bangkok.* New York: Vintage Departures, Random House.

Myerhoff, Barbara, and Jay Ruby
    1982   Introduction. In *A Crack in the Mirror,* ed. Jay Ruby, 1–35. Philadelphia: University of Pennsylvania Press.

Obeyesekere, Gananath
    1981   *Medusa's Hair: An Essay on Personal Symbols and Religious Experience.* Chicago: University of Chicago Press.

Ochs, Elinor
    1988   *Culture and Language Development: Language Acquisition and Language Socialization in a Samoan Village.* Studies in the Social and Cultural Foundations of Language. Vol. 6. Cambridge, England: Cambridge University Press.

Okely, Judith
    1992   Anthropology and Autobiography: Participatory Experience and Embodied Knowledge. In *Anthropology and Autobiography,* ed. Judith Okely and Helen Callaway, 1–28. ASA Monographs 29. London and New York: Routledge.

Okely, Judith, and Helen Callaway, eds.
    1992   *Anthropology and Autobiography.* ASA Monographs 29. London and New York: Routledge.

Petersen, Glenn
    1995   The Complexity of Power, the Subtlety of Kava. In *The Power of Kava,* ed. Nancy Pollock. Special issue of *Canberra Anthropologist* 18 (1 and 2):34–60.

Piaget, Jean, and Bärbel Inhelder
    1969   *The Psychology of the Child.* New York: Basic Books.

Powdermaker, Hortense
    1966   *Stranger and Friend: The Way of an Anthropologist.* New York: W. W. Norton & Co.

Powell, Anthony
    1995   *A dance to the music of time.* Chicago: University of Chicago Press. Originally published in 1951.

Ritchie, Jane and James
    1989   Socialization and Character Development. In *Developments in Polynesian Ethnology,* ed. Alan Howard and Robert Borofsky, 95–135. Honolulu: University of Hawai'i Press.

Rodman, William, and Margaret C. Rodman
    1989   To Die on Ambae: On the Possibility of Doing Fieldwork Forever. *Anthropologica* 31(1):25–44.

Rosaldo, Renato I.
    1984   Grief and a Headhunter's Rage: On the Cultural Force of Emotions. In *Text, Play, and Story: The Construction and Reconstruction of Self and Society,* ed. Edward Bruner and Stuart Plattner, 178–195. Washington, D.C.: American Ethnological Society.

1989 *Culture and Truth: The Remaking of Social Analysis.* Boston: Beacon Press.

Rudie, Ingrid

1993 A Hall of Mirrors: Autonomy Translated over Time in Malaysia. In *Gendered Fields: Women, Men, and Ethnography,* ed. Diane Bell, Pat Caplan, and Wazir Jahan Karim, 103–116. London and New York: Routledge.

Sahlins, Marshall

1985 *Islands of History.* Chicago: University of Chicago Press.

Sanjek, Roger, ed.

1990 *Fieldnotes: The Makings of Anthropology.* Ithaca, NY: Cornell University Press.

Sapir, Edward

1924 Culture, Genuine and Spurious. *American Journal of Sociology* 29:401–429.

Sartre, Jean-Paul

1956 *Being and Nothingness: An Essay on Phenomenological Ontology.* Hazel E. Barnes, trans. New York: Philosophical Library.

Scaletta (McPherson), Naomi

1985 Primogeniture and Primogenitor: Firstborn Child and Mortuary Ceremonies among the Kabana (Bariai) of West New Britain, Papua New Guinea. Ph.D. dissertation. McMaster University.

Scheper-Hughes, Nancy

1987a A Children's Diary in the Strict Sense of the Term: Managing Culture-Shocked Children in the Field. In *Children in the Field: Anthropological Experiences,* ed. Joan Cassell, 217–236. Philadelphia: Temple University Press.

Scheper-Hughes, Nancy, ed.

1987b *Child Survival: Anthropological Perspectives on the Treatment and Maltreatment of Children.* Boston: D. Reidel Publishing Co.

Schieffelin, Edward L., and Robert Crittenden

1991 *Like People You See in a Dream: First Contact in Six Papuan Societies.* Stanford: Stanford University Press.

Schneider, David M.

1980 *American Kinship: A Cultural Account.* 2d ed. Chicago: University of Chicago Press.

1984 *A Critique of the Study of Kinship.* Ann Arbor: University of Michigan Press.

Schrijvers, Joke

1993 Motherhood Experienced and Conceptualised: Changing Images in Sri Lanka and the Netherlands. In *Gendered Fields: Women, Men, and Ethnography,* ed. Diane Bell, Pat Caplan, and Wazir Jahan Karim, 143–158. London and New York: Routledge.

Schutz, Alfred
  1962 *Collected Papers, vol. I: The Problem of Social Reality*, ed. M. Natanson. The Hague: M. Nijhoff.
Seizer, Susan
  1995 Paradoxes of Visibility in the Field: Rites of Queer Passage in Anthropology. *Public Culture* 8(1):73–100.
Shore, Bradd
  1982 *Sala'ilua: A Samoan Mystery.* New York: Columbia University Press.
Shweder, Richard A., and Edmund J. Bourne
  1984 Does the Concept of the Person Vary Cross-Culturally? In *Culture Theory: Essays on Mind, Self, and Emotion*, ed. Richard A. Shweder and Robert A. LeVine, 158–199. Cambridge: Cambridge University Press.
Skomal, Susan N.
  1993 The Ethics of Fieldwork. *Anthropology Newsletter* 34(7):1, 26.
Super, Charles M., and S. Harkness
  1986 The Developmental Niche: A Conceptualization at the Interface of Child and Culture. *International Journal of Behavioral Development* 9: 545–569.
  1994 The Developmental Niche. In *Psychology and Culture*, ed. W. J. Lonner and R. Malpas, 95–99. Boston: Allyn and Bacon.
Thorne, Barrie
  1982 Feminist Rethinking of the Family: An Overview. In *Rethinking the Family: Some Feminist Questions*, ed. Barrie Thorne and Marilyn Yalom, 1–24. New York: Longman.
Thurston, William R.
  1994 The Legend of Titikolo: An Anêm Genesis. In *The Children of Kilibob: Creation, Cosmos, and Culture in Northeast New Guinea*, ed. Ali Pomponio, David Counts, and Thomas Harding. Special Issue of *Pacific Studies* 17(4):183–204.
Trawick, Margaret
  1990 *Notes on Love in a Tamil Family.* Berkeley: University of California Press.
Tronick, Edward, G. Morelli, and P. Ivey
  1992 The Efe Forager Infant and Toddler's Pattern of Social Relationships: Multiple and Simultaneous. *Developmental Psychology* 28:568–577.
Tumulty, Amanda Georgia
  1994 Gender, Fieldwork and the Construction of Knowledge: An Anthropology of Anthropologists. Senior Project manuscript. Bard College.
Turner, Diane Michalski
  1987 What Happened when My Daughter Became a Fijian. In *Children and Anthropological Research*, ed. Barbara Butler and Diane Michalski Turner, 97–114. New York and London: Plenum Press.

Vygotsky, L. S.
    1978   *Mind in Society.* Cambridge, Mass.: Harvard University Press.

Wagley, Charles
    1983   Learning Fieldwork: Guatemala. In *Fieldwork: The Human Experience,* ed. Robert Lawless, Vinson H. Sutlive, Jr., and Mario D. Zamora, 1–17. New York: Gordon and Breach Science Publishers.

Weiner, Annette
    1976   *Women of Value, Men of Renown: New Perspectives in Trobriand Exchange.* Austin: University of Texas Press.

Weston, Kath
    1991   *Families We Choose: Lesbians, Gays, and Kinship.* New York: Columbia University Press.

Whitehead, Tony Larry, and Mary Ellen Conaway, eds.
    1986   *Self, Sex, and Gender in Cross-Cultural Fieldwork.* Urbana and Chicago: University of Illinois Press.

Wolf, Margery
    1992   *A Thrice-Told Tale: Feminism, Postmodernism, and Ethnographic Responsibility.* Stanford: Stanford University Press.

Wylie, Jonathan
    1987   "Daddy's Little Wedges": On Being a Child in France. In *Children in the Field: Anthropological Experiences,* ed. Joan Cassell, 91–120. Philadelphia: Temple University Press.

Yanagisako, Sylvia
    1979   Family and Household: The Analysis of Domestic Groups. *Annual Review of Anthropology* 8:161–205.

Yanagisako, Sylvia Junko, and Jane Fishburne Collier
    1987   Toward a Unified Analysis of Gender and Kinship. In *Gender and Kinship: Essays toward a Unified Analysis,* ed. Jane Fishburne Collier and Sylvia Junko Yanagisako, 14-50. Stanford: Stanford University Press.

Zamora, Mario D.
    1983   Initial Encounter, Choice, and Change in Field Research. In *Fieldwork: The Human Experience,* ed. Robert Lawless, Vinson H. Sutlive, Jr., and Mario D. Zamora, 143–152. New York: Gordon and Breach Science Publishers.

Index

adolescence, 24, 33, 120–123, 186, 189, 194, 195, 207
adoption: in Euro-Western societies, 165; of fieldworker, 20, 172–176, 179–182, 196, 205; in Pacific Island societies, 11, 29, 38, 40, 146, 184, 203; request for, of fieldworker's child, 53, 185–186, 207
Anêm, 146–148, 150, 155–163, 200
anger: of child, 67, 120; and culture shock, 91, 132–133; of fieldworker at child, 53, 56, 80, 81; of host society friend, 159; learning appropriate expression of, 140
angst, 18, 52, 57, 74, 86
arrival in the field, 25–26, 37, 48, 63, 89–90
authority in ethnographic writing, 2, 46, 61–62, 83, 127, 130, 169, 208
autobiography, 198–200, 208, 210

baby-sitting, 49, 94, 95, 105, 161
Behar, Ruth, 128, 201
Berreman, Gerald, 71–72, 78, 80, 82, 94, 127, 168
Boas, Franz, 54, 59
Bowen, Elenore, 8, 61, 83, 127
breast-feeding, 48, 49, 78, 79, 146
Briggs, Jean, 8, 78, 127, 208

cargo beliefs, 148–149, 158
child custody, 12, 37, 106, 107, 201
children: attitudes of, toward fieldwork, 24, 31–34, 36, 48, 95, 116, 121; autonomy of, in the field, 29, 31, 50, 79, 94, 105, 127, 193; disciplining, 53, 56, 57, 65, 81, 111, 119; facilitating interaction with host community, 48, 68, 78, 81; failing to follow local patterns, 79–80, 116; friendships of, in the field, 28, 52, 111, 118, 119, 121, 123, 143, 194; guilty feelings of parents about, 2, 11, 22, 56, 209; host community attitudes toward, 118–122, 124; as informants, 57, 107, 121; lack of objectivity of, 16, 66–68; relevance of age of, 24, 33, 53, 56, 68, 94, 103, 107, 143, 191, 195, 196; role in ASAO symposium of, 3, 10. *See also* adolescence; infancy
church attendance, 50, 80, 95, 107, 137, 139
Chuuk, 23, 25, 33, 106–107. *See also* Namonuito; Pollap; Romonum
class. *See* social class
Clifford, James, 40, 44, 46, 70, 131, 169
confidentiality, 22, 68
control, sense of, 15–16, 65, 78, 197
courtship, 132, 133–135, 201, 207
cultural relativism: commitment to, 13, 18, 133, 207; expected of fieldworker, 10; lack of, among children, 57; questioning, 11, 18, 45–47, 53–56, 66, 140, 192. *See also* children, lack of objectivity of
culture shock, 16, 47, 73, 90, 132, 160
custody. *See* child custody

data collection, impact of family situation on, 3, 16–17, 52, 57, 68, 79, 81, 83

deception, 33, 72, 73, 82, 154, 156–157, 165. *See also* ethics; impression management
depression, 132
development, human, 66, 190, 192–194, 197, 206, 207
developmental niche, 193
divorce, 12, 37, 106, 137, 140, 166, 172, 201

empathy, 50, 65, 80, 130, 196
Enewetak. *See* Ujelang
entry into the field. *See* arrival in the field
ethics, 39, 42–43, 47, 55, 60, 72, 131, 133, 165, 168
ethnicity, 4, 11, 23, 96, 189
ethnocentrism, 10, 45–46, 54–55, 104, 142, 152
evolutionism, 54
exchange. *See* reciprocity
expatriates, 91, 92, 123

fa'aSamoa, 77
family, Euro-American model of, 4, 5, 10–13, 54, 96–97, 99, 152, 155, 165–167, 199, 203, 206
fatherhood, 98, 165
feminist ethnography, 128
fieldwork, prevailing model of, 3, 6–7, 10, 17, 19, 60–62, 73–75, 79, 81, 84, 126–127, 196–197. *See also* Malinowski, Bronislaw
fiu, 38–39, 206
frustration, 3, 49, 51, 56, 91, 93, 100, 145, 193

gendered fieldwork and ethnography, 74, 82, 126, 127, 202–203, 208, 210
Goffman, Erving, 71–72, 80, 170
Gottlieb, Alma, 5, 200, 201, 204, 208
guilt. *See* children, guilty feelings of parents about

Ha'apai, 47–48, 59
Hawai'i. *See* Maui
homesickness, 37–38, 133, 138, 206

homophobia, 167
housing: when accompanied, 26–27, 37, 47, 63–64, 77–78, 107, 127, 164, 167; when accompanied and childless, 99, 113, 182; when unaccompanied, 75, 85, 111, 131, 160, 172–173, 179, 181, 184, 205
husband. *See* spouse

identity: when accompanied, 15, 19, 34, 77, 88, 108–109, 122, 127, 130, 161–162; when alone in the field, 15, 204, 206–207; as anthropologist, 140, 167, 208; of child in the field, 14, 194, 203, 206; constructed by host society, 9, 17, 76, 117, 155–156, 159, 162, 169, 178, 182; as family member, 176, 184–185, 208; gay, 166–167; gender, 8; as ghost, 163–164, 166; hippie, 76–77; intensified in the field, 197; loss of, 15, 61, 86, 88, 109, 196–197; negotiating, 199; as parent in eyes of host community, 12, 77, 108, 143; of spouse in the field, 117; as wantok, 164; as whole "human," 9, 15, 34. *See also* personhood
illness: attempts to prevent, 105; of children in the field, 48, 111, 124, 127, 143; of family left at home, 31, 38–39; of fieldworker or spouse in the field, 27, 64, 159, 162, 173, 184; worries about, 75, 80, 103, 191
impression management: defined, 71–73, 78; demands of, 75; hindered when accompanied, 15, 18, 43, 56, 72, 80–83, 94–95, 195, 199, 208; questioning, 16, 73, 83, 168, 209
infancy, 192, 194
informed consent, 58, 62
interpretive approaches in anthropology, 7, 203
intimacy: attempts to achieve, 137, 207; differing models of, 19, 110, 133, 140; with host family and friends, 74, 94–95, 120, 126, 139; with hosts facilitated by children, 79, 80

joking, 56, 138, 140, 162, 176–178

Kaliai, 142–152, 155–156, 200
kava, 85, 87, 88–89, 90, 133, 139
kinship: fictive, challenging concept of, 152, 155, 165–168, 200, 203–204; fictive, fieldworker attempts to construct, 142–147, 156–157; fictive, incorporated into host society through, 52, 61; impact of host society, on fieldworker beliefs, 95, 101, 106; incorporation strategies, 20, 155–156, 164, 170–176, 180, 182, 186, 196, 204, 205; lesbian and gay constructions of, 166, 205; non-Western models of, 96, 143, 145–146, 152, 155–156, 165–166, 184; as organizing principle in Pacific Island societies, 4, 9, 12, 143–145, 155, 200. *See also* adoption; siblingship

language acquisition and proficiency: of children, 29, 49, 95, 185; of family, 27, 50, 101, 183, 186; of fieldworker, 41, 48, 51, 81, 111, 131, 133, 135, 162, 175; host society attitudes about, 92; impact of child's presence on, 56; impact of relationship with spouse on, 140; of spouse, 91, 92, 93, 183; of visitor from home, 81

maheni, 136, 137, 138
Malinowski, Bronislaw, 6–7, 127, 206
Manono, 77–80
Maori, 111–128
marae, 111–116, 118–121, 123, 125, 127
Maramatanga, 110–114, 124, 126, 128
Marcus, George, 6, 131
marriage, American egalitarian model of, 11, 97, 100, 177–178, 182
Marshall Islands, 169. *See also* Ujelang
matchmaking, 165, 170–172, 176–179, 181, 205
Maui, 74–77
Melanesia. *See* Anêm; Kaliai; New Britain; Papua New Guinea

Micronesia. *See* Chuuk; Marshall Islands; Namonuito; Pohnpei; Pollap; Saipan
missionaries, 46, 143, 172, 174
moral judgment, 66–68, 209. *See also* cultural relativism; ethnocentrism
Mormon church, 132, 135, 139
motherhood: attitude of fieldworker child about, 125; challenging Euro-American model of, 106, 202; Euro-American constructions of, 11, 45, 58, 96, 98; host society beliefs about, 101, 165; perceived deficiency in, 116, 177; and rapport, 65; threatened, 18, 52–53, 192
multivocality, 19, 22–23, 201

Namonuito, 98–103
neopositivism. *See* positivism
New Britain, 142, 148–149, 155–157, 164–165, 168, 200. *See also* Anêm; Kaliai
New Guinea. *See* Papua New Guinea
New Zealand, 111, 122, 204. *See also* Maori; Pakeha
Northern Marianas. *See* Saipan

objectivity, 5, 7, 9, 11, 15, 16, 62, 66, 73, 130, 133, 169, 188
Onoun. *See* Namonuito
other: attempts to become the, 9, 18, 130; challenging concept of the, 18, 39–43; children becoming the, 207; concept of, 8–9; repositioned, 39–43, 209

Pakeha, 110, 114, 116, 117, 119, 120, 122–123, 125, 127
Papua New Guinea, 142–144, 147, 155, 157, 164, 190. *See also* Anêm; Kaliai; New Britain
participant observation, 5, 46, 61, 66, 78, 142, 152–153
Peace Corps, 51, 91, 97–103, 105, 108, 134, 179, 188
performance risks. *See* impression management

228 *Index*

personal growth, 23, 62, 191, 196, 207
personhood: in the field, 130, 132, 152; gender differences in concept of, 10; sense of, when gay, 166; theories of, 10, 41, 74, 108, 143, 209; Western notion of, 73
pets, 102, 203
planning fieldwork, 23–25, 36–37, 47, 61–63, 103–104, 118, 143, 161
Pohnpei, 85, 89–91, 95
polite fictions. *See* impression management
Pollap, 104–106, 108
Polynesia. *See* Maori; Maui; New Zealand; Samoa; Tahiti; Tonga
positionality, defined, 9
positivism, 6, 7, 199
Powdermaker, Hortense, 8, 74, 83, 127
presentation of self. *See* impression management
privacy: gratitude or need for, 27, 64, 121, 194, 208; interpretation of, 182; lack of, 53, 78, 123, 160, 167–168; Polynesian sense of, 132; worries about, 107. *See also* confidentiality
professionalism: challenging, 5; maintaining, 133, 140, 199, 201, 202; perceived lack of, 2, 3, 6, 62, 64, 74, 130

ra, 112, 114
racism, 19, 116, 119, 120, 122–123, 128, 177
rank, 38, 59, 78, 133, 136, 138, 171, 185, 206
rapport, 5, 15–16, 19, 48, 65, 77, 130, 143, 151
reciprocity: in self-disclosure, 15, 94, 140; in social and material exchanges, 20, 99, 133, 146, 148, 150, 152
reflexivity, 5–8, 40, 58, 61–62, 71–72, 198, 202, 207
reliability in qualitative research, 61
returning home, 32, 37–40, 52, 68–69, 109, 115, 137–138, 197, 205
role conflict, 9, 10, 18, 45, 48, 53, 57, 183, 193

Romonum, 23–27
Rosaldo, Renato, 4, 5, 7, 41, 47, 54, 140, 141

safety: of children, 28, 77, 79–81, 94, 107, 116, 119–120, 191; of fieldworker, 134, 167. *See also* illness
Saipan, 107–109
Samoa, 40. *See also* Manono
Scheper-Hughes, Nancy, 7, 9, 66
Schneider, David, 4–5, 45, 54, 96, 146, 152, 165, 203–204
schooling, 23–25, 28–31, 37, 111, 118, 119, 120, 121, 191
science: as ideologically male, 7, 8; and objectivity, 5–7, 9, 83; and positivism, 6–7, 199
self-disclosure, 6, 65, 79, 94, 123, 136, 197, 207
separation from family, 25, 31–34, 35, 37–38, 40, 54, 73, 151, 209
sexuality, 167–168, 170, 172, 177, 179, 181–183, 189
siblingship: created in the field, 119, 147, 156, 159, 176, 182; Euro-American, 33, 65; Marshallese, 181; Tongan, 67, 135–137
social class: confronting differences in, 120, 122, 125, 126, 128; differences between fieldworker and spouse, 19, 96–99, 203; as embarrassment for fieldworker, 61; of fieldworker family, 23, 189; of host family, 131
socialization: American, 104, 189, 193; American versus Marshallese, 186; of fieldworker's child by hosts, 11, 49, 53, 143, 207
social support, 33, 93, 99, 193
spouse (of fieldworker): attitude of host community toward, 115, 117; collaboration with, 5, 45; identity of, in the field, 117; impact of expected gender roles on, 11, 14, 15, 65, 100; role in ASAO symposium of, 3, 10; role in the field of, 15, 29–30, 64, 74, 82, 89–95, 105–106, 112, 114–117, 123, 206

stress in the field, 72, 75, 78, 88–89, 92, 97–99, 153, 195, 207
subjectivity, 6, 7, 8, 9, 61, 130, 139, 210
supplies, 26, 28, 36, 99, 102, 146, 156, 173

Tahaa, 36, 42
Tahiti, 38–40. *See also* Tahaa
tapa, 136, 137
therapy, 1, 3, 17, 22, 31, 34, 190
time, demands on, 9, 79, 85, 88–89, 91, 109, 195
Titikolo, 158–159, 164, 166
Tok Pisin, 147, 157, 162, 163, 164
Tonga, 47–48, 59, 63–65, 67, 69, 131–140. *See also* Ha'apai; Vava'u
touching, 3, 48, 163

Trawick, Margaret, 198, 199, 201, 207, 208
Truk. *See* Chuuk

Ujelang, 170–188

vaulo, 150–151
Vava'u, 135–136
visitors from home, 51, 53, 78, 81–82

Waitangi Tribunal, 116
wantok, 20, 164–166
Weston, Kath, 166–167, 203, 204, 205
wife. *See* spouse
women: associated with emotion, irrationality, and subjectivity, 7–8; pressure on, to be professional, 62; research on, 117, 128; writing about personal experiences, 8, 22, 83, 127, 201, 202. *See also* gendered fieldwork and ethnography; motherhood; spouse